Common Sense in the Second Amendment

Common Sense *in* the Second Amendment

Eighteenth-Century English and the U.S. Bill of Rights

Margie Burns

Universitas Press
Montreal

Universitas Press

Montreal

U

www.universitaspress.com

First published in March 2020.

Library and Archives Canada Cataloguing in Publication

Title: Common sense in the Second Amendment : eighteenth-century English and the U.S. Bill of
  Rights / Margie Burns.
Names: Burns, Margie, author.
Description: Includes bibliographical references.
Identifiers: Canadiana 20200180479 | ISBN 9781988963273 (softcover)
Subjects: LCSH: United States. Constitution. 2nd Amendment. | LCSH: United States. Constitution.
  1st-10th Amendments. | LCSH: English language—18th century—Usage. | LCSH: English language—18th
  century—Etymology. | LCSH: Gun control—United States. | LCSH: Firearms—Law and legislation—
  United States.
Classification: LCC KF3941 .B87 2020 | DDC 344.7305/33—dc23

Contents

Preface

This book came about because of Newtown. After the mass shooting at Sandy Hook Elementary School, I decided to go through the U.S. Constitution and the Bill of Rights word by word, to look up each individual word, if necessary. The horror of the December 14, 2012, shootings was compounded by a paralyzing assumption among even well-meaning people that laws regulating deadly weapons would be 'unconstitutional.' My question was whether anything—anything at all— in these vital documents says that we cannot have gun control. I found that the second amendment is being misconstrued.

Gun control is constitutional. The statement is grounded partly on its own necessity and inherent reasonableness. After all, we join in society for the common good, as John Locke and others said. If we cannot control weapons of deadly force for the common good, then what *can* we control?

The statement is also grounded on the English of 1789, when the U.S. Bill of Rights was written. The vehicle of the first ten amendments was Anglo-American vocabulary in 1789—English words. While the English wording in the second amendment may sometimes be misunderstood today, Dr. Samuel Johnson—a source consulted by Supreme Court justices—would have understood it. He would have known that it did not confer on any individual an unlimited right to caches of deadly weapons. So did the framers of the Constitution and the members of the first federal Congress which wrote the Bill of Rights.

The second amendment needs rescue. The usage of its English words has been so altered in recent decades that its intent has been distorted. The difference between the first amendment and the second amendment is in danger of being lost to memory. Meanwhile, the difference between individual interest and the common good has become exaggerated and hardened and is in danger of becoming an unbridgeable gap. Reading documents from the first two centuries in America is a revelation. The founding documents explained things in terms of the general good. A shared common interest speaks from elite and ordinary. For the framers and their American forebears, the individual welfare and the general good did not necessarily conflict. The earliest settlers, then the colonies in the 1770s lived in communities where it behooved people to pull together. Differences and disputes there always were, and there was a new set of challenges for the states united after they split from Britain in 1782. But no influential writer, document, or population from the earliest settlements through the ratification of the Constitution voices a position of me-against-everyone-else. That may be the mindset of the mass shooter today. But it was not the mindset of the colonists—even at Concord and Middlesex—or of the framers.

A note about publication: the original title of this book was *Firearms Regulation in the Bill of Rights: Eighteenth-Century English Language and the U.S. Constitution*, and it came out in a much longer version in 2017—but self-published. Despite Newtown and every other school shooting, mass shooting, and pointless fatality by firearms after Newtown, I could not get an agent in the Washington, D.C., region to look at the manuscript. There was simply no appetite for pro-gun-control or anti-gun-violence material in the world of publishing. And from the perspective of 'political insiders'—a term used earnestly, by the way, ludicrous though it sounds—the very idea of regulating guns in the political process, from 2012 to 2017, was a non-starter.

For whatever reasons, the temper of the national political press has now changed. Mass shootings still occur, and an immense weapons commerce continues, but daily newspapers can now publish articles receptive to weapons regulation, where they could not in the eighties or in the nineties or pretty much any time from the eighties to 2017. The idea that we can regulate weapons of deadly force is not dismissed out of hand as 'fringe,' 'leftist,' or worse. A rational awareness that the right to weapons has limits that safeguard life, liberty, and property is allowable.

The title of this shortened book is *Common Sense in the Second Amendment*. Obviously, the issue of how to deal with gun violence has been difficult in the public discourse because of the strong passions raised. Some of the passion is misbegotten, based on an all-or-nothing misunderstanding of the second amendment, and some is shadily well-funded. But there is no denying it's out there. Anticipating the worst from an audience is not something an author wants to dwell on, but admittedly there are negative possibilities. So, a short anecdote is in order. In the process of writing the book, I considered several titles and subtitles, like *Gun Control in the Second Amendment: How the Bill of Rights Supports Common Sense*. An obvious precaution was to make sure no book with the same title had been published recently. On Saturday July 23, 2016, I googled the words, "how the bill of rights supports common sense." In an avalanche of paper and ink on the topic, the search turned up no results.

The simpler new title still turns up no results. The simple phrase "Common sense in the second amendment" does not exist on the Internet. Searching for it turns up no result, among billions of English phrases circulating in cyberspace as of September 30, 2019.

The reason the wording is not found is, of course, that the *idea* of common sense in the second amendment is not current. Nobody expects common sense in connection with our most radioactive amendment. "Second amendment" has become a bumper sticker. The very use of the phrase leads to misunderstanding. Reformers either cede the Bill of Rights and the second amendment to what we used to call—when I was growing up in Texas—the 'nut right' or fall back on arguments about "militia." Thus, we get well-meaning people arguing either that the second amendment should be repealed, or that the right to bear arms is not an individual right. Both propositions are false.

Certainly, the thesis of this book is that the second amendment itself provides for regulating military-grade weapons and hardware. But the provision is in "shall not be infringed" and in "well-regulated," not in "militia." The road to reform does not lie through militia. Granted, many Americans and Britons supported a well-regulated militia in the eighteenth century; anything was better than a large standing army, and a local defense composed of local citizens had more appeal than dragooning troops or paying taxes to support a large standing force. But people joined a militia as individuals, and there was supposed to be a floor under human conduct for anyone, whether alone or in a group. The classical model was the mythological Cadmus sowing the dragon's teeth—soldiers springing up from the ground, but preferably without turning on each other afterward, a sequel averted by the biblical model of beating swords into ploughshares among regular troops, and by the classical model of Cincinnatus returning to his farm among officers. The first president of the Society of the Cincinnati was George Washington.

"Militia" in the eighteenth century meant military service, and the right to bear arms was conceived as a public good, but it was still an individual right. These are not mutually exclusive principles and do not necessarily conflict. Abridging the absolute liberty of the individual mediates between being alone and being a member of society. The plan of government laid out in the U.S. Constitution was not intended to put the individual interest and the collective interest at odds with each other. To the contrary, the Constitution aligns the interests of the individual with the common interest. I hope that this short book may help clarify the alignment.

In doing the research, my main resource has been primary sources. I have gratefully used excellent secondary sources, but mainly to elucidate the primary documents. My contribution has been to read the primary documents and to check key wording against other primary sources including dictionaries. Simply put, the book approaches the topic of the second amendment by following the history of the wording.

I am grateful to the editors at Universitas Press for bringing this work forward in print.

November 2019

Overview:
"Infringed or Abridged"

> The freedom of opinion is one of the inalienable rights of man, and one of the great gifts of his creator; it is a privilege which no human power ought to infringe, and no state of society unnecessarily to abridge.
> Alexander Hamilton, 1812[1]

The first amendment is stronger than the second amendment. This point sometimes gets lost in the public discourse, especially when an all-or-nothing interpretation of the second amendment is being boosted. But as Alexander Hamilton understood, there is a key difference in how the two amendments are worded.

> Congress shall make no law respecting an establishment of religion, or prohibiting the free exercise thereof; or *abridging* the freedom of speech, or of the press; or the right of the people peaceably to assemble, and to petition the Government for a redress of grievances.[2]

> A well regulated Militia, being necessary to the security of a free State, the right of the people to keep and bear Arms, shall not be *infringed*.

In the first amendment, Congress may not even *abridge*—lessen—the freedoms of speech, press, and assembly. In the second amendment, Congress may not go so far as to *infringe*—break or destroy—a right to bear arms.

The key difference is the difference between the word *abridge* and the word *infringe*. Anyone who looks up the words in English dictionaries used in 1789—and for centuries before 1789—can find what the framers would have found. For all the centuries leading up to the Constitutional Convention in 1787 and the first federal Congress in 1789, the English word *infringe* meant to break, to violate. It still does; we still call "breaking the law" and "violating copyright" infringements. The word *abridge* meant to limit. It still does. A difference in degree can become a difference in kind, and abridgement severe enough could become infringement, but it is essential to understand that to abridge something—a power, a privilege, even a right—was qualitatively different in 1789 from infringement.

The difference is that we can abridge a right without infringing it. As the framers understood, human rights have human limits. A society can take customary and reasonable action against offenses and abuses. We can limit a right without destroying it, a line brightly and clearly drawn in the quotation from Hamilton.

Pointedly, the creators of the first ten amendments declined to say that the right to bear arms cannot be "abridged." If they had wanted to say so, they could have. They also had access to a large warehouse of longstanding English phrases that would have put bearing arms beyond the reach of law, if they had wanted to do so. But they chose to word the second amendment in a way that allows regulating. Congress is debarred only from violating, and the framers did not suggest that ordinances regulating weapons would violate anything. Such ordinances existed at the time. Nor does the second amendment say or imply that any and every abridgement is an infringement. That position in 1789 would have upended a century of political philosophy following Thomas Hobbes, John Locke, and David Hume among others.

For accurate understanding of the Bill of Rights, it is essential to use dictionaries and documents that existed when the Bill of Rights was written. The difference between the words *abridge* and *infringe* is findable. If this approach looks startling, it need not. One can combine political philosophy with practicality.

The framers were mostly admirable men—outside the abomination of slavery, of which they themselves knew the evil—but they were still fallible human beings, as they themselves knew. Along with a reasonable awareness of self and others, they supported reasonable self-interest. It is ridiculous to argue that they endowed the public with an unlimited, absolute right to take up arms against them. During the first federal Congress in 1789, there had already been a Shays' Rebellion, and a bloody revolution was beginning in France, inspired by the American Revolution, as members were aware. They hoped for better, not for a repeat. Witnessing events in France firsthand, Thomas Jefferson wrote to a friend, "A great political revolution will take place in your country, and that without bloodshed." "A king with 200,000 men at his orders, is disarmed by the force of the public opinion and the want of money."[3] Obviously, Jefferson's prediction was inaccurate. But his optimism accurately reflects the founders' non-avid view of bloodshed.

No records from the Constitutional Convention and the first federal Congress suggest that delegates welcomed a prospect of getting shot at by their own people. Recognizing the possibility of a future rebellion, they did as little as possible to encourage one. As the founders engaged proudly in setting up a new government—some of them having risked their lives, their fortunes, and their sacred honor for it—they left no suggestion that they looked forward to seeing it dismantled. No delegate claimed that firearms attested the vitality of basic freedoms or that unauthorized force vindicated the rights of humankind. More to the point, they did not leave taking up arms against the new government lawful or constitutional. They did not protect taking arms against judges or members of Congress or citizens voting in an election. To the contrary, the new American government outlawed both force and fraud.

An operating principle was "just rights." Throughout the seventeenth and eighteenth centuries, the phrase "just rights" was used by the framers and their forebears, in England and America, too many times to count. The Pennsylvania Assembly wrote about "just rights" to the governor in the 1750s.[4] The Continental Congress used it to try to induce British troops to desert—mostly unsuccessfully—in the 1770s.[5] The phrase was used privately and publicly—in letters, histories, commentaries, sermons, speeches. George Washington, John Adams, Benjamin Franklin, Thomas Jefferson, and James Monroe used it in private letters. "My first wish is for a restoration of our just rights," Jefferson wrote John Randolph in August, 1775.[6] Publicly, protesting against British treatment of Ethan Allen in January, 1776, Jefferson wrote, "When necessity compelled us to take arms against Great Britain in defence of our just rights," Americans had considered their British adversaries "brave and civilized."[7] But, Jefferson said, Americans changed their good opinion when the British shipped Ethan Allen to England in chains. He proposed that a captured British general be clapped into irons to see how it felt.

In the 1770s, leading up to the American Revolution, the phrase "just rights" circulated in print every year.[8] Americans protesting measures by king and Parliament spelled out that not just any rights were being violated. Americans were not squabbling over bagatelles. They were not demanding limitless license. They were not complaining about a reasonable abridgement of natural right, necessary to join in civil society. They were protecting their *just* rights. And on the other side of the line, British authorities denied infringing anyone's just rights.

Again, a big difference between the first two amendments is that the framers did not choose "shall not be abridged" for the second amendment. One way to draw the line between just rights and arbitrary power, or between a just right and excessive license, was to differentiate between abridgement and infringement. In political philosophy, *infringe* and *abridge* could both be applied to powers. Both were applied to royal authority and prerogatives, state powers, and laws. Both were also applied to rights. They applied to individual rights, common or special liberties, and privileges.

Thus, one difference between *infringe* and *abridge* is that only abridgement can be applied positively. *Infringe* could mean breaking a law or treaty or contract as well as violating rights. *Abridge* could mean abridging power or privilege, or it could mean abridging ordinary rights to enable people to live together in society. Either way, there was good abridgement;

there was no such thing as good infringement. Abridgement of individual rights for the sake of living in human society was not infinitely elastic—a just right would be important enough to safeguard—but it did mean an acceptable give-and-take.

The two terms are logically connected, as a British writer in 1733 made clear.

> In the first place then, I shall very readily agree, that the Test Act has set the Dissenters upon a different foot from the rest of the Society: the conclusion they draw from hence is, that their natural Privileges are infringed. If they say diminished, I allow that likewise to be true, for every Man's natural Privileges (such I mean as are his Rights in a State of Nature) are no doubt abridged exceedingly by his Entrance into Society: But when infringe implies to abridge unjustly, this I deny absolutely to be their case.[9]

A full and fair discussion of the first and second amendments to the U.S. Constitution will acknowledge the differences between the two. While public discourse in 2019 may confuse abridging and infringing, the eighteenth century differentiated clearly between them, as in the statement quoted from John Perceval (1711-1770), First Lord of the Admiralty, whose family tree included a sixteenth-century dictionary author and a seventeenth-century founder of Georgia.

When Congress sent the amendments to the states for ratification in 1789, the amendments applied the words *infringe* and *abridge* to different rights. Freedom of opinion and of conscience are unalienable. As Hamilton and Perceval recognized, some rights are unalienable—not something to carry around in the hand or advertise for sale on Craigslist or sell out of the trunk of the car. Unlike the natural rights of self-defense and discipline, freedom of opinion and of conscience cannot be partly given over to society to handle (unless someone tries to expand them to include, for example, human sacrifice). They shall not be abridged. This is one of the differences between infringing and abridging. Abridgement could be in the common good; infringement cannot. Changes and trends over time may have obscured these differences in the twenty-first century, but in the age of the Constitutional Convention, writers from John Adams to Noah Webster were familiar with it.

The difference itself is simple enough: an abridgement of rights pushed far enough becomes infringement, but not every abridgement is infringement. Nor does every abridgement of lawful powers infringe the law. And yet, by the end of the twentieth century, this clear distinction became obscured in America. In fact, it became so obscured that even a prominent law professor could confuse the action words of the first and second amendments:

> Despite its plausibility as a textual matter, the narrow interpretation of "prohibiting" should therefore, be rejected, and the term should be read as meaning approximately the same as "infringing" or "abridging."[10]

Look at the difference between Alexander Hamilton, publishing in 1812, and Professor Michael W. McConnell, published in the *Harvard Law Review* in 1990. It tells the story in a nutshell: in recent years, the "infringed" of the second amendment has too often been misconstrued as a synonym for the "abridging" of the first amendment.

The nutshell is not the whole story, of course. Hence this book. This introductory chapter presents the overview. First, the two action words *infringe* and *abridge* are different English words, with different meanings. (For convenience, the words will usually be discussed as *infringe* and *abridge*. However, discussion should be understood to refer to all forms—all tenses, the infinitive, use as participles or nouns—*to infringe* and *to abridge*, *infringed* and *abridged*, *infringement* and *abridgement*, etc.). It is essential to clarify that in the eighteenth century the words *abridge* and *infringe* were distinct and separate, that they had always been distinct and separate, and that to claim that the eighteenth century considered them synonyms will always be an anachronism. The two words never meant the same thing. While it is difficult to prove a negative, the evidence is clear. From the beginning of dictionaries in English through 1789, never at any time did English define infringement and abridgement to mean the same thing.

Therefore, no matter how absolutist some weapons supporters may feel, the second amendment itself is not absolutist. This point can be supported by analysis of the words—in simplest terms, by looking at the English the writers used. A view of the right to bear arms as limitless, sweeping, and absolute is contradicted by the vocabulary in which the Bill of Rights was written. In eighteenth-century English, and earlier, 'even to the meanest intelligence' as dictionary authors rather tactlessly used to put it, *abridge* was to limit; *infringe* was to break. Historical documentation for the distinction is voluminous and unassailable. The straightforward way to find it is to use English dictionaries, including ones used by the founders themselves. This is not to say that dictionaries were the only place the two words were defined differently. Their difference shows up in public documents and private letters from the eighteenth century. But dictionaries provide valuable evidence of the customary use. Chapter 2 discusses the history of the two words in dictionaries, which also show how their usage evolved over ten centuries.

A millennium of English dictionaries is not cherry-picking. The distinction between definitions of *infringe* and *abridge* is clear and consistent in English-language dictionaries from the eighth century to the ratification of the Bill of Rights, from Old English (Anglo-Saxon) through the eighteenth century. *Infringe* was destructive; *abridge* became constructive. Every dictionary that included *infringing* defined it as violating or breaking something, as in the famous Dr. Johnson's definition, "To violate; to break laws or contracts"; "To destroy; to hinder."[11] There are no exceptions in the entire history of English dictionaries before 1789. Dictionaries also used *infringe* to define other words for unacceptable, destructive acts—to violate, to break. Whether defined as a main entry (headword) itself, or used to define other words, *infringe* in all forms meant destruction. Either as infringement of a power, an authority—a law, a treaty, a constitution— or as infringement of a right, it remained destructive. To infringe a contract or treaty is to break it; to infringe a right is to destroy it.

The development of abridging as a concept was more complex. The linguistic history of infringement had no early turning points; abridgement had several. Before 1600, if dictionaries included the term *abridged* at all, the word referred to editing. *Abridged* meant condensed, synopsized, or shortened, as in abridged histories or abridgements of law like dictionary author and lawyer John Rastell's 1527 *Abridgment of the Statutes* of England. In the seventeenth and eighteenth centuries, and especially approaching 1789, more dictionaries in English included public-policy definitions for *abridge*. It was still a synonym for acts considered acceptable, necessary, often beneficial—to lessen, to limit, to contract. But now it went beyond editorial work. In philosophy and history, abridgement meant abridgement of power. Then it came to mean a voluntary abridgement of rights to form a society.

The difference still shows in contracts, as well as in social compact. A signed contract cannot usually be abridged; legitimate changes involve a codicil or rewriting the whole, where after-the-fact changes are breach. Abridging power or privilege, on the other hand, is not only possible but a good idea, and voluntary abridgement of individual rights to join in human society is beneficial. The consequence of voluntary abridgements of individual freedom is human society, as in the 1789 United States. However, abridgement of rights pushed to the point of infringement— as in 1774 America—was clearly a negative. When *abridge* came to refer to political acts, public policy, the difference between infringement and abridgement became overt. Infringing rights or laws was bad; abridging individual license or excess power was good. All of this is supported by Dr. Samuel Johnson's eighteenth-century dictionary.

To discuss Samuel Johnson's dictionary is not to imply that the eighteenth century used the words *infringe* and *abridge* with some abrupt innovation, unique to the era. Johnson's *Dictionary* aligned with the history of previous English dictionaries. The seventeenth and eighteenth centuries produced larger dictionaries and more dictionaries than ever before, but again, the words *abridge* and *infringe* were semantically separate before and after the period. They stayed semantically separate, from the eighth century through the next eleven centuries. While the language of the U.S. Constitution developed from English usage in its own time, the language, like the Constitution, was the development of more than a millennium.

Joining the terms

While infringed and *abridged* are and were different, in political philosophy they became logically connected. Where infringement always meant a wrong, the more subtle concept of abridgement evolved in meaning over centuries. Only in the seventeenth and eighteenth centuries, as human population increased, political philosophy branched out, and more attention was devoted in print to the concepts of rights and liberty, did abridging come to be used as Locke, Dr. Johnson, and the U.S. founders used it. As a limit but not a violation, in a careful distinction from infringing, it was juxtaposed with infringing in an English binomial—"infringed or abridged."

That the key action words in our first two amendments were a traditional binomial may need to be relearned now. Aside from a word-sleuth like Bill Bryson or a prominent scholar of U.S. history like Douglas Brinkley, most people would not recognize "infringed or abridged" as a traditional phrase. But it was. The two terms were paired in government, law, and policy, because their contrasting meanings complement each other. Rather than trace all the significant uses of *infringe* and *abridge* in English and American public documents, demonstrating their differences, in this book the trail will be narrowed to their use together as a binomial. The binomial is a good way to track their use in American public documents. To explain their difference—limited reasonably and voluntarily, versus limited to the breaking point—it is quicker and clearer to show that they became juxtaposed in political thought. Chapter 3 discusses the use of the infringe-or-abridge binomial in Britain and in America.

My theory is that such binomial phrases in English have been used, for millennia, for protection. This is the one theoretical aspect of the discussion. The dictionary definitions and the public and private documents using *infringe* and *abridge* are fact. The use of binomial phrases in legal documents from Anglo-Saxon to the present is fact, a matter of record. It is my inference that the binomial phrases used in government, law, and policy, including "infringed or abridged," were intended as protection.

Change and misunderstanding

Words change. As *abridge* changed in the eighteenth century, *infringe* changed in the nineteenth century. Previously, *infringe* had been the clearer term, and even today the dictionary definition has not entirely changed. But in the nineteenth century, usage shifted. It softened, began to be replaced by "infringe upon," lost its force. It was never used again in constitutional amendments after the second amendment. Chapter 4 deals with the changing usage of "infringed" over time and with its replacement in constitutional amendments by "denied or abridged." The binomial "denied or abridged" had its own history in public documents in America. As with earlier, traditional binomials, the purpose was protection of rights. In the U.S., the "denied or abridged" binomial has been used unambiguously to protect the right to vote.

Regrettably, when the traditional binomial was lost, its protection was lost. Chapter 5 deals with the loss of the infringed-or-abridged binomial, and the results. One result of losing the protective binomial in English is that we have had even some federal judges misconstruing the second amendment. Somehow, recent research on the second amendment seldom mentions English vocabulary in 1789 or pre-1789 definitions of *infringe*. We have had public exhortations to look at the original Constitution and to discover the founders' intent, yet little attention has gone to eighteenth-century language where it counts most. Rather than defining terms, most debate during the last thirty years has focused on militia membership versus non-membership, individual versus collective rights, new constitutional amendments versus repealing the second amendment, etc. 'Originalism,' 'strict construction,' and a 'structural constitution' developed political influence some years ago, but those views still have not translated into a thorough look at the precise but accessible terms *abridge* and *infringe*, in the eighteenth century and earlier, in the first two amendments. Given the stakes for the public when armed force is used, it is high time to take a careful look.

Background:
English Dictionaries

The difference examined here is the too-often disregarded shift from "abridging" in the first amendment to "infringed" in the second. The core rights of freedom of speech, the press, and assembly shall not be abridged, meaning limited; the more circumscribed right to bear arms shall not be infringed, meaning broken. This difference was not a sticking point for the 1789 Congress, which composed the amendments, working with Madison. Both amendments went through several rounds of crafting, and each clause and each phrase received due attention. None of the many documents recording the drafting and re-drafting of the Bill of Rights suggest that any faction tried to boost a private and individual right to military force. (Congressional debate over what is now the second amendment spent more time and ink on the rights of conscientious objectors than on the right to bear arms.) Never at any point did "shall not be infringed" mean 'untouchable.'

The difference is supported by word history (etymology), literary texts (philology), and law. The two words have separate etymologies, *infringe* from Latin and *abridge* from Anglo-Norman and Middle French. But the difference between the two words is not found in out-of-the-way sources; it is rooted in ordinary English and can be found in an ordinary, familiar category of book publishing—dictionaries. It is reflected in dictionaries in English from the eighth century through the eighteenth. The earliest Latin-English glossaries from the Middle Ages separated the two verbs; all early print dictionaries through the fifteenth and sixteenth centuries separated them, including Latin-English and English-Latin; they remained separate in English writing through the seventeenth and eighteenth centuries; and they were separate and distinct when the Constitution was produced.

The large history of English dictionaries exceeds the scope of one book; this chapter traces only the history of two words through their appearance in dictionaries, and the discussion could be expanded. The words evolved in general dictionaries, Latin dictionaries, dictionaries for translating modern European languages, and especially in law dictionaries. In the century of the Constitutional Convention, Samuel Johnson's dictionary, owned by the founders, defined the key terms.

Not every English dictionary from the first Latin-English word lists to 1789 included both *abridge* and *infringe*. But every dictionary up to 1789 that did include the words differentiated between them. Infringement meant "a breach, a violation," from before Robert Cawdrey's *Table*

Alphabeticall in 1604, through seventeenth-century and eighteenth-century editions of Edward Phillips' *New World of Words*—"To infringe (properly to break to pieces) to violate, transgress, or break a Law, Custom, Privilege." In America, multiple editions of John Entick's *New Spelling Dictionary* provided the same definition—"Infringe, v.a. to violate, hinder, destroy." Entick's dictionary was first published in 1764, was revamped by Noah Webster, and was widely used in America before Webster published his own game-changing dictionary.[12] *Abridge*, in the same dictionaries, was defined mainly as editing—to abbreviate, "to make short," "to contract," "to retrench." Abridging did not mean an infringement, and in no way was an infringement just a limitation. The distinction between *abridge* and *infringe* is widespread, accessible, and consistent.

The history of English dictionaries (lexicography) has been covered by global experts including DeWitt Starnes and Gertrude Noyes in the forties and Gabriele Stein, Jurgen Schaefer, and Werner Huellen more recently. An overview is offered by the 2009 *Oxford History of English Lexicography*. Many dictionaries are archived in searchable text in the *Lexicons of Early Modern English* database (LEME). Catalogues of dictionaries from the Early Modern period to 1900 include works by Robert O'Neill and David Vancil.

In overview, the English language and English dictionaries changed and grew from the Anglo-Saxons to the fourteenth century; changed and grew after the invention of printing in the fifteenth century; changed and grew after paper became more available; after an expansion of literacy, education, and commerce paved the way for a rising middle class and for the market for books in Britain and America; and as the sheer number of books grew, from the sixteenth century through the eighteenth century. During the same centuries the English lexicon itself expanded, and English vocabulary grew beyond even Chaucer and Shakespeare's lexicons. Even the English alphabet expanded; in the early seventeenth century, *I* and *J* became separate letters. As book publishing in general grew, the range, availability, and accessibility of reference books grew. In the later eighteenth century, basic dictionaries were augmented or supplanted by encyclopedias; when the first *Encyclopedia Britannica* appeared in 1771, it was subtitled *a Dictionary of Arts and Sciences*.

For the world of letters, the English expansion was a good thing. English literature and language studies had some catch-up ball to play in Western culture. Geographical features that protected England from military invasion (after 1066) could distance it from European cultural developments, and English philology lagged Italian and French. The British thus provided with natural defenses were naturally sometimes defensive. Johnson's dictionary was popular as a one-man substitute for the work of an entire national academy, like the French and Italian academies, which England did not have, and Johnson was touted by British chauvinists as living proof that Britain could do with one man what it took other nations (the French) a whole academy to produce.[13] That Johnson worked with a team of studious compilers for eight years seems not to have deterred this patriotic talking point.

Latin-to-English word lists, glossaries, and teaching aids or study aids for translating had existed since the eighth century, but the development of full English dictionaries took several publishing eons. English-to-Latin glossaries did not appear until the fifteenth century. English books with the word 'dictionary' in the title (usually spelled *dictionarie* before 1600) did not appear until the sixteenth century. Dictionaries published before the seventeenth century were likely to be translating dictionaries or law dictionaries. Everyday English words were the last category added to English dictionaries. Ordinary English words entered dictionaries as main entries after words from other languages, 'hard words,' and the terminology of specialized fields (herbalism, navigation, medicine).

Eighth century through tenth century

Entries for *infringe* and *abridge* barely existed in the earliest English dictionaries and glossaries dating from the eighth through the tenth centuries. These faint and separate early trails are a given: *abridge* was not a word in Latin. Since *abridge* did not exist in the time of early Latin-to-Old English (Anglo-Saxon) manuscripts, it naturally would not appear in manuscript word lists or glossaries which translated Latin into Anglo-Saxon. Unlike *infringe*, direct from Latin, *abridge* came to English by the knobbier feudal route of Anglo-Norman and Middle French. It originated in the Middle Ages rather than antiquity, entering the English language much later than *infringe*; they are different etymological vintages.

The *Oxford English Dictionary*, the world's most comprehensive compilation of English usage from Old English to now, lists nine different spellings for the French etymology of *abridge*—Anglo-Norman *abbregger, abbrigger, abregger, abriger, abrigger, abrigier,* Anglo-Norman and Middle French *abbreger, abreger, abregier*. English being notorious as the language its own speakers could not spell, the *OED* lists even more spellings for the English etymology of *abbrege*. In Middle English, the language of Geoffrey Chaucer and *Gawain and the Green Knight*, *abridge* could appear as *abbrege, abbregge, abbrige, abbrigge, abregge, abrige, abrigge, abryge*; and *obrege, obregge, obrygge*. Through the fifteenth and sixteenth centuries it was spelled *abrege, abrydge, abbredge, abredge, abridg, abbridge, abridge*; and for good measure *abbryge, abreage,* and *abredge*.

Old spellings for *infringe* are far fewer—*enfring, infrynge, infring*. The word *infringe* is a simpler term all around—easy to translate from Latin on sight, simple to spell, simple to define. To break outright, to violate, is a simpler concept than to limit or to moderate by degrees.

A form of *infringe* can be found in England's 'oldest dictionary,' a manuscript from the eighth century called the *Corpus Glossary*. The entry is *infractus*, from the Latin *infringere*, translated into Old English (Anglo-Saxon) as 'injured,' *giwaemmid*.[14] (The glossary contains several words using and not using the prefix *in-* almost interchangeably, quasi-synonyms like the modern *flammable* and *inflammable* or *valuable* and *invaluable*.) The *Corpus Glossary* has no entry for abridging. Nor does it have an entry for *abbreviate*.

Another glossary from the eighth century, the *Latin-Anglo Saxon Glossary*, also includes *infractus* and provides the same definition in Old English, meaning injured.[15] It has no entry for *abridging*, but there is an important development. While it has no entry for *abbreviate*, or for the Latin verb *breviare*, there are entries for the Latin *adbreviatio, abbreviated*. More importantly, it uses Latin forms of *abbreviate* to define other words including the words *Ephitomos* and *Epigramma*. The eighth-century *Latin-Anglo Saxon Glossary* is thus the earliest example of an English dictionary using the key word to define other terms without defining the word itself—showing that the word was itself understood clearly. For the next ten centuries, dictionaries in English often did the same—not bothering to define *infringe* or *abridge*, although using either or both in definitions of other words.

Twelfth century through fourteenth century

In the eighth century, *abridge* was not yet a word in any language. It first appeared in the first half of the twelfth century, in the Anglo-Norman *abrejer*, meaning to shorten a duration of time, as in feudal obligation—"*diminuer les services attachés à un fief*," "*diminuer la valeur ou les services d'un fief*." To abridge was to shorten one's servitude in fiefdom. A few decades later, in the late twelfth century, *abbregger* had broadened somewhat to mean reducing more things in magnitude or extent. The French word meant "to curtail, lessen, or diminish (a right or privilege, etc)," "to reduce the extent or scope of (authority, power, etc)." The definition also again applied to reducing the feudal services attached to a fief.[16] Soon followed the editorial sense—to shorten, condense, summarize a text, to make it shorter while keeping the essentials.

The French *abridge* as shortening duration relates to constitutional history; the early French term already applied to reducing rights or privileges and to reducing power. Hence the term could develop as a form of protection under law in French and then in English. In Anglo-Norman as in English, it applied early to law. In the law dictionaries, *to abridge* in a legal case meant to omit parts of a writ, a claim, etc., reducing the total redress demanded without invalidating the whole. This meaning of *abridge* became connected to the post-classical Latin *abbreviare*, meaning to abridge or write in brief, as in legal briefs.

The word *abregge* came into use somewhat later in England than in France. With less direct reference to fiefs, in England the word still pointedly applied to lessening rights or powers, as well as to editing or shortening a text. Both meanings were current in the literary world of Middle English. The University of Michigan *Middle English Dictionary* online, a searchable electronic archive of more than 15,000 pages of Middle English vocabulary, yields scores of citations for both *abridge* and *infringe*.[17]

The *Middle English Dictionary* defines the public-policy sense of *abridge* as

(a) To limit (sth.) in scope or power, reduce in strength, curtail;
(b) to assuage (pain, sorrow, etc.), reduce the severity of; also, to shorten the duration of (penance, purgatory); ~ labour, to lessen or shorten (someone's) labour.

Authors cited include some of the most famous writers of the age—Gower, Wycliffe, Chaucer. The concept also applied in religion. An advisory for clergy from 1425 recommended, "Yef he be sory for hys synne [. . .] Abregge hys penaunce then by myche" (If he is sorry for his sin, then much abridge his penance). The 1450 *Secret of Secrets* (*Secreta Secretorum*) reads, "Sum tyme must be doon rigoure of lawe, and sum tyme it must be abreggid aftir that the persone be of estate" (Sometimes the law must be applied rigorously, and sometimes it must be abridged, if the person has enough estate).

The *Middle English Dictionary* defines *abbreggen* as

(a) To reduce (sth.) in number or amount, diminish; (b) to shorten (sth.) in space, decrease the length of (a journey, a rod); (c) to make (sth.) of shorter duration, to shorten (the time that something lasts), to cut short (someone's life); also, to set a limit of (seventy weeks); (d) to become shorter in time.

Again, the examples refer to lightening someone's load, or not—reducing obligations or privileges, or not—in public policy. At this point, one can also see the key term used as part of a binomial phrase. Sixteen Middle English examples include an edict of 1433 from the Rolls of Parliament, which required "the Bailliffs [. . .] abbregge ne pardon no maner of dute" (Bailiffs are not to *abridge or exempt* any duty). A 1450 act included the provision "That this Acte, Resumption and Ordenaunce, or eny of theym, extende noght or in any maner *abbrege or abate* xx marcs yerely [. . .] which we late graunted by oure Letters Patentes." (This Act shall neither expand nor *abridge or abate* the annual twenty marks previously granted.) Use of a binomial such as "abridge or abate" became typical for grants, proclamations, and charters for the next several centuries. Binomials continued to protect titles, appointments, and land grants given by successive monarchs.

Broadly, abridging meant lessening—sins, numbers of people, time spent in correction, the length of a passage or way, periods of time. As defined in the 1440 *Promptorium Parvolorum*, it meant "Dockyd, lessyd or obryggyd: Abbreviatus, minoratus." This example is particularly appealing because of its lastingness. In late Middle English, to abridge money or time or labor was to subtract, to cost it out—or as in the English-Latin translation quoted, to "dock" pay, etc., maybe a colloquialism today but professional vocabulary in the 1400s. The *Middle English Dictionary* defines the verb *dokken* as "1. (a) To cut (a tail, beard, hair) short; dock the tail of (a horse); (b) *fig.* ~ the tail, to curtail (someone's) power or freedom" and "2. (a) To abridge or reduce (sth.); also, mutilate, impair; (b) to curtail the activities or privileges of (sb.); (c) ~ of *promis*, to deny (sb.) that which has been promised."

Entries for either *infringe* or *abridge* in late Medieval English dictionaries are scant. There is no discernible connection between the two words in medieval dictionaries, in the tenth through thirteenth centuries. However, other Middle English binomials did use forms of abridge, and both *infringe* and *abridge* appeared in English literature and in public documents of the period. Several *MED* citations for *abridge* come from three of the most influential authors of the fourteenth century—poets Geoffrey Chaucer (1343-1400) and John Gower (1330-1408), and theologian John Wycliffe (1330-1384). Chaucer used forms of the word in the *Canterbury Tales* and elsewhere, several times referring to abridging burdens such as labor, sorrow, or punishment.

Wyclif's bible—or English bible translations inspired by Wyclif—used several forms of *abridge*, as do other works by Wyclif. Wyclif's bible uses *abridge* in connection with God's power, as in Isaiah 59—"Ther is not abreggid the hond of the Lord, that sauen he mai not, ne agreggid." This passage couples two terms not only related but alliterative *and* rhyming—"abreggid" and "agreggid"—to say that divine power is neither too little nor too great. The Wyclifite documents thus neatly couple the opposites of contracting and expanding, like later documents in literature and law. Wyclif's bible also included binomials. In the context of abridging powers and rights, Wyclif instructed parish priests, "Criste [. . .] techith us in all his lawe to kepe & to mayntene this ordenance *with-owten addynge ther-to or abregynge ther-fro*." (Christ teaches us in all his laws to keep and to maintain this ordinance without adding to it or abridging it.) Binomials about adding to and subtracting from something continued to be used in law well after Wyclif. They are still used today. The principle of neither adding to nor subtracting from an existing text became significant early in literature and in law. The principle is a lasting interface between editing and public policy, where adding to or subtracting from the wording of a law has consequences.

The *Oxford English Dictionary* dates the earliest English use of *abridge* to 1393, in Book 7 of John Gower's *Confessio Amantis*: "Largesse it is, whos privilegge Ther mai non Avarice abregge."[18] (The *Middle English Dictionary* gives earlier examples, from Wyclif's bible dated 1384 and from Chaucer in

1385 and 1390, and two other examples of "abregged" or "abreggede" in the editorial sense, dated 1387.) Gower's line is apt: a king's most important attribute besides honesty is "largesse"—generosity—not to be abridged by avarice. In a line of thought that Hobbes would have appreciated, Gower expounds the traditional commonplace that mankind's wealth was at first common, until the greed and stinginess of great lineages led them to take from others too much for themselves, forgetting the common good. The attribute of giving to others is kingly, according to Gower, and avarice should not abridge the will to help others survive and thrive. Regardless of which author used it first, *abridge* as used in the U.S. Bill of Rights is about six hundred years newer to English, or younger, than the simpler *infringe*.

The *Middle English Dictionary* does not define the English *infringe* as an entry. The word *infringe* appears in the *MED* only to define other words—verbs including *break* (*breken*), *annull* (*annullen*), and *trespass* (*trespassen*); and nouns including *transgression* (*transgressioun*). Medieval citations of the word indicate only a few variant spellings. The *MED* does define a French version, *enfrainen*: "To break (a commandment), to violate (the marriage vows)."

One example of infringement cited by the *MED* comes from a 1350 legal glossary. In it, an Old English term, *Gridbriche*, is translated into French (*pais enfrainte*). The language of law has some interesting byways. Obviously, we no longer use the ancient word *gridbriche* or search it out in Old Icelandic. However, we do still have the concept itself—"breaking the peace," or "breach of peace." A full definition is provided by the *MED*:

> grith-briche (n.) Also -brice, -bruche, -breche, -brece, gridbriche, -breche, gritbruch, -breche & (errors) grithbruthe, grichbreche. Pl. -briches, -brēches. [OE griþbryce; cp. OI griða-brek. Also cp. ME brēche n.]: *Law.* (a) Disturbances or violence committed toward persons, at places, or during specific periods that were under special protection of the king; also (after 1200), any breach of the peace; (b) jurisdiction over cases involving such offenses; the right to try such cases, levy and collect fines; also, a fine for such offenses.

The English term had been translated into Latin by 1120, the translation serving as definition and probably as ordinance:

> Si quis a uicecomite uel a minstro pacem regis habeat, si infringatur in eo, gri[ð]breche sit, et Centum sol. emendetur." (If a sheriff's or a king's peace is breached, it is gridbreche.)

Here the spelling of *gridbreche* approaches that of *breach*.

The definition for *infringe* in the *Oxford English Dictionary* is simple: "To commit a breach or infraction of (a law, obligation, right, etc.); to violate or break (an oath, pledge, treaty, etc.); to transgress, contravene." The earliest example of *infringe* in English cited by the *OED* dates back only to 1533, from the Merchants Guild, "Whatsooewer brothir or brethir attempte to infring or breke this sayde lawe." Since the *OED* entry for *infringe* has not been updated recently, comparison to the entry for *abridge* is inexact; researchers continue to unearth evidence and may update further. Even so, probably fewer Middle English examples of *infringe* will turn up than Middle English examples of *abridge*. The Latin *infringere* did not require translating into English to be clear. And when it was translated, its clarity was done better justice to by forceful English words like "break" and "breach" than by the Latinate "infringe."

Gower also used *infringe* in his 1393 *Confessio Amantis*. Fittingly, therefore, an early example of *abridge* and an early example of *infringe* appeared in the same chapter of the same book on ethics and governance. The context for *infringe* was a marginal note on the classical figure Lycurgus, legendary lawgiver of Sparta.[19]

> [Here he presents an instructive example concerning those Rulers who not only having established a law preserve it, but also in order that they might augment the common good diminish their own power. And he tells that Ligurgius the ruler of the Athenians had established his subjects in every abundance of prosperity, wealth, and unanimity by means of appropriate laws, when, wishing those laws to be more firmly observed for the utility of the commonwealth, caused himself to depart to foreign lands. But first he extracted a solemn oath from his lieges in this manner: that they would not break [*infringerent*] his laws in any way until he returned. With these things sworn, he commuted his pilgrimage into exile to be permanent, without return.][20]

Gower's use of *infringe* was in Latin, not English, but the moral of the story is relevant. Gower's classical exemplar of a good king, Lycurgus, was a ruler who passed laws of incremental reform for the common good, followed them himself, and caused all equally to obey them. Lycurgus was admired by eighteenth-century Americans; his portrait features among bas-reliefs of famous lawgivers in the U.S. House of Representatives.

For the framers, these classical figures were prototypes. On June 2, 1777, John Adams wrote affectionately to Abigail Adams, "I suppose you will have a Constitution formed this Year"—you'll get that Constitution you've been wanting. He went on,

> Who will be the Moses, the Lycurgus, the Solon? Or have you a score or two of such? Whoever they may be and whatever Form may be adopted, I am perswaded there is among the Mass of our People a Fund of Wisdom, Integrity and Humanity, which will preserve their Happiness, in a tolerable Measure.[21]

Adams' prediction was premature—too optimistic by ten years. He may have written in a hurry, since things were rushed. In the same letter, Adams warned his wife, "If the Enemy come to Boston again, fly with your little ones all of them to Philadelphia. But they [the British] will scarcely get to Boston, this Campaign."

English dictionaries through the sixteenth century

With the invention of the printing press, dictionaries proliferated along with other books. The earliest print dictionaries in English date from 1440 to 1500. They were translating aids, bilingual rather than monolingual; of the five earliest dictionaries or vocabularies in England, two were Latin-English, two were English-Latin, and the other dictionary translated French—Caxton's *Vocabulary in French and English*. None of them included *infringe*, either as a main entry or to define other words. Of the five, only one included an entry for either infringing or abridging. Only the English-to-Latin *Promptorium Parvulorum*, c. 1440, contained an entry for *abridge*, concisely translated—"abbryggen: *Abbreuio*."[22] There might be reasons why an English author writing in Latin in 1440, and needing a translating dictionary, would want to look up *abridge*. Would-be authors had their opportunity, since the book was printed at least six times by 1528. An English dictionary definition for *infringe* is not found in print before 1500.

It remained hard to find in the early sixteenth century. Only two definitions for *infringe* appeared in English dictionaries for the next thirty-five years. Both are intriguing. One appeared in Wynken de Worde's 1532 edition of the Latin-to-English dictionary *Hortus Vocabulorum* (garden of vocabulary), a much-valued manuscript dating back to 1430 and first printed in 1500. The *Hortus Vocabulorum* had an entry for *infringe*, but with no English definition or translation for the entry. Instead de Worde gave the Latin word a Latin definition: "Infringo/gis. *[in]frigendo illudere*."[23] Figuratively this translates 'to roll over and play dead,' as one would say about an inert or useless authority figure, a sleeping judge.

Probably *infringere* was seldom translated into English because it was not considered a hard word. The Latin for *infringe* would lend itself to easy understanding even for non-Latin readers. Still, it is interesting to find this cryptic gloss of the word in 1532, at a critical time of high tensions in Henry VIII's court, squeezed toward the margin of the page. The original looks as though someone had hesitated to translate *infringo* too directly or too clearly.

Just one other English definition for infringement appeared in the same period: in 1530, in John Palsgrave's massive English-French dictionary, *L'esclarcissement de la langue francoyse*. The well-connected Palsgrave, a Londoner who tutored Henry VIII's sister Mary in French, produced an enormous scholarly work, the high-water mark for English-French dictionaries for a century. A rarity among early dictionary authors, Palsgrave gave ample scope to *infringe*. It appeared under the archaic spelling *refrynge*—"I Refrynge I breake up agayne ie infringe."[24] Palsgrave provided a colorful illustration, interesting in the context of the court of Henry VIII, and translated it into French: "I am nat aboute nor neuer was to refrynge your lybertyes Ie ne taiche poynt ne ne tachoye iamays dinfringer voz libertez." Palsgrave also used *infringe* in French to translate and clarify the English word *break*:

> I Breake my Superiors comaundment/ [. . .] que *ienfraigne, enfraindre* [. . .] you haue broken your princes commaundement: Vous aues *enfraynt*, vous aues transgress, vous aues irrite le comandement de vostre prince.

Palsgrave thus not only defined the word infringe but used it to define another word in a separate entry, using two different French forms of the word to do so.

Palsgrave also defined abridge, but only in its editorial sense—"Abridge or make short a thing"—translated "abrege." Palsgrave's 1530 *L'esclarcissement* was thus the first English dictionary to define both *abridge* and *infringe* in some form. Palsgrave was drawn upon by compilers of English-French dictionaries for more than a century, but the dictionary was not re-published until the nineteenth century, partly because its size made it expensive.

One other English dictionary also defined abridgement in the same period, and only one—a 1527 law dictionary by barrister, printer, and author John Rastell. This was the *Exposicions of the termys of the law of England*, later better known as *Les Termes de la Ley*. Rastell's first edition contained the French and Latin used in legal writing of the time (Law French and Law Latin). Rastell did not include a definition for *infringe*. But he explained fully the entry "Abridgement of a plaint or demaund":

> Abridgement of a plaint or demaund is wher one bringeth an Assise, writte of dower, writte of warde, or such lyke, [. . .] then the plaintif or demandant, may abridge hys plaint or demaund to that parcel, that is to say, he may leave that part out and pray that the tenaunt shall aunsweare the rest to which he hath not yet pleded any thing.
>
> [. . .] and notwithstanding the demandant hath abridged his plaint or demaund in part, yet the writte remaineth good stil, de libero tenemento for the rest.[25]

The definition remained constant for the next century. In 1530, Rastell's son William, also a barrister, added an English translation to the dictionary. Its popularity and use are thoroughly attested; the dictionary went through seven editions by 1576. A landmark in English lexicography as well as law, it went through 29 editions over 292 years, with a last American edition in 1819.

There had been earlier continental dictionaries of civil law, but the *Termes de la Ley* was the first in English. As legal historians point out, the law dictionary preceded by a decade Sir Thomas Elyot's *Dictionarie* of 1538, regarded as the first general dictionary printed in English. "Rastell's work

[. . .] was the first of its kind to appear in England and probably had as long a life as any other English law book."[26] Later augmented by expanded antiquarian and historical explanations, it became the standard reference work in Anglo-Norman for law students. Following in the great footsteps of William Caxton as well as the giant footprint of civil law, Rastell wrote that he had translated the French himself.[27]

Likely it is not coincidental that Rastell had published an abridgement of English statute law before publishing his dictionary. Abridging the statutes would alert him to the need for defining law terms. Abridging might even remind him to include an entry for *abridgement*. Rastell also produced a practical compilation of legal forms, *Collection of Entrees: of Declarations*, edited and re-published by his son. Thomas Jefferson owned the *Collection*.[28] So did John Adams, whose copy is in the Adams holdings in the Boston Public Library.

Despite the differences separating the three priceless early sixteenth-century dictionaries from de Worde, Rastell, and Palsgrave, the entries using the terms *abridge* or *infringe* have a common denominator. All three dictionaries defined the terms in ways that connect them with their future use in public policy and governance.

Dictionaries and ordinary use

During the rest of the sixteenth century, England under the Tudors produced quite a few dictionaries. Most served as translating aids, some for Latin and some for vernaculars, mainly French and Spanish. Three patterns emerge in the sixteenth-century English dictionaries. First, none of the friendly aids to travelers defined either *infringe* or *abridge*. Second, if the terms were defined, it was only in scholarly dictionaries or law dictionaries. And third, only the law dictionaries defined abridge in the public-policy sense.

Naturally, the sixteenth-century dictionaries reflect sixteenth-century geopolitics. Palsgrave's French-English dictionary appeared on the market in England the year Francis I declared French rather than Latin the national language of France (1530). Two years later, Giles Du Wes' *Introductory* for French came out.[29] Henry VIII and the Boleyn faction at court sometimes pursued warmer relations with France—where Anne Boleyn, fluent in French, had served as lady-in-waiting—to counterbalance European alliances of Spain, the Papacy, and the Holy Roman Empire. Du Wes did not define *infringe* or *abridge* in French or English.

The sixteenth-century dictionaries provide information on social history as well as on political history. Given their trove of insights into what the authors perceived as audience, need, or market demand, their inclusion or omission of words provides an index to usage. The author picked and chose according to what he deemed useful for a British citizen dealing with other nations. Some were intended to make Britons better acquainted with each other. In 1547 William Salesbury styled his *Dictionary in English and Welsh* "necessary to all suche Welshemen as will spedly learne the englyshe tongue thought unto the kynges majestie very mete to be sette forthe to the use of his graces subjectes in Wales."[30] Dedicated to Henry VIII and produced at the king's behest, the dictionary followed the new Wales laws of 1535 and 1542. Its purpose was to help Henry and Wales by bringing the Welsh into a sense of nationhood with the English; Salesbury included "a little treatyse" on English pronunciation of the letters of the alphabet, further to help the Welsh speak English.

Salesbury's dictionary is one of few original sources and is one of the best sources for sixteenth-century Welsh. It also contains valuable information about contemporaneous daily life. Partly because Salesbury was catering to his audience, partly because courtly words were often French-Latin imports, it tends toward the homespun. Henry VIII may have been focused on enabling the Welsh to understand English laws, but the un-alphabetized pages of Salesbury's dictionary do not expound law terminology. Instead, they run columns of simple Welsh like the words for "blacke bery" and "a hammer," translated into English. At times the dictionary has the flavor of J. R. R. Tolkien's Hobbiton, with kitchen nouns and food nouns joining reduplicative English translations for Welsh words like *smoke* and *smolder*. Should a Welsh citizen visiting London want to order breakfast, Salesbury translates the Welsh phrase for "colloppes and egges"—loosely, bacon and eggs—and elsewhere translates "collops" and "An egge," the latter twice. Salesbury must have warmed to his task. In a little flourish, his last entry is "The ende" in Welsh, translated into English. Notwithstanding English laws for Wales and the imprimatur of Henry VIII, Salesbury did not include *infringe* or abridge. The dictionary did not define either willful violation of law or moderating a privilege by degrees. Predictably, Henry VIII's laws did not entirely transmute the Welsh populace into Englishness.[31]

Several sixteenth-century English translating dictionaries were anonymous. One was the 1550 *Very Necessary Boke both in Englyshe & in Frenche wherein you mayste learne to speake & wryte Frenche truly in a litle space*, a short English-to-French dictionary. The unknown author published under the young Edward VI on the throne in England and Henry II in France. The *Very Necessary Boke* included less vocabulary than Palsgrave's massive work twenty years earlier but was far more portable and affordable, to aid English merchants and other travelers to France. The author tried to kill two birds with one stone; along with the language lessons, he provided several pages as a "boke of Courtesy," a string of etiquette reminders for English travelers, translated into French on alternate lines. With an eye to the vaunted polish and sophistication of Paris, he relayed simple advice like "Cut not thy breed to thynne"—to keep sopped-up gravy from dribbling off the table, into the lap, or down the chin. In mnemonic rhymes, Englishmen traveling in France are advised, for example, not to double-dip at the communal table —"The morsel that thou begynnest to touch /Cut it clene, and not to moch." The helpful dictionary did not include *infringe* or *abridge*. The merchant's friend, it was not the legislator's friend, the jurist's friend, or the ruler's friend—aside from facilitating commerce profitable to the crown.

Dictionary publishing likewise reflected the temper of the moment when relations between England and Spain occasionally warmed up, or officially warmed up. Two English-Spanish dictionaries came out—the *Book of English and Spanish*, and *A Very Profitable Boke to Learn* [. . .] *English and Spanish*—when Mary Tudor married Philip of Spain in 1554. Both were anonymous; the omission of an author's name may have reflected the widespread suspicion about the Spanish marriage, if not doubts about Mary's ill-fated reign. Like the English-French dictionaries, the English-Spanish dictionaries were portable, lightweight, and accessible. Word lists in the scantier *Boke of Englysshe and Spanysshe* are short. Prevalent religious terms are translated into Spanish. So are some terms from government— "treason," "To make peace"—and several from commerce—"A knave," "Companies," and "knavery." Longer, more colorful segments translate commercial items of trade, merchandise or cargo such as spices— "Incense," "Nutmegges," "Cynamom." The more interesting *Very Profitable Book* tried to live up to its title. Short, simple English dialogues (colloquia) are paired in left-to-right columns with their Spanish translation: "I will. Gyve me money." "I cannot [give] it for that price." The dialogue also includes "You offer me losse" and "You offer to litle money." The next entry pursues the issue, translated, "I will shewe you an other sorte, which I will sell, for lesse price. But it is not always profitable to consider the lessar price. There is nothyng better, than to buie that is good." Neither book included *infringe* or *abridge*.

Commerce between England and main trading partner France fluctuated over the century. Relations between English Protestants and French Huguenots involved commerce as well as religion, and the commerce included book publishing, which increased when the Company of Stationers was chartered in 1557 and when Elizabeth I ascended the throne in 1558. A spate of English-French dictionaries appeared in the 1570s, after the Protestant Henry III of Navarre married the French king's sister in 1572 and became heir to the throne of France (pledging to convert to Catholicism), and after the St. Bartholomew's Day massacre of French Huguenots in August 1572 intensified sympathy for French Protestants among English Protestants. Huguenot refugees in London joined the ranks of dictionary authors.

Under Elizabeth I, dictionaries published in England were no longer anonymous. Some contemporaneous dictionaries on the continent were anonymous, as were some published later in England under the Stuarts, but whether because of Elizabeth's encouragement or because of the new Stationers' Register, Elizabethan authors seem to have been willing to define terms—something that became an issue under James I—and to put their names to their work. Understandably, some of the names were anglicized. Huguenot refugee Claude de Sainliens, living in London, became Hollyband or Holyband and Latinized his first name to Claudius. He produced the *French School-maister* in 1573, *A Plaine Pathway to the French Tongue* in 1575, and the *French Littelton* in 1576.

Holyband's *Plaine Pathway* was another short, portable reference work that tried to live up to its title. As in a guide book, chapter titles indicate use for travel and commerce, providing French translations for "to demaund the waye," and "Of the Inne or lodging." The *Plaine Pathway* has a laudably clear layout, with French and English translations on facing pages or in facing columns. The readability carries over into the vocabulary lists and short samples of business conversation. The book also included a section of sample business letters, a sixteenth-century version of Microsoft templates. One form letter begins,

> Welbeloved brother, it may please you to send me by the first Ship that you shall finde sayling heatherwardes 7. pieces of grene velvets [. . .] with 5. pieces of unwatred chamblets, fourthermore one bousayne of pieces of linnen cloth [. . .] with advertising me of the price and cost, and I will paye and content you agayne, I have sent you long agoe the pepper, suger, and cloves that you demanded of me by your last letter together.

For writing "To a debtour," the template begins,

> Sir Thomas my welbeloved frend after my humble commendations this present shalbe to beseache you earnestly that it please you quickly without more delay that you will send me by the expresse bearer hereof the two hundred crownes of golde that you know to be dew unto me for because that I have necessarily to do there with.

None of Holyband's dictionaries contained an entry for forms of *infringe* or *abridge*. Nor did the next English-French dictionaries, by Guillaume la Pichonnaye in 1576 and Jacques (James) Bellot in 1578.[32]

Publication of Spanish dictionaries and grammars did not revive until after the Armada was defeated in 1588. One, the influential *Bibliothecae Hispanicae* of 1591, was authored by Richard Perceval, ancestor of precisionist and pamphleteer John Perceval, quoted at the beginning of this book.[33] The ancestral Perceval had put his knowledge of Spanish to good use, from an English perspective; employed by Lord Burghley to spy on Spain, in 1586 he deciphered Spanish intelligence on planning the Armada. The earliest edition of Perceval's dictionary did not contain entries for either *infringe* or *abridge*. At the end of the century, John Minsheu's 1599 expanded edition of Perceval's Spanish-English, English-Spanish dictionary contains a full entry for *abridge*, and for *infringe* in English and Latin.[34] Minsheu also used *abridge* to translate and define several Spanish words for abbreviating or abstracting.

Richard Mulcaster's famous schoolbook, the *Elementarie*, in 1582, included entries for both *infringe* and *abridge*, but for spelling only, not for definition.[35] Reading sixteenth-century dictionaries makes clear that the developing English lexicon needed help with spelling; ordinary words could be spelled different ways, within the same book and sometimes on the same page. However, in the same colorful publishing universe, English was expanding its range, its comprehensiveness, and its contacts with other cultures, and the English lexicon flourished.

These English sixteenth-century dictionaries have in common their usability, portability, and accessibility. They were guides and translating aids, intended for a more general audience than a circle of scholars, clerics, or bibliophiles. Therefore, they provided snippets of useful, natural dialogue along with the vocabulary lists, intended for sixteenth-century businesspeople, distance learners engaged in what today might be called continuing education. They contain lessons for adult learners, teaching exercises without the classroom. Aids to scholarship are one thing; self-improvement is another. Oversimplifying somewhat, one difference between Palsgrave's ponderous 1530 English-French dictionary and the portable dictionaries for merchants and travelers later in the sixteenth century is the difference between dictionaries meant for reading, writing, or study, and dictionaries meant for speaking. Until almost the end of the sixteenth century, the latter do not include either *infringe* or *abridge*. Throughout the sixteenth century, the two words were not the language of ordinary conversation but—where they appeared at all—mainly of written discourse, including the discourse of law.

The one partial exception to the over-all pattern was translating dictionaries for Italian. Both *abridge* and *infringe* were used in dictionary entries to explain or translate Italian words. Perhaps because Italian was the Romance language closest to Latin, the language of law and the church, some Italian translators also provided entries for the two terms themselves, late in the century. John Rider's English-Italian dictionary in 1589 contained comprehensive entries for both terms as well as using *abridge* to translate other words.[36] John Florio's Italian-English dictionary in 1598 used *abridge* to translate other words, without including an entry for *abridge* itself in Italian, but Florio did provide an entry for *infringe* in Italian as well as using it to translate other words.[37] The concepts were clear enough to use in translating, even when they were not particularly current in English.

Dictionaries and scholarship

Aside from the partial exceptions mentioned, the only dictionaries defining either *infringe* or *abridge* as entries in the sixteenth century were dictionaries for scholars or law dictionaries. The next prominent scholarly works after Palsgrave's French dictionary in 1530 appeared in 1552, Richard Huloet's English-Latin dictionary and Robert Estienne's three-language dictionary of English, Latin and French. The two 1552 dictionaries continue the early pattern for Latin dictionaries in English: Huloet's English-to-Latin dictionary did have an entry for *abridge*, while Estienne's Latin-to-English dictionary did not. (Again, *abridge* was not a word in Latin, as Robert Ainsworth later pointed out.) Estienne's large three-language dictionary was particularly influential, as its author was from a prominent publishing family and founded a publishing house. While it has no entry for *abridge*, it does translate the Latin *infringere* into brief English and French: "to breake. *Rompre*."[38]

Huloet's English-to-Latin *Abecedarium* included both *abridge* and *infringe*. Huloet's and Estienne's mid-century dictionaries demonstrate that size is only one difference between the portable manuals for travelers and these larger works. While Huloet's definitions are terse, the entries for *infringe* as a headword and using it to define other words cover the ground:

"Infringe. Luke [look] in Breake.

Infrynge a custome. Soluere morem.

Infrynge a lawe. Legem refigere, uel rumpere uel uiolare, Vide in breake."

"Breake in pieces. [. . .] infringo, is."[39]

Like Dr. Johnson two centuries later, Huloet in 1552 could use *infringe* to define other words without spending much space on defining the word itself; it was self-evidently understandable.

The dictionaries for English and Latin share several patterns. While they tend to contain scant information on the two words, where they include either word, they attest its clarity. Peter Levens' dictionary of 1570 is another English-Latin dictionary that includes an entry for *abridge* but not one for *infringe*. On the other hand, Thomas Thomas's Latin-English dictionary of 1587 has an entry for *infringe*, does not have an entry for *abridge*, but uses *abridge* to translate other words. The same is true for his 1596 dictionary.[40] The English-Latin dictionaries continued to translate *abridge* only, and the Latin-English dictionaries continued to translate *infringe* only. All the early dictionaries for English and Latin separate *to infringe* from *to abridge*. No early dictionary connects them, let alone as synonyms.

Law dictionaries

Throughout the sixteenth century, general dictionaries defined *abridge* only as editing. English general dictionaries did not yet use *abridge* in the context of political philosophy. During the sixteenth century, however, the word in dictionaries approached political philosophy through its use in law. The legal meanings of *abridge* were important—and still are—and law dictionaries contained definitions significant for public policy.

Reference books were significant and influential in law. The earliest in English was Rastell's *Termes de la Leye* in 1527, previously discussed, which then reappeared in several more editions. In 1590, attorney William West published the *Symbolaeographia*.[41] Not exactly a dictionary, the *Symbolaeographia* has been considered a guide to legal forms, a book of conveyancing precedents, and the standard work on forms of fines. By whatever name, it was a popular and widely used reference work, re-published several times by the end of the 1590s. Shakespeare's last will and testament was modeled on one of West's forms. Over four hundred years, countless law students have read West's use of "abridged" to define a *release*.

> Releases. What a Release is. A Release is an instrument whereby estates, rights, titles, entries, actions, and other things be some times extinguished, sometimes transferred, sometimes abridged, and sometimes enlarged, of which see these examples.

(The *OED* cites West to illustrate *abridge*, but from an edition four years later than West's first edition quoted here.)

However, West did not define *abridge* as a headword. His reference work is another example that includes the word only to define other terms. West's matter-of-fact use of "abridged" corroborates the sixteenth-century understanding of abridgement, attests that clearly it was understood. West's use also corroborates that unlike infringement, it was not synonymous with offense or abuse. It represented not a destructive constraint but acts necessary, acceptable, or practical. Like the law dictionaries, West's book does not define the word *infringe*.

Rastell and West's use of *abridged* in law aligns with later use connecting it to rights and powers. Earlier, abridging could be damaging, wielded by the powerful, like the abridging by Chaucer's cruel lordships, or Gower's maxim that a ruler's generosity should not be abridged, or provisions that a patent or charter not be abridged after the fact. Where punishment or obligation was abridged, on the other hand, obviously the abridgement was beneficial. It was desirable that Satan's power be abridged, in late medieval writing; it was desirable that the power of tyrants or of monarchs should be abridged, in early modern writing. After Rastell and West, by the time Hobbes, Locke, and Hume used the term, it was desirable that the absolute rights of the individual in a state of nature be abridged. By the apogee of the Enlightenment, the course of *abridge* made it increasingly secular, practical, and ordinary, as in law dictionaries and then in political philosophy. Through all centuries, the broad underlying concept is protection.

James I and *Ignoramus*: John Cowell's *Interpreter*

While defining terms, dictionaries also reflect usage. Either way, they shed light on the public discourse. Reading a dictionary showed Britons how they were speaking to each other; if common language did not necessarily lead to common views, the dictionaries still reinforced a sense of being on the same page. In the sixteenth and seventeenth centuries, dictionaries for ordinary use paralleled use of the vernacular bible. The individual's use of dictionaries is rooted small-scale in a principle of applying individual reason, of looking things up for self-help or self-improvement, an unfiltered grass-roots auto-didacticism, analogous to an individual's consulting scripture. Many dictionaries were published during the Reformation and throughout the seventeenth century, and dictionary entries had heft even when kept as short and neutral as possible.

From the monarch's perspective, dictionaries including law dictionaries could also seem threatening. They could become politically charged in tense times, as in England during the seventeenth century, both before and after the nation beheaded King Charles I in 1649. The century got off to a particularly bad start for dictionary author John Cowell (1554-1611). In 1610, Cowell was hauled before the Star Chamber over his law dictionary, *The Interpreter*.

Cowell is a sad case whose story illustrates the cynical axiom that no good deed goes unpunished. The full title of Cowell's book ran,

> *The Interpreter* Or Booke Containing the Signification of Words: Wherein is Set Forth the True Meaning of All, or the Most Part of Such Words and Termes, as are Mentioned in the Law Writers, or Statutes of This Victorious and Renowned Kingdom, Requiring Any Exposition or Interpretation. A Work not Onely Profitable, but Necessary for Such as Desire Throughly to be Instructed in the Knowledge of Our Laws, Statutes, and Other Antiquities.[42]

To abide by the law, people living under it must know the law; the English principle goes back to Alfred the Great. It was boosted even by Henry VIII, no democrat, through Salisbury's dictionary for Henry's Welsh citizens.

Cowell was a professor of civil law—a 'civilian'—an earnest Cambridge scholar who undertook his dictionary project at the request of his Anglican bishop. Supporting the position that civil law, canon law, and common law were not necessarily at odds, he defined terms from all three.[43] Theoretically inoffensive, the project of defining the vocabulary of government, law, and politics can be dicey during conflict between branches of government, and Cowell strove—unfortunately for himself—to make his definitions clear, fair, and comprehensive. As a result, his dictionary provoked a chilling admonition from James I, via the royal spokesman, that it was "dangerous to submit the power of a king to definition."[44] Worse, stumbling into the ongoing crossfire between crown and Parliament, the author displeased Parliament as well as the monarch. The House of Commons charged that his definitions of *Parliament*, *King*, and *Prerogative* amounted to absolute sovereignty for the king. Cowell also incurred the wrath of Sir Edward Coke (1552-1634), the legendary barrister who at the time was Chief Justice of the Common Pleas. Books were licensed by the crown, and Coke tried to get Cowell in trouble with the king. James saved Cowell from being impeached by Parliament and executed—but suppressed the dictionary. The day after the king's proclamation, according to lore, Cowell's dictionary was publicly burned by the royal hangman.

The "Proclamation touching D. Cowels booke called the Interpreter" was issued March 25, 1610. Nowadays, the proclamation would be said to have a chilling effect. In seventeenth-century Britain, there was such a thing as bad publicity, especially in the person of the public hangman. Adding to the emphasis, most royal proclamations came out as "By the King,"—who, again, licensed publication of books—as James told Parliament in 1621; "Most of them myself doth dictate every word. Never any proclamation of state and weight which I did not direct."[45]

The proclamation began with wholesale criticism of writers. Like other public officials complaining about 'the media' over the last fifty years, in tone if not in diction, James lashed out against "such an itching in the tongues and pennes of most men, as nothing is left unsearched to the bottome, both in talking and writing."[46] He directed his fire particularly against political inquiry:

> And Therefore, it is no wonder, that men in these our dayes doe not spare to wade in all the deepest mysteries that belong to the persons or State of Kings or Princes, that are gods upon Earth: since we see, (as we have said) that they spare not God himselfe.

In keeping with James' preference for mysteries, the proclamation does not define the "State of Kings or Princes," or the difference between their persons and their state, or the description of monarchs as "gods upon Earth."

From inveighing against writers in general, the king went on to criticize unauthorized writers, in tone if not in vocabulary like more recent public figures attacking bloggers or academics. As James recognized, the threat was that such writers might have influence;

Whereupon it cannot otherwise fall out, but that when men goe out of their element, and meddle with things above their capacitie; themselves shall not onlely goe astray, and stumble in darknesse, but will mislead also divers others with themselves into many mistakings and errours.

Here the king narrowed the focus again. Having moved from criticism of writers in general to criticism of under-qualified writers meddling above their pay grade, he moved against the author in his sights: "The proofe whereof wee have lately had by a Booke written by Doctour Cowell, called THE INTERPRETER." James' problem with Cowell's law dictionary was that it defined terms, including terms relating to Parliament and "the supreme power of this Crown,"

In some things disputing so nicely upon the Mysteries of this our Monarchie, that it may receive doubtfull interpretations: yea in some poynts very derogatory to the supreme power of this Crowne: In other cases mistaking the true state of the Parliament of this Kingdome, and the fundamentall Constitutions and priviledges thereof: And in some other points speaking unreverently of the Common Law of England, and of the works of some of the most famous and ancient Judges therein.[47]

The proclamation was sweeping, to say the least. Speaking unreverently of the law is something that Britons and Americans traditionally take pride in, and generally it has not been outlawed aside from restricting jokes about airport security.

"Wherefore," James moved to suppress Cowell's book;

We doe hereby not onely prohibite the buying, uttering or reading of the sayd Books, but doe also will and straitly commaund all and singular persons whatsoever, who have or shall have any of them in their hands or custody,

to turn the dictionary over to the authorities. Anyone who had copies of the book was to turn them over to the Lord Mayor of London if a city resident, or to the local sheriff if a resident of a county, or to the Chancellor or Vice-chancellor if "in the two universities" (Oxford and Cambridge). Presumably the two bastions of the free marketplace of ideas would convey the offending books to the hangman. Cowell resigned his Cambridge professorship and died the following year.

Although Cowell was a Cambridge scholar and had been Vice-Chancellor at Cambridge in 1604 and 1605, the university seems not to have resisted the proclamation. A few years later, however, the campus took scholarly revenge for the attack on one of its own. When James I visited Cambridge in 1615, students performed a play for him titled *Ignoramus*. The title was a little law-student joke, playing on the word for an indictment not true-billed by a grand jury. At the time, a grand jury was empaneled from local citizens, who might know circumstances relevant to a case. An indictment not considered worthy of proceeding to trial would come back to prosecutors marked "Ignoramus"—'Uh, we don't know about this.'[48] In the skit performed for the king, "Most of the technical phrases of the common law used in the play were those explained in Cowell's *Interpreter.*"[49] Furthermore, the lead character, 'Ignoramus,' was played by a student imitating Chief Justice Coke, who dressed "like Chief Justice Coke and cutt his beard like him and feigned his voyce."[50] The king like the audience enjoyed the play—he was displeased with Coke—and the word *ignoramus* passed into common use, in the sense still used four hundred years later.

Cowell's book also lived on. Despite the proclamation, copies of the first edition exist; the bonfire did not get all of them. Apparently, trying to keep students at Oxford and Cambridge from reading it went about as well as trying to keep them from reading Machiavelli a century earlier.[51] Later editions of Cowell's dictionary appeared at significant junctures. In 1637, the year the English Civil War began, when Charles I tried to impose the English Prayer Book on religious services in Scotland, the *Interpreter* was reprinted twice. Another reprint came out after the second Civil War, in 1658, the year Protector Oliver Cromwell died. In 1672, Thomas Manley of the Middle Temple published an enlarged edition of the *Interpreter*, confirming its acceptance in the legal profession. This one was reprinted or published in new editions in 1684, 1701, 1708, and 1727. The final 1727 edition was owned by John Adams and is housed in the Adams collection in the Boston Public Library. In fact, Cowell's dictionary was so useful that it was already in its second edition by the time James issued his proclamation. It went through ten editions by the early eighteenth century.

Cowell's actual definitions show that the author was dealt with unjustly. The House of Commons specifically objected to three entries, "Subsidy, Parliament, and Prerogative, in that booke of his called the Interpreter."[52] One term especially—subsidy—concerned the Commons, which spelled out the potential problem: "That the King might make lawes of hymself, and demand subsidies *de jure* without consent of Parliament." Here Cowell ran afoul of Parliament but not of the king; it is unlikely that James would find this concept problematic, and the royal proclamation against Cowell did not mention "subsidy."

Yet Cowell defined *subsidy* as "assessed by Parlament," not by royal dictate. It was Cowell's next comment that offended Commons;

> Some hold opinion, that this subsidie is graunted by the subject to the Prince, in recompence or consideration, that whereas the Prince of his absolute power, might make lawes of himselfe, he doth of favour admit the consent of his subjects therein, that all things in their owne confession may be done with the greater indifferencie.

Cowell did not uphold the king as a subsidy-receiving god on earth. With the cautious "Some hold opinion," Cowell nods to the sovereign to avoid overstating Parliamentary power, but it is subjects who grant subsidy to the king. The crown admits "the consent of his subjects therein" for the sake of the commonwealth; Cowell was merely applying the traditional concept of rational authority, delegated from populace to chief executive. Farther along, he affirmed Parliament's power to determine the tax rate, and by law: "whence you may gather that there is no certaine rate, but even as the two houses shall thinke good to conclude. Subsidie is in the statute of the land, sometime confounded with custome."

Unfortunately for Cowell, Commons seized on one clause—"whereas the Prince of his absolute power, might make lawes of himselfe"—to attack him. The proclamations do often look like ordinances by the king, or at best one-man resolutions by the king. Many royal proclamations concerned finance. Some were reasonable—edicts after the Great Fire that London buildings should be constructed of stone or brick, attempts to rein in counterfeiting and tampering with the currency, an attempt to protect food supply for the hungry by prohibiting the manufacture of starch (which used up potatoes, although the starch manufacturers claimed to be using only peels and scrap).[53] Defining touchy terms of economics and power, and following his training, Cowell included all sides in his definitions—maximizing his exposure to jeopardy in the ongoing battle between Parliament and king.

An astute defense of Cowell came from a sympathizer early in the eighteenth century. As the anonymous editor of the 1708 edition prefaces the *Interpreter*,

> I know of no offence, that was immediately taken at this first Edition: tho' it was infinitely hard to speak of Prerogative, Property, Government, Laws, and mutual Rights, with that caution and regard, as not to make some to murmur, and others to insult; especially where Parties and their Passions were even then prevailing.[54]

Much of the difficulty arose from Cowell's conscientious effort to be clear and balanced. Cowell's definition of the king's prerogative, for example, was near-fatally clear:

> Prerogative of the King (*praerogativa regis*) is that especiall power, preeminence, or priviledge that the King hath in any kinde, over and above other persons, and above the ordinarie course of the common lawe, in the right of his crowne.

As with some of Cowell's other language, the definition might seem self-evident: to be 'prerogative,' a power or privilege must be 'especiall'; otherwise, it wouldn't be prerogative. Cowell was defining on the sharp points of two horns of a dilemma; either the king is above the laws, or he is not an absolute king. But neither this simple observation nor five pages of careful discussion of royal prerogative made Cowell safe. Either the king is above Parliament, or he is not an absolute monarch; the *Interpreter* summed up the English Civil War, the grounds of the seventeenth-century revolution, in a nutshell, and caught (as Hamlet puts it) "between the pass and fell incensed points of mighty opposites," Cowell paid the price. Later, other parties, outside crown and Parliament, were more humane and more grateful. Publication and sales of Cowell's useful dictionary continued for more than a century, and as his unnamed 1708 editor points out, Cowell was buried with honor under the altar in the chapel of Trinity Hall, a benefactor to the university.[55]

One thing the unhappy object lesson of Cowell shows is that people paid attention to dictionaries in the seventeenth century. The king, the Chief Justice, and Parliament paid explicit attention to Cowell's dictionary. In fact, the legal profession itself adopted it—somewhat ironically, given Cowell's severe legal difficulties. Cowell was not an outlier.

Like other law dictionaries in Cowell's lifetime, Cowell's *Interpreter* did not define *infringe* in any form. Cowell defined only words "requiring any Exposition or Interpretation," as he said, and neither his nor other law dictionaries treated infringement as requiring exposition. That a word like *infringe* is missing from a dictionary of legal terms might seem anomalous, but again, the omission signals that the concept was clear enough not to require defining. However, Cowell provided an extensive entry for *abridge*:

> *Abridge* (*Abbreuiare*) cometh of the French (*abreger*) and in one generall language signifieth as much as to make shorter in words, holding still the whole substance. But in the common lawe it seemeth (at the least for the most part) to be more particularly used for making a declaration or count shorter by subtracting or severing some of the substance therein comprised. As: a man is said to abridge his plaint in an Assize. So that here (*abridger*) is not (*contrahere*) but rather *subtrahere*. Termes of the lawe. *Broke. titulo, Abridgement*. and *anno* 21. *Hen*.8.*cap*.3. Of this the Civilians have no use, by reason of certaine cautelous clauses, they ordinarily have at the end of every position or article of their libell or declaration to this effect. By vertue of which clauses the plaintiffe faileth not in the end by any over or under demand, neither is driven to begin his action againe, but obtaineth for so much as he proveth to be due, though not to the heithe of his demaund.

Cowell's definition is a fuller version of Rastell's, which it contains. Cowell gives the sense of *abridge* in "generall language" first, then moves on to the legal sense, and then touches on the possible legal outcome of abridgement—that a plaintiff might obtain a partial victory without having to start over. Despite Cowell's legal difficulties, nothing suggests that the definition of abridgement troubled either king or Parliament. The reasonable underlying idea that we don't have to go back to the egg to guide every action in a law case was apparently not considered subversive.

Seventeenth century

Ironically, despite Cowell's problems, English dictionaries developed expansively over the rest of the seventeenth century and began to resemble modern dictionaries. More English-to-English (monolingual) dictionaries appeared, alongside the translating dictionaries. Among the most prominent were Robert Cawdrey's *Table Alphabeticall of Hard Usual English Words* in 1604; John Bullokar's *English Expositor* in 1616; Henry Cockeram's *English Dictionarie: Or an Interpreter of Hard English Words* in 1623; Thomas Blount's *Glossographia* in 1656; Edward Phillips' *New World of English Words* in 1658 (plagiarizing Blount's dictionary); and Elisha Coles' *English Dictionary* in 1676. All were drawn upon by subsequent dictionary authors. All included some form of both *infringe* and *abridge*, although not quite all defined both terms as entries.

Robert Cawdrey's *Table Alphabeticall of Hard Usual English Words* in 1604, often billed as the first non-Latin English dictionary, had clear if short definitions for both *abridge* and *infringe*: "abbridge" is "to shorten, or make short"; *infringe* is "to breake, to make weake, or feeble."[56] Cawdrey listed *abbridge* jointly with *abbreuiat* (abbreviate), defining both at once. That Cawdrey included both *infringe* and *abridge* suggests both his thoroughness and a change in the times. His main sources were word lists from the sixteenth century, and the model most closely followed was Edmund Coote's *English Schoole-Maister* of 1596.[57] It had no entry for *infringe*. Coote's book did include "abbridge," defined with utmost concision. For *abridge*, "see abbreuiat" (abbreviate); for "Abbreuiat," the entry just above it, the definition is "shorten."[58] Locke later criticized authors who defined words by providing synonyms rather than definitions, but the practice was widespread.

Like dictionaries before and after, those of the seventeenth century distinguish between the two key words. When *infringe* and *abridge* appear in seventeenth-century dictionaries, they appear separately. As in earlier periods, some seventeenth-century dictionaries omitted one or the other. Bullokar's *English Expositor*, Cockeram's *English Dictionarie*, and Phillips' *New World of English Words* all appeared between 1616 and 1658. All three defined both *infringe* and *abridge*, with separate and distinct entries—short and minimal—for each.

The next major dictionary, Thomas Blount's *Glossographia* in 1656, did not include either word as a headword. However, Blount's dictionary does use *abridge*, not itself defined, to define related terms:

Abbreviator (Lat.) one that abridges or makes a brief draught of a thing. In Rome there are Officers belonging to the Pope called *Abbreviators de parco majori* (whose Office is to endite Letters at request of suppliants, which inditing is termed a rough draught, or copy of the Request) And *Abbreviators*, also *de parco minori*, whom the Italians call *Giannizzeri*, who also attend on the expedition of Letters, I. *Part Treasury of Times.*

Abbreviature (*abbreviatura*) a brief writing, an Abridgment or brief of a thing.[59]

Blount offered to interpret "all such hard words as are used in our refined English tongue," but Cawdrey, Bullokar, Cockeram, and Phillips also claimed to define 'hard words.' The difference is that Blount could bring specialized knowledge to bear; like Cowell earlier, he had legal training. In 1670, he published a scholarly law dictionary, *Nomo-Lexikon*, which like Cowell's offers the standard legal definition for *abridge* and no definition for *infringe*.[60]

Both of Blount's dictionaries contained more historical information and more references than other dictionaries at the time, a fact that partly explains why Edward Phillips, an unworthy nephew of John Milton, pirated both books. "A beggarly half-witted scholar, hir'd for the purpose by some of the law-booksellers," the aggrieved Blount described Phillips, "to transcribe that in four or five months, which cost me twice as many years in compiling." In revenge, or in self-defense, Blount brought out *A World of Errors Discovered* in Phillips' pirated dictionaries. It must have been some consolation to Blount that the book sold well. Blount needed to make a living as an author, since he was debarred from making a living through the legal profession; "though a barrister and a member of the Inner Temple, he was, as a Roman Catholic, prevented from practising at the Bar."[61]

The heated competition among authors arose from heated demand for books. British book publishing grew at a phenomenal rate during the century of revolution. In spite of—or because of—ongoing turmoil including civil wars, the book-buying public continued to grow as British population grew; towns, cities and the middle class grew; and commerce, exploration, and empire further extended the range of subjects. Pride in the English tongue manifested in a growing number of books on language, English, writing in English, and cleaning up English spelling, not an overnight process. Samuel Johnson called the growing communications industry in Britain the "superfoetation" of the press—a word that has not lasted but which celebrated immense development during Johnson's life. The development of a press prolific if not free was well under way, and dictionaries were a growing category of publishing. Aside from trends of British national pride, an interest in history, and steady interest in the vernacular, the language itself was growing; while jettisoning some archaisms, English vocabulary was augmented by developments in medicine and law among other fields. The Oxford English Dictionary has estimated that, from 1500 to mid-seventeenth century, the number of words in English doubled.

When Blount followed up his general dictionary in 1656 with a law dictionary in 1670, he was meeting a perceived need. His 1670 *Nomo-Lexikon* defined *abridge* differently from the earlier *Glossographia*.

Abridge (from the Fr. *Abreger*) to make shorter in words, holding still the whole substance: But in Law it seems to signifie, for the most part, the making a *Declaration* or *Count* shorter, by subtracting or severing some of its substance. For example, a Man is said to *abridge* his Plaint in an Assize [. . .]. The cause is, for that in such Writs the certainty is not set down, but they run in general. And though the Demandant hath *abridged* his Plaint or Demand in part, yet the Writ remains good still for the rest. *Brook, tit. Abridgment. An. 21 H. 8. cap. 3.*

Unlike his earlier entry on *abbreviate* for general use, Blount's definition of *abridge* for lawyers comes almost verbatim from other law dictionaries, including Rastell's 1527 *Exposition* and Cowell's 1607 *Interpreter*. Before producing his own law dictionary, Blount in 1667 had published a revised edition of Rastell's, which stayed in use; Blount's version of Rastell was reprinted in 1671 and 1685.

Like authors of law dictionaries before and after, Blount omitted any entry for *infringe*. Not until the eighteenth century did *infringe* appear as a main entry in a law dictionary. The omission might strike a reader today as odd; more recent law dictionaries include the term, although they mainly limit it to intellectual property. But the seventeenth-century lawyers were not alone. While more general dictionaries of the seventeenth century had begun to include an entry for *infringe*, often a terse entry of synonyms, several prominent dictionaries omitted it, including one praised by Locke as one of the best dictionaries of his time, the 1671 *Etymologicon Linguæ Anglicanæ* of Stephen Skinner. Again, neither the etymology nor the meaning of *infringe* seems to have needed clarification.

Remaining seventeenth-century English dictionaries include Phillips' *New World of English Words*, first published two years after Blount's work and drawing heavily upon it.[62] While Phillips' derivation of Blount was egregious, Phillips was following established tradition by treating previous dictionaries—including very recent ones—like a supply room with the door left open. "The student who is squeamish about plagiarism had simply better not study the old wordbooks, to which the concepts of plagiarism and literary property are hardly applicable. Dictionaries were gathered one from another."[63] Even so, Phillips' treatment of Blount was graceless. Phillips copied entries from Blount's dictionary, part of Blount's title, and parts of Blount's preface, and so soon after Blount's book that his would now violate trade practices as well as fair use. At least the ensuing print controversy livened up book sales.

Like other popular dictionaries, Phillips' went through multiple editions. Phillips' core definitions of *infringe* are like those earlier and later: "To Infringe, (properly to break to pieces) to violate, transgress, or break a Law, Custom, Privilege, etc."; "Infringement, such infringing, Violation, or Breach." Like Blount before him and Johnson after, Phillips used *infringe* to define other words including *contravene*—"to act contrary to an Agreement; to infringe, or break a Law"; and *violate*—"to infringe, breach, or transgress; to ravish, or force a Woman." The concept could hardly be mistaken for, or confused with, that of 'abridging.'

Abridging applied to editing. Phillips defined *abridge* as a synonym for *abbreviate*—"(Lat.) to abridge, to make short"—which like Cawdrey and Coote he uses circularly as a synonym for *abridge*—"To Abridge, (Fr.) to make short, to abbreviate." He also used *abridge* to define *contract*, *epitomize*, and *retrench*; for the last, "(Fr.) to cut off or abridge; to diminish, or lessen." Thus, Phillips' derivative dictionary, like dictionaries before and after, differentiated between *infringe* and *abridge* and further established the difference. Phillips did add some headwords not included by the authors he imitated most, including an archaic form of abridging—*bredgen*—"(old word) to abridge, to shorten."

The missing link: law dictionaries

As must be apparent by now, general dictionaries were being influenced by the law dictionaries. While the older law dictionaries did not explain the concept of infringement, they did articulate connections between different senses of the word *abridge* and explain its etymology. In the seventeenth century, law dictionaries began to intersect with other dictionaries dramatically. At the same time, from 1600 into the eighteenth century, the vocabulary for political issues in dictionaries began to emphasize a concept of liberty. The over-all pattern is simple, once you look at enough old dictionaries. In the 1600s, whenever a law dictionary connects the meaning of *abridge* with rights and powers, that dictionary will likely emphasize words for liberty. Blount's 1670 *Nomo-Lexikon* is an on-point example; it contains "liberty" at least 66 times and "liberties" at least nineteen times. The trend continued in later dictionaries.

Blount's law dictionary defined the headword *abridge* only as abridging a filing—shortening or condensing a plaint. However, the 1670, 1691, and 1717 editions of Blount's law dictionary also defined other words by referring explicitly to power or privilege "abridged," citing Magna Carta. Blount's re-published law dictionary is thus another example of using the word to define other words without defining it or without defining it in the same sense. Blount's dictionary also used the word *infringe* to define other entries, still with no entry for infringement itself. Again, infringement and abridgement must have seemed clear enough not to need defining, even to a dictionary author.

Furthermore, Blount's law dictionary marks a transition point. Where Blount uses "abridged" to define or explain other terms, abridging power or privilege takes on a favorable association. The definition of "County Court" includes a comment that the court "was abridged by *Magna Carta*."

"Entail" or fee tail "is abridged, curtailed, or limited, and tied to certain conditions." Statutes of Mortmain are "something abridged by" later laws, permitting donations to hospitals without a license of mortmain. Thus, Blount's dictionary marks an interim point joining the relatively neutral legal definition of abridgement, abridging a plaint, which had held constant since Rastell and West in the sixteenth century, and its favorable light in political philosophy in the seventeenth and eighteenth centuries. The uses in Blount seem to be partly related to very old senses in French feudal law. However, his sources included recent ones; Blount cited John Cowell many times and praised him.

As said, Blount's law dictionary was freely drawn on by Edward Phillips, and Phillips borrowed Blount's highlighting the word *liberty*. Phillips uses the word "liberty" at least ninety times in the *New World of English Words*, and "liberties" at least nineteen times, with the same definitions and with the same uses for *abridge*, in a favorable sense of abridging power. Blount's law dictionary was at least as influential as his English dictionary and was drawn on by later dictionary authors.

Blount and Phillips among others thus paved the way for Samuel Johnson, whose dictionary occasionally cites Blount for law words and cites Phillips many times. When Johnson also linked liberty with abridgement, following Blount and Phillips, the link was firmly established in English dictionaries. The difference between Blount in 1670 and Johnson in 1755 is that Johnson added a definition for abridgement in the Lockean sense of acceptably abridging individual liberty. Limitation of the king's prerogative, on behalf of subjects, was followed by voluntary limitation of individual prerogative, on behalf of fellow citizens.

Small wonder Dr. Johnson quoted and cited John Locke with enthusiasm. Locke was not only a famous philosopher and an author recommended by star poet and precisionist Alexander Pope, he was a major supporter of dictionaries. In fact, he was one seventeenth-century philosopher who gave dictionary authors an explicit thumbs-up. In "Some Thoughts Concerning Reading and Study for a Gentleman," Locke reminds himself, "There is another sort of books, which I had almost forgot, with which a gentleman's study ought to be well furnished, viz. dictionaries of all kinds."[64] He goes on to list authors and titles of fifteen reference books.

Eighteenth-century dictionaries before Samuel Johnson

At the beginning of the eighteenth century, a large new dictionary came out, the *Glossographia Anglicana Nova* of 1707. It was attributed to Thomas Blount—who had been dead for twenty-seven years—but was published anonymously.[65] Like Dr. Johnson's dictionary fifty years later, it used passages from prominent authors to illustrate the definitions. This was an innovation; law dictionaries had used citations from the beginning, but most general English dictionaries had not. Similarities between the *Glossographia* and Johnson's dictionary include the 1707 definition of *infringe*: "Infringe, (Lat.) to break to pieces, to break a Law, Custom, or Privilege." The reference to law, custom, and privilege is significant. Like Johnson later, the *Glossographia* also used *infringe* to define several other words having to do with rights and powers, including *contravene*—"to infringe or break a Law or Agreement"; the old Saxon word *Mundbretch*—"an Infringement of Privileges"; and *violate*—"(Lat.) to break, infringe, or deflower."

The *Glossographia* has no entry for *abridge*. However, it did define *abridgement* as a headword—"Abridgment, commonly signifies the same thing with Abreviation, which see." The *Glossographia Anglicana Nova* itself is called an "abridgment" on the title page. Without defining *abridge* itself, the dictionary also uses the term to define several other terms. "Abreviate" is defined as "to abridge or make short." Forms of *abridge* also define *retrench*—"to cut off, to abridge, diminish, or lessen"; an archaic Chaucerian word, *agrutched*; *commentary*—"a brief abstract, or historical abridgment of things"; *epitome*; and *extraction*.

The *Glossographia* also uses *abridge* to define terms in law. "Release, in Law, an Instrument whereby Estates, Rights, Titles, Entrys, Actions, and other things, are sometimes Extinguished, sometimes transferred, sometimes abridged and sometimes enlarged," repeats the definition in West's 1590 *Symbolaeographia*. As in older law dictionaries and legal handbooks, "Entayl, in Common Law, signifies Fee-Tail, or Fee intayled or abridged," and "Abridgment of a Plaint in Law, is when one part of the Plaintiff's Demand is left out, and it is pray'd that the Defendant may answer to the other." The distinction between infringing and abridging is as clear and consistent in 1707 as in Johnson's dictionary fifty years later.

The two other major dictionaries of the eighteenth century before Johnson were by John Kersey and Nathan Bailey. Kersey, a philologist, had authored a smaller *New English Dictionary* (bylined 'J.K.') in 1702; revamped and enlarged Edward Phillips' *New World of Words* in 1706; and produced his own *Dictionarium Anglo-Britannicum, or A General English Dictionary*, the first abridged dictionary, in 1708.[66] Kersey's big *General English Dictionary* defines *to infringe* as "to transgress, or break a Law, Privilege, Custom, &c." Like earlier dictionaries, it also uses infringement to define *to violate*—"to infringe, break, or transgress, to ravish, or force."

Kersey defines *to abridge* in editorial and legal contexts—"to shorten in Words, still retaining the Sense and Substance. In Law, to make a Declaration or Count shorter, by leaving out part of the Plaint or Demand." He includes the old *to bredgen*—"to abridge or shorten," and throws in the archaic *agrutched*—"abridged," as well as *to abbreviate*—"to abridge, or make short." Kersey had defined each word the same way in the 1706 Kersey-Phillips *New World of Words*, except that the definition of *infringe* retained Phillips' parenthetical "(properly to break to pieces)." Unlike Johnson's, Kersey's dictionaries did not define *abridge* as limiting rights, power, or privilege, whether favorably or unfavorably.

Nathan Bailey, who died in 1742, was the most important eighteenth-century lexicographer aside from Johnson. He published his first dictionary, the *Dictionarium Rusticum, Urbanicum & Botanicum*, in 1704, produced a popular *Universal Etymological English Dictionary* in 1721, and published the large *Dictionarium Britannicum* in 1730, further enlarged in 1736. All of Bailey's dictionaries were re-published in successive editions. Bailey's *Dictionarium* of 1730 defines *to infringe* like Kersey's dictionary before and Johnson's afterward: "to break a Law, Custom or Privilege."[67] *Violating* is defined alternatively as "infringing, transgressing, or breaking;" and "to force or ravish a Woman." Like Kersey, Bailey defined *abridge* in the *Dictionarium* only in the editorial and legal senses, not in connection with rights or powers. He also used forms of *abridge* in the editorial sense to define other words from editing.

In the larger *Universal Etymological English Dictionary* of 1737, Bailey added to definitions of *abridge* a further definition: "also to restrain a Person from some Liberty, &c. before enjoyed."[68] At this point, in dictionaries, the word *abridge* explicitly enters the realm of public policy, not just narrowly in law as in abridging a complaint but more broadly in the relationship between governing and governed. This was a further turning point in dictionary definitions of the concepts. Bailey retained the uses of *infringe* to define "contravene" and "violate."

By this time, Bailey had begun to draw upon law dictionaries for his general dictionary. Like the older law dictionaries and the anonymous *Glossographia*, he applies "abridged" to define *entail*, "or Fee entailed or abridged, by which means the heir is limited and tied up to certain Conditions." He also applies "abridged" to define *counties*, like the Counties Palatine, "the Jurisdiction of which was formerly very great, but their power now is very much abridged." Bailey had used the same example in his *Dictionarium*, but without defining the term *abridge* this way as an entry. Bailey's is another example among many, through the history of English dictionaries, of *abridge* or *infringe* used to define other words in a dictionary where either it is not listed as an entry itself, or its entry as a headword does not include the pertinent definition. The inconspicuous details give evidence of the usage of the two words.

Robert Ainsworth's *Latin Dictionary*

By 1736, translating the word *abridge* involved mistakes so typical that they drew corrections from Latin scholar Robert Ainsworth (1660-1743), author of the highly regarded, authoritative *Thesaurus Linguae Latinae Compendiarius*, better known by generations of Latin students as *Ainsworth's Latin Dictionary*. The work was republished, updated, and expanded or abridged in many successive editions. In the preface to the first edition, Ainsworth tried to set the record straight on translating *abridge*. Ainsworth pointed out five errors attached to the one word alone, in "the best of our Latin and English dictionaries," devoting more than two pages of fine print to identifying errors translating *abridge* and related words.[69]

Part of the problem was that *abridge* had no direct Latin equivalent, unlike *infringe*. Therefore, its editorial synonym, "To abbreviate, or shorten," was sometimes translated into what Ainsworth called bad Latin. Ainsworth gives the example "Abbreviare, contrahere, in compendium redigere":

> The first of these *Latin* words must be acknowledged to be bad, and yet is neither here, nor in their classical part, marked as such; and *abbreviatus*, which followeth in the next article, is not inserted at all in their classical part, neither is *abbreviatio*; and *abbreviatura* is unquestionably bad, and yet all inferred here as good *Latin* words.[70]

Much language from classical antiquity could be translated into English. Still, a gap of two thousand years made for difficulties even in a neoclassical period. Eighteenth-century England had far more use for the concept of editorial abridging than had the Romans with their dearth of paper, ink, literacy, middle-class readers, leisure time, editorial freedom, and print.

So eighteenth-century readers mistakenly translated the English "To abstract, or abridge," into "Abstrahere, &c."—which as Ainsworth points out did not actually mean "*contract or abridge*, neither indeed is this sense of it to be supported by the classic writers." Most authors of English-Latin dictionaries or Latin-English dictionaries were not Latin scholars like Ainsworth, and most drew upon scant libraries. In translating, they sometimes mistook easy words. "An abstract, or short draught of a thing," was translated into "Compendium, abstractum"; "moreover, *breviarium, summarium, *epitome*, the words used by classic writers to denote this sense, are intirely omitted." (Ainsworth uses the apostrophe to mark a Latin word borrowed from Greek.) The result was simple mistranslation, into or from Latin. "To abbridge, or lessen one's charges," Ainsworth notes, was translated into Latin "denoting rather *to put one's self to charges*" (the right translation, he suggests, should have been *minuere sumptus*, not *contrahere sumptus*).

One mistranslation Ainsworth corrected was that of abridgement of liberty. Ainsworth quotes the mistranslation and corrects it, inserting an editorial bracket for clarity:

> *To abbridge*, or *keep one short of his liberty*, Coercere, in ordinem redigere.] Instead of the latter, which signifieth *to reduce into rank or order*, should have been inferred *fraenare, refraenare, cohibere, inhibere, reprimare, comprimare*, or *compescere*.

As Ainsworth remarked, it is erroneous to translate "To abbridge, or keep one short of his liberty" into "Coercere, in ordinem redigere." The Latin phrase has a different meaning—"to reduce into rank or order." The voluntary abridgement of liberty to enter human society, written about by Locke, was more like refraining (*refraenare*) than like coercion. Ainsworth emphasized this mistranslation because it had appeared in several recent dictionaries. In an extended discussion, Ainsworth singled out Coles' dictionary of 1677, "designed chiefly for the use of scholars of a lower class," and remarked with displeasure that despite its flaws, Coles' dictionary, "being not half the price of Dr. *Littleton*'s, hath gone through twelve impressions."

Ainsworth himself defined two senses of *abridge*, with translations. The editorial definitions are extensive:

> "*To abridge* [shorten] Arcto I. contraho xi, 3. in compendium cogere, in summum redigere, rhultum in pauca conferre."
>
> "*Abridged* [shortened] Arcatus, contractus, in compendium redactus.
>
> *An abridger*, Qui in compendium redigit.
>
> *An abridging* [shortening] Contractio, 3.
>
> *An abridgement*, Compendium, 2. commentariolus; summa negotii, *epitome, *es, f.* *synopsis, *is, f.*"

The other sense was the less current *abridge of*, meaning to deprive: "*To abridge* [deprive of] Privo, I. orbo, spolio." "*Abridged of*, Orbatus, privatus, spoliatus." "*An abridging of*, Privatio, 3. spoliatio."

Among the generations of scholars who used Ainsworth's dictionary was John Adams, who owned the 1773 edition. In 1788, in his *Defence of the Constitutions* of the United States, Adams included Ainsworth in a short list of "any of the common dictionaries," dictionaries commonly used.[71] The scholarly Adams himself learned from what he read; he did not use *abridge* for 'reducing to order.' In his own writing, Adams like the other framers used *abridge* favorably to mean reducing power or privilege, and favorably or not to mean limiting rights or liberties, depending on necessity.

"To abridge ones Liberty"

Throughout the seventeenth and eighteenth centuries, both *abridge* and *infringe* were often used to define words foreign to English speakers. Whatever their other uses, their use in bilingual and poly-lingual dictionaries attests their clarity. In the seventeenth century the word *infringe* was used to translate and to explain words in Randle Cotgrave's French-English dictionary in 1611, John Florio's Italian-English dictionary in 1611, John Minsheu's multi-language (polyglot) dictionary in 1617, Perceval-Minsheu's Spanish-English dictionary in 1623, and Henry Hexham's Dutch-English dictionary in 1658, among others. As discussed, it was also used in Latin-English dictionaries. English dictionaries used *infringe* to define violation and breach in English; foreign-language dictionaries used it to translate words for violation in other languages. The customary meaning of *infringe* was summarized as violation, and the word was understood readily enough to be used frequently, even routinely, in translating.

In the eighteenth century, with the floodgates opened for printing and book publishing, the stream of new publications and continual re-issues brought more bilingual dictionaries. Forms of *infringe* provided definitions in most of them. Languages with words translated as *infringe* included Danish, French, Gaelic, German, Hindustani, Irish, Italian, Latin, Malabar, Norman French, Portuguese, Spanish, Swedish, and Welsh. All these eighteenth-century bilingual dictionaries also contained forms of *abridge*—defined, defining, or both.

Backtracking, the first sophisticated use of *abridge* in a bilingual dictionary had appeared much earlier, in Randle Cotgrave's 1611 *Dictionarie of the French and English Tongues*. Cotgrave's dictionary is remarkable for more than one reason. It is "The chief source of what we know about Renaissance French" in a single book.[72] It was exceptionally thorough for its time, with separate French-to-English and English-to-French sections. And it introduced liberty as a context for the word *abridged*:

"Destrainct: "Strained, pressed, wrung, vexed extremely; also straitened, restrained, abridged of libertie."

Destraincte: "A narrow strait, or pinch; a hard, or extreme wring; also, a restraint of libertie.

Destraindre: "To straine, presse, wring, vex extremely; also, to straiten, restrain, or abridge of libertie."

Restrainct. "Restrained, shortened, or abridged of libertie, shut or kept up, held or closed in."

Restraincte. "A restraint, restraining, shortening or abridging of libertie, holding or keeping in."

Restraindre. "To restrain, straiten or bind in, abridge or shorten of libertie, shut or keepe up, hold or close in."

Regrettably, little is known about Cotgrave. He was educated at Cambridge and worked for William Cecil, Lord Burghley, to whom he dedicated the dictionary. The range of the dictionary and the comprehensive definitions suggest that the author had strong motivation.

Cotgrave's joining the concept of abridgement with that of liberty had no immediate provenance in dictionaries. If it had any provenance in dictionaries at all, it was indirectly in Palsgrave's 1530 French dictionary. A century earlier, to interpret *restrain*, Palsgrave had written, "It is a sore thyng to restrayne a man of his lybertye."

"I Restrayne one of their lybertye

Je restrains, conjugate lyke ie constrayns, and ie cohibe. It is a sore thyng to restrayne a man of his lybertye: Cest une dure chose que de restraindre ung homme de sa liberte, or de le cohiber de sa liberte."

The direct connection between Cotgrave and Palsgrave is that Cotgrave used Palsgrave, a major influence, extensively.[73] No dictionary between 1530 and 1611 links the concept of liberty with constraint, restraint, or abridgement as do Palsgrave's and Cotgrave's.

Outside the law dictionaries, Cotgrave's 1611 dictionary is the earliest in which the concept of abridgement moves into the lexicon of political philosophy. In 1611, however, abridging liberty did not have a Lockean acceptability. When Cotgrave's dictionary was published, Locke had not been born; when Palsgrave and Cotgrave define restraint, they mean coercion, restraint imposed, not voluntary. Nor does the linkage appear for decades in dictionaries following after Cotgrave's. It shows up again only toward the end of the seventeenth century, then in some eighteenth-century dictionaries and from seventeenth-century and eighteenth-century philosophers, as when Johnson quotes Locke with a different perspective.

If Palsgrave's "I Restrayne one of their lybertye" in 1530 and Cotgrave's "abridge of libertie" in 1611 are joined in a line, it is less by English dictionaries than by political philosophy. In the seventeenth and the eighteenth centuries, negative representations of abridging liberty morphed into positive representations of voluntary abridgement. There is a lexical shift from coercion to function, from restraint to building a society. In philosophy, the shift is marked by the writing of Thomas Hobbes, John Locke, and David Hume. In his essay on human understanding in 1689, Locke clearly uses abridgement to mean a reasonable pulling in of elbows to coexist with other humans. So did Hobbes before him and Hume after. Where exactly the shift is marked in dictionaries is harder to pinpoint. Cotgrave in 1611 used the phrase "abridged of libertie" in a way that does not sound the note sounded by Locke; Johnson in 1755 used the phrase in a way that does. Clearly a turning point occurred between the two. A handful of dictionaries between Cotgrave and Johnson, and only a handful, mark the transition—William Robertson's in 1681, Elisha Coles' in 1699, Abel Boyer's in 1700, and especially Robert Ainsworth's in 1736.

William Robertson's *Phraseologia Generalis* (general phrase book) of 1681 was the next dictionary after Cotgrave's to refer to abridging liberty. Scots lexicographer Robertson (d. 1686), educated at the University of Edinburgh, was a noted Hebrew scholar and teacher, part of a seventeenth-century Protestant movement to search out meaning in the bible by pursuing the original language.[74] He published a grammar of Hebrew, the *Gate or Door to the Holy Tongue*, in 1653, followed in the next two years by a Hebrew-English dictionary, and he contributed the Hebrew scholarship in the 1674 and 1678 editions of Gouldman's *Copious Dictionary*.[75] He then published his general English dictionary, the copious *General Phrase Book*.[76]

Robertson's entry for *abridge* and *abridgement* runs more than half of a two-column page, with separate definitions for each sense. Each definition is followed by Latin translations. The first is editorial, expanding earlier editorial definitions of the term and edging into law—"An abridgement, breviate, or, brief, or abbreviation of things, matter, discourse, or writing, &c." The next is financial retrenchment—"To make an abridgement of, i.e. to lessen ones charges." The next is the sense from political philosophy, "To cause an abridgement of, or to keep one short and straitened of his liberty," (wrongly) translated *"Coercere, in ordinem redigere aliquem."* Robertson's definition of *abridge* still does not have the same ring as in Hobbes or Locke; abridgement is not yet voluntary. There is no entry for either *infringe* or *violate*, although Robertson's entry for *to break* runs more than a page.

The next dictionary connecting *abridge* to liberty appeared in 1699, a republished edition of Elisha Coles' English-Latin, Latin-English dictionary, which includes "To abridge ones libertie," translated *"Coerces, in ordinem redigere."*[77] This was the faulty Latin translation criticized and corrected by Ainsworth. Coles' English dictionary of 1676 and the earlier editions of his Latin dictionary did not contain it, but the 1699 edition was posthumous; Coles' "Fourth Edition, Enlarged" was brought out by bookseller Peter Parker, an early publisher of Milton's *Paradise Lost*. Parker's title page claims that errors in previous editions of the dictionary have been "Rectified," "many Superfluities Retrenched," and "very many Defects Supplied"—"all suited to the meanest Capacities, in a plainer Method than heretofore."

Coles-Parker's 1699 Latin dictionary did insert a correct translation for *"Coerces, in ordinem redigere"*—'to reduce to order' or 'to humble, to degrade,' as in rank. It is also translated as "To compell men to live according to their estate and profession." So, the same Latin phrase is translated to mean "To abridge ones libertie," "to reduce to order," and to compel people "to live according to their estate and profession." Here again is a turning point. Reduction to order might be mandatory, but conceivably it could be a good idea. Further defining abridgement, Coles-Parker also included "To abridge ones charges," meaning to reduce one's expenditures, to retrench in a financial sense. The context is practices, or policy—again, not just editing. The common denominator in the jumbled translations is that they all have significance for the body politic. Even the erroneous translations of *abridge* go beyond editorship.

A gap of seventy years remains between Cotgrave and Robertson, and besides Robertson's (1681) and Parker-Coles' (1699), just one more dictionary entry for *abridgement*, at the end of the century, marks its transition into public policy. In 1699-1700, Huguenot refugee Abel Boyer published the first edition of his French-English, English-French *Royal Dictionary*. Like earlier dictionaries, it translates "To abridge" into French terms for abbreviating. But to illustrate, Boyer then quotes a sentence from the famous Puritan minister Jeremiah Burroughs (1599-1646), "Christian Religion abridges us of no lawful Pleasures."[78]

The line in Boyer's dictionary comes from Burroughs' *Moses His Choice, with his Eye Fixed upon Heaven.*[79] While Burroughs used the word "abridges" in a religious context, his logic was analogous to Locke's. Burroughs argues that godliness does not mean undue abridgement, as Locke argues that civil law does not mean undue abridgement. Locke does not refer to Burroughs, but in Burroughs, religion is not an infringement of natural right, and in Locke, civil law is not an infringement of natural right. Boyer's *Royal Dictionary* came out in numerous editions and became the premier authority in French-English dictionaries. When Boyer adapted Burroughs to explain abridgement, the inclusion probably reinforced Locke's influence.

In the dictionaries, in the seventeenth and early eighteenth centuries, abridgement in political thought evolved largely in bilingual dictionaries. Boyer's French dictionary is one example. No all-English dictionaries before Johnson in 1755 contained the same public-policy definitions for abridgement; in Britain the public-policy definitions were recognized, recorded, and established by Samuel Johnson. In the bilingual dictionaries, in contrast, *abridge* became linked with liberty by the 1730s, although not positively. The Swedish-English-Latin dictionary of two bishops, Jacob Serenius and Eric Benzelius, published in 1734, defines *abridge* with "liberty" near the top. A brief translation in the editorial sense is followed with the more emphatic quotations from Coles and Boyer, "To abridge one's liberty," "To abridge one's charges," and "The Christian religion abridges us no lawful pleasures."[80]

The larger picture is that 'foreign'-English dictionaries in the eighteenth century emphasized liberty, obviously a concept relevant to political philosophy. The bilingual dictionaries tended to boost liberty earlier than did the English dictionaries, which did so later in the eighteenth century. The Swedish-English-Latin dictionary of Serenius and Benzelius contained more than a dozen entries with forms of the word *liberty*. Sometimes the headword defined has little immediate association with the word—suggesting that the compilers wanted to insert the concept of liberty wherever they could. The entry *pretender*, for example, is illustrated by "We have beheld the greatest pretenders to publick Liberty, turn the greatest Tyrants themselves," helpfully translated into Swedish.

By the middle of the eighteenth century, bilingual dictionaries seem to have adopted liberty as a pet project. The 1754 Danish-English dictionary of Andreas Berthelson, like the Swedish dictionary before, contains more than a dozen uses of "liberty."[81] Each is translated into Danish. It is as though Berthelson was trying to reinforce liberty by presenting the word in print. Perhaps the dictionaries in northern Europe played the self-nominated role of beacon light played by colonial newspapers in America. By mid-eighteenth century, "liberty" was a marquee term in the dictionaries of Scandinavia and the Netherlands.

Berthelson's dictionary translates *abridge* briefly and then gives three uses, the first two being "To abridge ones liberty" and "Christian religion abridges us no lawful pleasures," and the third "To abridge a Discourse." Like recent English dictionaries in their emphasis on "liberty," but going beyond the English dictionaries, the dictionaries translating European languages did not reflect Locke's use of abridgement as an acceptable trade-off of individual rights for mutual protection. The step linking liberty to abridgement in English dictionaries as in political philosophy remained for Samuel Johnson.

Samuel Johnson's *Dictionary*

Samuel Johnson's epochal *Dictionary of the English Language* landed in public with a splash in 1755. While Johnson's was not the first modern English dictionary, and some entries might strike a reader today as either too derivative or too creative, it was by any measure a phenomenal feat and remains a landmark in the history of dictionaries. It also enhanced Britain and the English language in the world of letters in an age when, on the continent, even Voltaire and Rousseau compiled dictionaries.

Johnson's title page announced his key innovation, using quotations as examples to explain the words—*A Dictionary of the English Language: In which the Words are Deduced from Their Originals, and Illustrated in Their Different Significations by Examples from the Best Writers*. Living up to the claim, Johnson and his team worked on the project for eight years; the result was an honest effort as well as a milestone in scholarship and English social history.[82] The *Dictionary* was well-regarded in America, despite Johnson's criticisms of Americans and his attempts to discourage rebellion through pamphleteering. (His 1775 *Taxation No Tyranny* failed to turn the tide of history.) Benjamin Franklin ordered copies of the *Dictionary* for the Library

Company and the College of Philadelphia in the 1750s.[83] Alexander Hamilton cited it in his revolutionary articles in the 1770s.[84]

Johnson included full entries for both *infringe* and *abridge*, defining each sense of each word, with relevant quotations from authors Johnson admired. As always before, the two words had different definitions. What Johnson's dictionary demonstrates is that by 1755 the term *abridge* was established in political philosophy. Johnson defined *abridge* in one sense from editing, then in two senses from political philosophy; and he progressed from editing to political philosophy in defining both the verb *to abridge* and the noun *abridgement.*

To ABRIDGE v.a. [. . .]

2. To contract, to diminish, to cut short.

The determination of the will, upon enquiry, is following the direction of that guide; and he, that has a power to act or not to act, according as such determination directs, is free. Such determination *abridges* not that power wherein liberty consists.

Locke.

As indicated, furthermore, the definition from political philosophy was that of privilege or power abridged. To clarify forms of *abridge*, the author Johnson invoked most was John Locke. For both the verb and the noun, he thus cited the preeminent authority on abridgement of natural right to join human society.

ABRIDGMENT. *n.s.* [*abregement, Fr.*]

1. The contraction of a large work into a small compass [. . .]   3. Restraint, or abridgment of liberty.

The constant desire of happiness, and the constraint it puts upon us, no body, I think, accounts an *abridgment* of liberty, or at least an *abridgment* of liberty, to be complained of.

Locke.

Johnson's public policy definition of *abridgement* is concise and cleanly written—"restraint, or abridgment of liberty." It becomes clearer yet when Johnson quotes Locke.

Both Locke quotations come from the 1689 *Essay on Human Understanding*, which Johnson turned to repeatedly. Scholars have thoroughly documented Johnson's use of Locke; a researcher in 1930 found that Johnson cited Locke 1,674 times in just the first volume of the *Dictionary.*[85] The philosophical sense of *abridgement* as a check on absolute liberty was established by Johnson's time partly by earlier dictionaries and largely by philosophers. The concepts of infringement and abridgement each characterize relations between a people and its government; each term can be associated with both rights and powers; both are found in eighteenth-century moral philosophy and political philosophy; and it is no accident that Johnson chose Locke to define one of the terms.

In a nutshell, for Locke as for other writers, abridgement and excessive abridgement were two different things. As Locke put it, the only constraint put upon us by "The constant desire of happiness" is "to act for it."[86] Acting in our own best interest is not an excessive abridgement of liberty. "If to break loose from the conduct of reason, and to want that restraint of examination and judgment, which keeps us from chusing or doing the worst, be liberty, true liberty, only madmen or fools are the only freemen: But yet, I think, no-body would chuse to be mad for the sake of such liberty but he that is mad already."[87] Arguing point-blank that not every abridgement is something to complain of, Locke differentiated abridgement from a wrong *per se*. For Locke, the higher aim is true liberty—different from both absolute monarchism and irrational license. In short, Locke reasoned that not every abridgement is a grievance, a view that aligns him with other Enlightenment authors and which influenced Samuel Johnson and the framers.

Johnson could not use Locke to define *infringe*—Locke eschewed the word—but he repeatedly used Locke to define *abridge*. Johnson's *Dictionary* also cites three passages from Locke to define the word *liberty*—one of which would become very familiar to Americans. The chapter heading read, "A constant determination to a pursuit of happiness no abridgment to liberty." Used both as a chapter heading and as a margin note, Locke's "pursuit of happiness" was readily visible to anyone (like Thomas Jefferson) thumbing through Locke's work.[88] That phrase "pursuit of happiness" in the Declaration of Independence is not coincidence; obviously the founders were familiar with Locke's *Essay*. Benjamin Franklin praised it, writing as 'Poor Richard,' in a tribute to Locke in 1748.[89] Jefferson recommended it to a young reader in 1773.[90] George Washington specifically ordered the two-volume title in 1783.[91] Johnson himself thought so well of these passages in Locke that he quoted one again to define the simple word *act*. "The desire of happiness, and the constraint it puts upon us to *act* for it, no body accounts an abridgment of liberty."

Like the definitions for *abridge* and *infringe* themselves, the words defined by *abridge* and *infringe* are differentiated clearly and consistently in Johnson's dictionary. Words defined by *abridge* are modulated; words defined by *infringe* are destructive. Forms of *abridge* explain editing terms like *epitome, compendium, breviary, summary, abbreviator*—"One who abbreviates, or abridges"; "*abbreviature*"—"A compendium or abridgement"; and *to contract*—"To shorten; to abridge; to epitomize." Johnson applied *abridge* in a restrictive sense only in editing, not in political philosophy. He did not use *abridge* to mean lessening, diminishing, or reducing in general; nor did he use abridgement to define a stringent, forcibly confining or subduing.

In contrast, Johnson used the draconian *infringe* to define *violate*—"To infringe; to break anything venerable"; *violation*—"Infringement or injury of something sacred"; and *violator*—"One who injures or infringes something sacred." Johnson defined even *violence* as "Injury; infringement." Naturally, he used infringement to define the transitive verb *to break*; Johnson's 38 definitions included "To infringe a law," still used today. Since Johnson used forms of *infringe* and *abridge* to define other words more than a dozen times, again, their meanings must have been accessible in 1755.

By 1787 Johnson's dictionary had come out in eight editions. Despite any revisions, all editions kept intact the distinction between the two key words. All the eighteenth-century editions retain the connection between infringement and destruction, the editorial meanings of *abridge*, the meaning in political philosophy, and the quotations from Locke. These include the editions that came out in 1773, when revolution was brewing in America, and in 1785, after Johnson's death, in the Federal period.

Johnson was a man of encyclopedic studies. He defined 'easy' words (as with the 38 definitions for *break*) as well as 'hard words,' and he had a practice of choosing passages from authors he liked—relying on recommendations from Alexander Pope, among others—and then using the same authors, including Locke, again and again.[92] No other dictionary quoted writers as much as Johnson's did, and Johnson went beyond citing writers for illustration, to relying on them for his sense of the words.[93] Johnson's dictionary was a landmark, but Johnson did not write in a vacuum. In separating *infringe* and *abridge*, as discussed, Johnson's dictionary fell within solidly established tradition and was also solidly aligned with eighteenth-century writing. In citing Locke, however, and in defining *abridge* as a limitation of rights, power, or privilege, Johnson included a meaning not routinely included in dictionaries. His third, political definition of "abridge" was established, clear, and straightforward, but had been used more in law, philosophy, and history than in ordinary dictionaries.

The big dictionary establishes that, by the middle of the eighteenth century, abridgment had joined infringement in political philosophy to characterize connections between human society, government, and human rights. The short summary is that society, government, and rights were not intrinsically at odds. In a successful human endeavor, they were joined. Defining the terms helped to clarify the relationships, and clarifying the relations helped to perpetuate the success.

Tracking the language of the amendments: synopsis

In this thread of English usage, the short synopsis is that *infringe* and *abridge* were not synonyms in any age, from the beginnings of English through the eighteenth century. The two English words had separate tracks, recorded in print dictionaries from the fifteenth century through the eighteenth. Seen in the rear-view mirror from the perspective of the Bill of Rights, each track is interesting. The verb *to infringe* changed from a routine omission to a constant in dictionaries. It appeared only once in the earliest Latin-English dictionaries; it appeared a few times in early English print dictionaries including the Latin dictionaries; by the seventeenth century it appeared often; in the eighteenth century, most English dictionaries included it. Omitted in early dictionaries, in the eighteenth century it was translated into every language from Dutch to Malabar to Swedish. Part of this increasing entry into dictionaries came from the simple fact that later dictionaries tapped earlier ones, each new dictionary incorporating work by prior compilers. Dictionaries also became more inclusive, adding ordinary English words to prior lists of 'hard' words. However, the over-all trend is more than just a linear increase over time. *Infringe* was used to translate foreign words, or to define other English words, more often than it was defined as an entry itself. It was used more often, in dictionaries, than it needed definition. Meanwhile, its definition and translation remained consistent.

Entries for forms of the word *abridge* also increased from earlier dictionaries to later dictionaries, further increasing in the eighteenth century. To that extent its etymology paralleled that of *infringe*. However, the track of the word *abridge* is more complex. The Anglo-Norman word did not appear in Old English or Anglo-Saxon dictionaries; it appeared in early English-to-Latin dictionaries but not in Latin-to-English dictionaries; in the sixteenth century its appearance was hit-or-miss; in the seventeenth century more frequent; in eighteenth-century dictionaries it was everywhere. In the nineteenth century it featured in the titles of dictionaries like Noah Webster's.

As with *infringe*, part of the story is that as the English language grew, and dictionary publishing grew, dictionaries themselves grew, incorporating entries from previous dictionaries and becoming more extensive over time. Uses of each meaning of abridgement also grew over time. The editorial verb *to abridge* as a synonym for *abbreviate, epitomize*, etc., was used much more in the seventeenth century than it had been in the sixteenth. One of the rare appearances in sixteenth-century literature comes in Shakespeare—"look where my abridgement comes," Hamlet jokes as the players enter in Act 2. By the eighteenth century, as the volume of published books, pamphlets, periodicals, and papers increased, so did the practice and the vocabulary of editorial abridging.

In the seventeenth and eighteenth centuries, the use of *abridge* developed in the field of political philosophy. The policy sense of *abridge* associated with rights, powers, and privileges became a makeweight in political philosophy. The word had had such associations since the Middle Ages, but the application to rights, powers, and privileges grew in the seventeenth century and more in the eighteenth. The association was surely strengthened by the fact that the word's editorial sense meant to shorten or reduce something without loss of essentials; it was strengthened further by the etymology of 'fief abridged,' originally limiting the privileges of a fief, in law; and by numerous published abridgements of law—statute, case, custom, commentary—a practice well established in the eighteenth century.

In political philosophy, in the writing of Locke and others, the word underwent a semantic development, from a sense of abridgement as constraint in the sixteenth century to a sense of abridgement as practicality, as trade-off, in the eighteenth century. Both senses mean limits, but one is compelled while the other is voluntary, and this concept of voluntary self-restraint for the individual aligned with a concept of imposing some restraint on figures of authority. The usage—the concept of rights, power, and privilege abridged—is the glue on the play for the social compact.

In every century, the two words remained differentiated. From the earliest dictionaries through 1789, not one English dictionary, not one, gives either word as a synonym for the other. They were never interchangeable. The two words do not appear as synonyms even in Latin-English dictionaries by scholars, with multiple Latin synonyms and translations for both terms. Paradoxically, the difference between the two key verbs is so simple that its very simplicity may have had a regrettable effect on scholarship. The distinction is easy, and easy things can be easy to overlook. To document an easy distinction with a mountain of evidence might seem over-the-top, but given the firearms carnage of the twenty-first century, the cause is worth it.

English Binomial Phrases

Binomial phrases contain two words traditionally paired, like "night and day," "hearth and home," "life and limb." They are a traditional way to convey separate but related concepts. As defined in linguistics, "Binomials, also known as word-pairs, doublet, twin formulae or freezes, are pairs of coordinated members of the same grammatical category, e.g. *man and wife, to have and to hold, dead or alive, for and against*, etc."[94] Often the binomial phrases are irreversible binomials, also called fixed collocations or 'freezes.' Despite the specialized nomenclature, the description simply means that the two terms usually come in the same order, as in ordinary conversation—"odds and ends" rather than "ends and odds," "to and from" rather than "from and to."[95]

Binomials are part of the music, color, and texture of everyday life and are important in English as in other languages. They do not usually appear in dictionaries, but linguistics experts study them with great interest. "A large part of the language we produce is pre-patterned and formulaic. What follows is that language cannot be solely understood as a product of regular grammar rules paired up with creative and spontaneous vocabulary use."[96] They are now considered part of a language; "without the knowledge and appropriate employment of fixed expressions, proficiency in a given language cannot be attained in a satisfactory manner."[97]

British and American history abound with binomials—opposites or closely related, positive or negative, sometimes alliterative or rhyming, often rhythmic. Binomials appeared in Anglo-Saxon wills, they appear in the public statements of English monarchs through the centuries, and they appear in unpoetic documents like Powers of Attorney. Many binomials have taken on legal heft, like "force or fraud," the two basic categories of all injustice according to Aristotle, Aquinas, Dante, and their philosophical descendants who made kidnapping illegal: "The crime of seizing and taking away a person by force or fraud, often with a demand for ransom."[98]

Binomials join two words of the same part of speech—two verbs, nouns, prepositions or modifiers. Adjective binomials include "entire and complete," "legal and valid," "free and clear," "clear and present (danger)," and "customary and appropriate," or "reasonable and customary." Adverb binomials include "jointly and severally," "diligently and faithfully," and "fully and freely."

Noun binomials—two nouns with a conjunction—include universals like "work and play." Others include "rights and responsibilities," "rights and powers," "rights and liberties," "(without) fear or favor," and "peace and prosperity." The old "friend or foe" is a noun binomial. So are the familiar "full faith and credit," "sale or transfer," and "(in) whole or part." English binomials structure and color U.S. government, history, and popular culture. In 1863, in the Gettysburg address, Abraham Lincoln created "with liberty and justice (for all)"—a binomial so suited in sound and sense to a millennium of existing phrases that it instantly entered the popular verbal storehouse.

In 1976, Watergate prosecutor Leon Jaworski titled his book *The Right and the Power*, using the age-old binomial for constitutional authority. Jaworski seems to have changed the thinking of one Elvis Presley. Famously, Presley had visited the Nixon White House in 1970. Less famously, he later gave Jaworski's book to a hometown friend. Exhibited at the Elvis Presley birthplace museum in Tupelo, Mississippi, the copy is inscribed by Elvis: "Dear Janelle, I hope you enjoy reading this book. I did!" Some Elvis hits themselves contain binomials—"(It's) Now or Never"—although Presley seems to have preferred extended metaphors as in Mae Axton's "Heartbreak Hotel."

Irreversible binomials

Irreversible binomials keep the two words in the same order. One good example among verb binomials is "rock and roll"; English users do not say "roll and rock." Using ordinary noun binomials, English speakers do not customarily say "prosperity and peace," "fraud or force," "foe or friend," or "wrong and right." Fixed prepositional binomials include "back and forth," "up and down," "to and fro" in English—not "forth and back" or "down and up."

Even a quick overview of English binomials indicates that the word order tends to fall into patterns. The question is why they do. People see, hear, and use familiar binomials that seem natural; the question is why they seem natural. Factors that can influence the order in binomials include sound, rhythm, meaning, and frequency of word usage.[99] The simple binomial "crime and punishment," for example, fulfills several likelihoods. *Crime* is the shorter word, and the short word often comes first. *Crime* is the word stressed, and the punchier stressed word often comes first. Crime theoretically precedes punishment, and time can be a factor. Presumably crimes outnumber their punishments—since not all offenses are caught—and frequency is a factor.[100]

Often the order is logical. "Arm" in "arm and hammer" is closer to hand, and proximity can be a factor, as in "near and far." "Dollars" in "dollars and cents" is the larger amount, and size or importance can be a factor. "Publish" in "publish or perish" comes first in time, and chronology can be a factor. The first word in "wait and see" is the action that comes first.[101] Order is often chronological, as in "born and bred," or "out and about."

The general rules are not airtight, and sometimes they come into conflict. The events that happen first in actuality do not always come first in binomials. The familiar binomial "thunder and lightning" conflicts with time. As we know from elementary school, we see lightning before we hear thunder, because light travels faster than sound. But *thunder* is a shorter, punchier word than *lightning*, and in binomials shorter often comes first.

In other factors, animate precedes inanimate ("horse and buggy"), and positive precedes negative ("good and evil"). For good or ill, linguistics experts also apply the "condiment rule"; the main dish precedes the condiment. This guiding principle "applies to food, people, and other things," two examples being "eating and drinking" and "principal and interest."[102] The condiment rule suggests that linguistics conferences may be more fun than popularly imagined, if not a hoot and a holler. It also explains "turkey and dressing," "chicken and dumplings," and "scotch and soda." A related rule is that the alcohol term precedes the non-alcoholic in cocktails.[103]

"Real-world relations" often apply in binomials, including degrees of priority or dominance.[104] The Lone Ranger comes before Tonto although Tonto's name is shorter and punchier. Binomials arranged in pecking order include "guys and dolls," "prince and pauper," and "gold and silver." Even priority and power are not airtight determinants, however. *North* may come first in "north and south" because north determines the compass, but the compass does not explain why *east* comes first in "east and west." If east tops west on the totem pole, it may mimic the seeming direction of the sun in a flat-earth view, or a clockwise movement on the compass, starting wheel-of-fortune from North.

One real-world relation is gender, and in gendered binomials, the male term often comes first.[105] Easy examples include "male and female" or "man and woman," the somewhat old-fashioned "man and wife," "husband and wife," and the 1950s-style "his and hers," as on towel sets. When gender asymmetry combines with rank, the binomials are predictably "king and queen," "prince and princess," "duke and duchess."[106] "Princess" and "duchess" are also the longer words, and longer words tend to come second, and they have more frills and furbelows, and the more complex word tends to come second. Setting priority aside, the more generic word tends to come first—"bells and whistles," "fair and accurate"—and the generic term is often shorter, simpler, and older to boot.

However, the male-first rule has many exceptions among gendered pairs. In "ladies and gentlemen," *ladies* precedes *gentlemen* as a courtesy;

the word *ladies* is also shorter and simpler. "He and she" is male-first, but "mom and dad" is female-first, perhaps because "mom" is more closely associated with parenting. However, both "mother and father" and "father and mother" are frequently used, and if parenting explains why "mom" comes first in "mom and dad," it does not explain why "mom" comes first in "mom and pop business," where the primary function is not parenting. That "Bride and groom" and "bride and bridegroom" place the female first is understandable; they refer to the wedding, where the bride is the main dish or centerpiece—another example of the condiment rule, also called the accessory rule. The word *bridegroom* is also longer, more complex, and derivative.[107] "Barbie and Ken" is another female-male binomial. Barbie's name usually precedes Ken's, although Barbie is female, and Ken's name is shorter, simpler, punchier, and less marked than Barbie's. Presumably "Barbie and Ken" fulfills the condiment rule, with Ken as sidekick or accessory. The less essential term also comes second in "shoes and handbags" and "shoes and stockings."

Sounds often come into play in binomials—rhyme and alliteration, stress and length, vowel and consonant sounds. "Mine and thine," "twice or thrice," and "hither and thither" are old rhyming binomials. "Chip and dip" is a new one. Pairing words with the same first letters (alliteration) is frequent—"do or die," "black and blue," "wash and wear," "signed and sealed." "Drink and drive" is a more recent example, like "down and dirty"; "push and pull" is older. Auctioneers still use the alliterative "any and all," as in "with any and all faults," heard on the television program *Texas Flip and Move.*

"Infringed or abridged" as a binomial

Clearly, the vast terrain of law employs a vast number of binomials. According to linguistics scholars, proficiency in legal discourse can depend on "the appropriate use of fixed expressions, including binomials." In law, for centuries, "Binomials have been associated with formulaic and conventional usage."[108] More broadly, in the interface between everyday life and law, for more than a millennium, the English binomial form has been used in public affairs. For more than twelve centuries, Anglo-American law, history, and political philosophy in Britain and America have framed abuses of power in usefully clear and concise English phrases—binomials. Throughout the millennia, the purpose has been to identify offenses and abuses and to guard against them, to ward them off. The binomial "infringe or abridge" is one example. "Infringed or abridged" used to be joined in a single traditional phrase. It was used in several tenses and sometimes with the verb nominalized—"infringement or abridgement," "abridge or infringe," "infringing or abridging," etc. Sometimes it used "and" instead of "or"—"abridged and infringed." (Binomials containing different forms of *infringe* and *abridge* will be discussed as the same binomial from here on; quotation marks will indicate specific forms where necessary.) These two action words, connected with the rights in the first two amendments, are separated in the Bill of Rights. They also became largely separated in British usage at the end of the eighteenth century. However, they were joined in British English before 1789, were joined in American English before and after 1789, and are still found joined in state documents of British Commonwealth nations including Canada and Jamaica today. The binomial "infringed or abridged" was so used in the nineteenth-century United States that it became a cliché, sometimes satirized.

Less famous now than the "denied or delayed" of legal maxim or the "denied or abridged" of later constitutional amendments, versions of "infringed or abridged" can nonetheless be found through four centuries of English print. An early example turns up in a 1592 pamphlet by Elizabethan playwright Thomas Nashe (1567-1601). Nashe asked rhetorically, "if monarchies must suffer popular states to enjoy their free liberties and amplest fraunchises, without the least infringment or abridgment," should not royal prerogatives be allowed full function?[109] The phrasing can be found in Britain through the eighteenth century.

When Europeans settled in the new world, the binomial was used on both sides of the Atlantic. A few examples provide a quick overview. As American printing became established, use of the infringe-or-abridge phrasing increased in America. In one colonial example, in 1693 Samuel Willis, a Connecticut founder, wrote Major-General Fitz-John Winthrop to urge ratification of an updated charter for Connecticut, "That Therefore, they declare that all their subjects here who desire the benifit of Common and Statute Laws of England may enjoy them without the least infringement or abridgement."[110]

In 1751 an erudite Dubliner named Charles Lucas wrote to defend Ireland by placing Ireland into the context of the British constitution. Going back to the Norman Conquest, and using an argument used by English historians as well, Lucas pointed out that even William the Conqueror kept up the English system of local representation. After the 1066 Norman Conquest, Lucas wrote, the "Difficulties and Inconveniences" of enmity between Normans and Saxons and different languages and cultures "were obviated, without any Infringement, or Abridgement of the Rights, or Privileges of any Individual, and for the general Emolument of the whole Community."[111] The English addressed the "difficulties" of occupying a territory by allowing the Saxons to choose their own representatives for their cities, boroughs, and counties.

In May 1767 the *Gentleman's and London Magazine* published a letter of "Instructions from the Town of Boston to their Representatives," dated March 9.[112] James Otis, Thomas Cushing, Samuel Adams, and John Hancock, the representatives, thoughtfully shared their instructions (which they probably helped compose) with the British public. With an eye to closing loopholes against liberty, the letter included a final instruction that "you openly profess our duty and loyalty to the King, and a constitutional subordination to Parliament," "being at the same time vigilant and jealous of our just rights, liberties, and privileges; in all cases protesting against and counteracting, with decent firmness, every attempt in the least to abridge or infringe them."

The letter also instructed Adams and the others to ask Britain "to prohibit the importation and purchasing of slaves." The request would have been a smashing blow against slavery if it had succeeded; Britain was the second-largest slave trading nation after Portugal. However, every attempt by colonists to stop the importation of slaves was disallowed by the British crown, which stood to lose revenue if the commerce diminished. It may be pointed out that the slaveholding landowners stood to profit from reducing the supply, raising the value of enslaved persons already in America. The point is accurate as far as it goes. However, the benefit to future shiploads of enslaved people—who would not have been brought over—would have been incalculable. The letter was published more than once, like most public documents. James Boswell, Dr. Johnson's biographer, reprinted it in the *Scots Magazine* later in 1767.[113]

On December 31, 1768, the New York House of Representatives passed several resolves (resolutions).

> The House (according to order) resolved itself into a committee of the whole House, to consider of, and draw up proper and constitutional resolves, asserting the rights and privileges of his Majesty's subjects within this colony, which they conceive have been greatly *abridged*, and *infringed*, by several acts passed by the last parliament of Great Britain.[114]

The resolutions passed by the General Assembly of the Colony of New York were published in New York and were soon reprinted in Britain.

The same binomial was used in other colonies, not to the joy of crown and Parliament. On February 22, 1770, the privy council of Jamaica "asserted," in the repressive comment of a British writer, "That their body have at least an equal power and right of legislation with the house of representatives, which they will never suffer to be abridged or infringed."[115] On November 7, 1773, the Reverend Hugh Knox preached a sermon before "his excellency General Clausen," just arrived in St. Croix, the Virgin Islands, where the Presbyterian Knox served as minister. Knox, Alexander Hamilton's early mentor and supporter, reminded the congregation "that if mankind would obey the dictates of Christianity, the rights of the magistrate would never be encroached on, nor those of the subject ever infringed or abridged."[116] Hamilton later used the same terms with the same precision, as quoted.

The infringe-or-abridge phrasing continued to be used after the Revolutionary War. On February 25, 1783, the General Assembly of Vermont published a set of resolutions.

> Resolved, that neither the Executive, or Legislative authority of this State have ever entered into any negotiation, truce or combination with the enemies of this and the United States, except that only of an exchange of Prisoners, and they are still determined, at the risque of their lives and fortunes to continue their opposition to any attempts made, or that may hereafter be made to infringe or abridge the rights to [or] the freedom and Independence of this and the United States. [117]

Independent from the United States as well as from Britain at this point, and eager to join the U.S., Vermonters were stung by insinuations that their state had tried to make a separate peace with Britain in the Revolutionary War.

Infringe-or-abridge binomials continued to be used in America throughout the nineteenth century, in connection with both rights and powers. Concerns could be larger or smaller. In January 1809, two members of a Connecticut Methodist Episcopal Church wrote to outgoing President Thomas Jefferson, to express relief that he had not abolished religion in America.

> Being situated in a part of the Union where Republican principles were not very popular we were (just prior to your election) frequently told that your avowed opposition to the Christian Religion was such, that should you be elected, all Religious Institutions would be utterly subverted—but to the confounding the Authors of this unjust calumny it is with the greatest pleasure we can state that our Religious Rights & priviledges have not in the least been abridged or infringed upon.[118]

The kudo was a premier example of damning with faint praise. American history buffs may recall that Jefferson wanted to be remembered specifically for three things, to be engraved on his tombstone, one being the Virginia Statute of Religious Freedom.[119]

Joseph Hamilton Daveiss on the Bill of Rights

In 1810, the infringe-abridge binomial was applied by U.S. lawyer Joseph Hamilton Daveiss (1774-1811), who prosecuted Aaron Burr.

Daviess is a particularly apt source, because he applied the phrase specifically to regulating guns.

> Again, "The right of the people to keep and bear arms, shall not be infringed." This is a freedom of the very same holy nature with the other; but will any man venture to say that congress *abridges* or *infringes* the sacred freedom by saying that none shall come armed to an election, or into a court of justice, or a place of divine worship; the freedom of using arms as in speech is a rational liberty, and to be used, but it has its bounds.[120]

Daviess' rhetorical question is pertinent today: "Will any man venture to say that congress abridges or infringes the sacred freedom by saying that none shall come armed to an election, or into a court of justice, or a place of divine worship"?

As shown, Daviess in 1810 discussed the right to bear arms by using the right of speech as analogy; "the freedom of using arms as in speech is a rational liberty." Each right is "to be used, but it has its bounds." He went on to lay out the argument in some detail, quoting the first and second amendments and closely paraphrasing John Locke.

> "Nor abridging the *freedom of speech*"—Now when the word freedom is used, I understand it to mean a rational liberty comporting with the social condition of mankind in a community. It never can mean especially in a social compact, that exemption from all restraint and control, which implies the state of nature and tends to reproduce it.[121]

In this particularly interesting passage, Daveiss went on not just to compare speech and bearing arms, but hypothetically to link the two: "Let us be more explanatory—Is a speech calling upon the people to take arms and oppose the government out of the reach of congress? Cannot this be punished, or is a law for that purpose an abridgement of the freedom of speech?"

Here Daveiss differentiated between abridging and infringing, as quoted. He went on,

> This shews you I hope, that my view is correct in saying that the negative words which say *Congress shall not abridge the freedom of speech or of the press give them a positive right to pass any law comporting with the national power of their duty, upon either of these points, correcting any abuses, and which leave their true political freedom uninfringed.*

Daveiss made a good point in a somewhat off-the-cuff, laconic way. There was no need to dwell on it; it was accepted in 1810 that keeping guns out of a polling place keeps "true political freedom uninfringed." More accurately, it protects political freedom. For Daveiss, as for other Americans of his time, "true political freedom" involves not being shot at while voting. Guns could be used to infringe it.

Daveiss' discussion of language and actions—words and deeds, connected to force—is unusually good. The topic of 'just words,' of distinguishing between speech acts and other acts, has been a vexed one. Daveiss discussed it in terms of the rule of law: "no lawyer will deny that in a constitution as in a statute, introducing a new law, affirmative words imply a negative, and *e converso*."

> When it says the people have a right peaceably to assemble and petition for redress of grievances, a negative is implied that they shall not assemble with force and arms for that purpose, or that under color of this right they shall not assemble in such a manner as to excite to insurrection against the government.

He went on to challenge his own logic.

> It will here be asked, can congress make laws to forbid profane swearing, as not comprised within the freedom of speech—Can they say how arms shall be worn, and what and when—Can they say what solemnities shall be observed to render lawful a meeting of the people?
>
> I answer—No. The duties or powers of congress cannot be extended to local police: those of a national nature only are within their sphere.

But Daveiss makes clear that the national powers of Congress include public safety. And as he said, a negative in law or constitution implies an affirmative.

> Congress shall not point out *how* arms are to be worn; but they may say there are certain times and places in *which the citizens shall not wear arms*; and there is a certain kind of popular assemblage which shall not be lawful.

While Daveiss did not spell out forms of unlawful assemblage, grim examples include book-burnings, barn-burnings, tarring and feathering, and lynch mobs. Daveiss was a seasoned combat veteran who enlisted in the American army in his teens and died at thirty-eight after being mortally wounded in the battle of Tippecanoe. His writing does not present bellicosity or militarism as ends in themselves.

The binomial language was recognized and used across party lines, opposing parties could and did use the same lexicon, and it was used on both sides of the Atlantic and for lofty purposes and lesser. In England, a Justice of the Peace argued in 1811 that "All the Acts of Parliament that have passed for raising Rates for particular purposes are all in the affirmative, but not one of them either infringing or abridging the inherent, ancient and long usaged right in the Justices" to use tax revenues "for the Public Purposes of the County."[122] The "long usaged right" referred to by the judge was housing expenses for judges.

Back in America, in 1818 preacher Benjamin Trumbull (1735-1850) recorded in his history of Connecticut a statement from the "commissioners of the united colonies" of Massachusetts, Rhode Island, and Connecticut.

> The commissioners replied, that they found their [Rhode Island's] present state to be full of confusion and danger, and that they were desirous of giving them both advice and help. They however observed, that as the plantation made at Rhode Island, fell within the limits of the ancient patent granted to the colony of New-Plymouth, they could not receive them as a distinct confederate. They represented, that it was the design of the honourable committee of parliament, that the limits of that colony should not be abridged or infringed.[123]

The passage quoted is from Trumbull's narrative about alleged "perfidy of the Narragansett Indians" in 1648. But Trumbull in 1818 revised the commissioners' original statement. In records from the Massachusetts General Court in 1648, the same statement reads,

> To which mocion the Comis's returned this answer under all theire hands [. . .] they finde Roade Iland upon which your plantacions are setled to fall within theire line and bounds, which the honourable Comittie of parlement thinke not fitt to Straighten or infringe.[124]

Trumbull's edit was sensible. The "straighten" of 1648 would be archaic in 1818, by which time "straighten" meant, as now, to straighten out rather than to lessen. Trumbull captured the meaning of the original seventeenth-century binomial, "straighten or infringe," by converting it to the binomial preferred in the nineteenth century, "abridged or infringed."

In the first half of the nineteenth century, young readers in America were clearly expected to understand the infringe-abridge vocabulary. They ran across it in textbooks and histories. An example appears in the 1820 *History of Chelmsford* (Massachusetts). The author recommended that for a congregation,

> it is better to dismiss malcontents regularly than to retain them in uneasiness, or force them into disorderly steps. Besides the denial of the principle would infringe the rights of conscience, and abridge the religious liberties claimed by protestants as their divinely secured right, and guaranteed by the laws of the Commonwealth.[125]

The phrasing continued to appear, in books and periodicals focused on history or public policy, and in newspapers, and sometimes in laws. Again, the function of the binomial was protection, though the focus of protection was not always religion. An 1830 Connecticut statute used it to protect resources for the state's asylum: "That nothing in this act is intended, or shall be construed to infringe or abridge the grants of lotteries heretofore made to the president and directors of the Retreat for the Insane and the Enfield Bridge Company."[126]

Among the newspapers, William Leggett's short-lived *Plaindealer* of 1836-1837 used the phrasing in a larger context. Leggett (1801-1839), a popular and populist journalist, served several years as editor at the *New York Evening Post* and wrote for other papers before founding his own. His *Plaindealer* was a Democratic weekly, passionately anti-slavery. In 1836, Leggett editorialized that the District of Columbia had power to free slaves in Washington, D.C., whether Congress liked it or not.

> These rights are all expressly acknowledged in the Constitution, and Congress has Therefore, no power to pass any law infringing or abridging them. But the power of Congress over the inhabitants of the District of Columbia is as absolute as was that of Virginia and Maryland over the inhabitants of that territory, before it was ceded to the federal government. The right of either of those states to abolish slavery within its limits has not, that we are aware, ever been denied.[127]

Leggett had gone to college at Georgetown. He argued ingeniously that if Virginia and Maryland had the power to emancipate their slaves, then the territory they ceded to Congress to create Washington, D.C., had the same power. Regrettably, the argument went nowhere. Leggett died untimely at the age of thirty-eight, his health weakened by malaria contracted during his U.S. naval service. The District did not emancipate slaves until 1862, twenty-three years after Leggett's death and just months before the broader Emancipation Proclamation.

Historical American newspapers and periodicals from the nineteenth century consistently display use of the same binomial. An open letter to Vermont's congressional delegation in 1839 urged the state's delegates "to remonstrate, in the name of the people, and as a sovereign State, against any abridgement of, or infringement upon, the right of petition"—meaning anti-slavery petitions in Congress, prohibited under the Gag Rule. By the middle of the nineteenth century, the binomial was standard newspaper phrasing in various contexts, some less heated than others. A letter to the editor in the June 25, 1845, *Ypsilanti Sentinel* (Michigan), about land use, said, "I ask not that any man's rights shall be abridged or infringed."[128] A piece in the July 8, 1847, Brattleboro *Vermont Phoenix* called for a speedy end to "hostilities with Mexico," "without abridging her territory, or infringing her right of possession." Invariably, even the most mundane use of the infringe-abridge binomial in nineteenth-century newspapers distinguishes between the two words.

Occasionally the phrase became part of a trinomial that further reinforced the protections. A long, thoughtful piece on suspending *habeas corpus* in invasion or rebellion, in the May 8, 1851, *Vermont Watchman and State Journal*, referred carefully to "abridging, interfering with, or infringing" *habeas corpus*. The writer repeated the trinomial with some emphasis, carefully spelling out the protections against suspending the ancient and precious right. At other times, the old binomial remained tight. A piece in the March 4, 1857, *True American* (Steubenville, Ohio), criticized an attempt by Pennsylvania to keep non-naturalized foreigners from serving as officers in private companies. Had the law related only to public office, the writer argued, it would have been acceptable; "No man's right is infringed or abridged" by such a restriction.

The 1857 Lecompton Constitution and the 1859 Republican Party

Two prominent uses of the infringe-abridge binomial in nineteenth-century America were opening shots in an increasingly deadly conflict. Both were linked with slavery and the approaching Civil War. The first was the 1858 Lecompton Bill, the pro-slavery "Bill for the Admission of the State of Kansas into the Union," presented in the Senate on February 17, 1858. The other was the platform passed by the state convention of the Ohio Republican Party the following year, partly in response to Lecompton. As in the eighteenth century, the language of protective binomials featured in dueling public documents in the nineteenth century, used pro- and anti-slavery as it had been used pro- and anti-independence.

The bill admitting Kansas to the Union included an amendment by Senator James Green of Missouri, which passed the Senate on March 23, 1858:

> nothing in this act shall be construed to abridge or infringe any right of the people asserted in the constitution of Kansas at all times to alter, reform, or abolish their form of government in such manner as they may think proper. Congress hereby disclaiming any authority to intervene or declare the construction of the constitution of any State, except to say that it be republican in form, and not in conflict with the constitution of the United States.[129]

In other words, Kansas should enter the union under the infamous Lecompton Constitution of September 1857.

The Lecompton constitution had been designed to bring the territory of Kansas into the union as a slave state, to prevent diminishing the power of the slave states. The constitution ultimately lost in Kansas by a substantial majority. In the interim and afterward, Green's language was reported nationally, in newspapers and other periodicals including *Harper's* (then called *Harper's New Monthly Magazine*); the *Prairie Farmer*; the Raleigh, North Carolina *Weekly Standard*; the Altoona, Pennsylvania, *Tribune*; the *Tribune Almanac*; and the *National Magazine*. The Morrisville,

New York, *Madison Observer* led off its March 25, 1858, issue with "Passage of the Lecompton Bill in the Senate." The *Observer* homed in on the key language.

> We learn that the bill for the admission of Kansas into the Union as a State, with the Lecompton constitution, passed the Senate of the United States, last Tuesday, by a majority of eight votes. The bill was amended by adding the declaration that nothing therein contained should be construed to abridge or infringe any right of the people of Kansas at all times to alter, reform or abolish their form of government.[130]

The Lecompton constitution provoked strident opposition and strident support. Green's amendment, with its none-too-veiled threat of internal state revolution, was reported even in Great Britain. In fact, the infringe-abridge binomial in nineteenth-century British newspapers appeared mainly in reference to America's Lecompton issue.

The Lecompton Bill also provoked direct response in the election cycle of 1860, in which Abraham Lincoln was elected president. The new Republican Party had arisen in the first place largely in reaction to the Kansas-Nebraska Act of 1854, which opened Kansas to slavery. In 1859, the platform adopted by delegates to the Ohio state Republican convention stated that

> We claim for all citizens, native or naturalized, liberty of conscience, equality of rights, and the freest exercise of the right of suffrage; we favor whatever legislative or administrative reforms may be necessary to protect these rights, and guard against their infringement or abuse; and we oppose any abridgement whatever of the right of naturalization, now secured by law to immigrants.[131]

Newspapers across the country carried the Ohio party platform, as they did other such declarations. The state conventions in turn influenced the 1860 Republican national platform. While Ohio's exact language did not become a national party plank, the national platform did contain a similar plank protecting immigrants, using the familiar lexicon.

> That the Republican party is opposed to any change in our naturalization laws or any state legislation by which the rights of citizens hitherto accorded to immigrants from foreign lands shall be abridged or impaired; and in favor of giving a full and efficient protection to the rights of all classes of citizens, whether native or naturalized, both at home and abroad.[132]

The national party platform denounced the resumption of the African slave trade, denounced the Kansas-Nebraska Bill, and castigated the Democrats for their "desperate exertions to force the infamous Lecompton Constitution upon the protesting people of Kansas." The Republican Party has changed since 1860.

As for the Lecompton Bill itself, it passed 33 to 25. Senator Green was born in Virginia, and his brother Martin later became a Confederate general; all the members from Southern states voted Aye, joined by a few other senators, with members from border states split. The text of the bill flooded the nation. Other periodicals carrying it included the *New York Times*, the *United States Democratic Review*, and the *National Magazine*. Horace Greeley published and denounced it in his *Tribune Almanac and Political Register*, with a full account of its passage. It appeared as an entry in an 1859 reference work titled *The Political Text-book, or Encyclopedia; Containing Everything Necessary for the Reference of the Politicians and Statesmen of the United States*. Kansas ended up joining the Union as a free state in 1861, but the national Democratic Party was fractured by the conflict, with anti-slavery Democrats weakened and increasingly marginalized.

In the years just before the Civil War, polarities sharpened and intensified. The heightened tensions were continually reflected, and transmitted, in newsprint. The language of communiqué used in the eighteenth century to build the new nation was used in the nineteenth century to divide it. June 1859 was a typical month. On June 22, the Raleigh, North Carolina, *Weekly Standard* quoted the key language from Green's amendment in the Lecompton Bill, with the infringe-or-abridge binomial. On June 23, the *Highland Weekly News* (Hillsborough, Highland County, Ohio) quoted the above passage from the Ohio Republican Party platform.

In a conflict, the accepted binomials could be invoked by both sides, and they were. Amid bitter polarities, a cutting issue could underlie use of binomials like "abridged or infringed," on both sides of the issue. One such issue was slavery. The use of the infringe-abridge binomial in the hated Lecompton bill was probably enough to taint or compromise the phrase for use in any constitutional amendments after the Civil War.

Alongside newspapers, the old binomial with its variations also continued to be used officially. In 1861, the Supreme Judicial Court of Massachusetts used it in denying an appeal in *Commonwealth v. Henry Weymouth*. "This is certainly a safe and reasonable exercise of judicial discretion, which cannot be used to abridge or infringe upon the rights of any one."[133] Weymouth, the unhappy prisoner, had been convicted of larceny and sentenced to two years in prison on February 18, 1861—just days after seven seceding slave states had formed the Confederacy. Before Weymouth was incarcerated, Massachusetts revised the sentence and gave him three and a half years instead. The state supreme court upheld the increased sentence, ruling that it was legal because it occurred during the same court term, no error was found in the record, and no rights of third parties were affected: "there is no good reason for refusing to vacate a judgment for sufficient cause, and substituting a new one in its place. This is certainly a safe and reasonable exercise of judicial discretion, which cannot be used to abridge or infringe upon the rights of any one."[134] As the Massachusetts Supreme Court reports summarized the takeaway, "A judge of the superior court has power to revise and increase a sentence passed upon a convict, during the same term of court, and before the original sentence has gone into operation, or any action has been had upon it."

The court seems to have been rather hostile to the prisoner. Additional circumstances that may have influenced the increased sentence are not recorded; there is no mention of violence. It would be interesting to know whether anger stemming from the secession and the impending Civil War influenced Weymouth's situation. Some people in Massachusetts considered the act of secession itself larcenous; in 1861, the *Atlantic Monthly* magazine explicitly analogized rebellion and secession to larceny.[135]

Mr. Justice Catron

The function of public-policy binomials was protection, but sometimes protection lapsed, particularly when the same binomial was used by opposing sides. On the other side of the Mason-Dixon line, another unsavory use of the infringe-abridge binomial also appeared in print in 1861. On July 21, the *Daily Nashville Patriot* reported instructions to a grand jury by U.S. Supreme Court Justice John Catron. The grand jury had met in St. Louis, Missouri, on July 10. What Catron said was that an armed assembly cannot be considered treasonable, and the Nashville paper quoted Catron at length:

> As it is both the right and duty of every citizen to become fully informed upon all governmental affairs so as to discharge his many political obligations intelligently at the ballot-box, and in other legitimate ways, and the freedom of the press and of speech are guaranteed to him for that as well as other essential purposes; and as the right of the people peaceably to assemble and petition for redress of grievances, and to keep and bear arms, cannot be lawfully abridged or infringed, it is evident that an assemblage for the mere purpose of procuring peaceable redress for supposed grievances, cannot be considered treasonable.[136]

Catron (1786-1865) was a Supreme Court justice from 1837 to his death. His federal judgeship and his standing to rule on cases involving slavery were not jeopardized by his being a slaveholder or by the fact that his only child was fathered with an enslaved woman. In 1857, Catron had sided with the majority in the infamous *Dred Scott* case, barring federal protection from enslaved persons.

Conveniently, in July 1861, Catron allowed wide latitude to gatherings—even to armed gatherings. Specifically, he extended the latitude to "a military gathering," and to armed gatherings if the men present were not assembled "in military array":

> nor can a free and full discussion of the acts of public men and public measures, whether such discussions be in private conversations, public meetings or the press; nor can a military gathering, when assembled for no purpose or design of interfering, by force or intimidation, with the lawful functions of the government or of its constituted authorities, or of preventing the execution of any law, or of extorting its alteration or repeal, or of overthrowing the lawful supremacy of the United States government in any State or Territory. Hence a conspiracy to be treasonable must be for a *public or general*, and not a mere private object; it must contemplate force in the pursuit of its ends; it must, in order to ripen into treason, be accompanied or followed by some warlike act, such as the assembling of men in military array, and in the posture of war, or in a forcible and threatening attitude, for the furtherance of the treasonable design.

Fort Sumter had been fired on three months earlier, the U.S. Civil War had begun, and Missouri had stayed in the Union, keeping the Missouri River under federal control. By the end of the Civil War, Tennessee was the state with the second-largest number of battles fought on its soil, although Tennessee did not promote its participation afterward, in tourism, as much as did Virginia and some Deep South states.

Remarkably, Catron drew a distinction between conspiring to commit treason, and actually committing treason:

> However flagitious may be the crime of conspiracy to subvert by force the Government of our country, such conspiracy is not treason. To conspire to levy war, and actually to levy war, are distinct offenses.

As quoted, Catron then named specific activities, pretty much drawing a road map for local Confederates of what they could get away with. Traveling to a meeting or assemblage, as for example to a secret meeting to conspire, was "not an actual levying of war" and was therefore not treasonable. However, gathering men together in uniform was treasonable. (It would also be dangerously overt.) In a nod to law and order, Catron warned against misprision of treason—failing to report treasonous activities—but without comment. Most people recalling the Civil War would consider Catron's definition of treason lenient to the point of aiding and abetting.

It is important to recognize that to arrive at his ruling, Catron reworded the second amendment: "the right of the people peaceably to assemble and petition for redress of grievances, and to keep and bear arms, cannot be lawfully abridged or infringed." Apparently for the purpose of rewording it, he even linked it to the first amendment, to speech—"free and full discussion." Catron's instruction to the grand jury is the only print example, so early, of inserting "abridged" into the second amendment. Clearly it was meant to facilitate Confederate assemblages early in the Civil War.

Race, Reconstruction, and the language of later amendments

That the infringe-abridge binomial had become connected with racial justice before the Civil War should be apparent. It was used as dueling phraseology north and south of the Mason-Dixon line and in slave and non-slave territories; it was applied to oppose the Gag Rule and to support anti-slavery petitions to Congress but also showed up in the Lecompton Bill and in Judge Catron's grand jury instruction protecting local Confederate assemblages. After the Civil War, it continued to be used in the U.S., in newspapers and elsewhere, but its direct use for race matters such as the right to vote receded. The older infringe-abridge binomial was replaced by the shorter, clearer "denied or abridged," as in later Constitutional amendments.

In the context of racial justice, the replacement of the older phrasing by the newer binomial becomes explicit during Reconstruction, when both sets of terms were sometimes used side-by-side. On January 1, 1868, newspapers in the South and in Washington, D.C., reported on the Louisiana constitutional convention, being held in New Orleans. One item quoted by the press, including two papers in Washington, was that "The right of all persons to travel on the common carriers, and be entertained at all places, shall not be infringed, or in any manner abridged."[137] The motion had been offered by Pinckney Benton Stewart Pinchback. It became part of the state constitution adopted in March 1868, since known as one of the best constitutions in the history of Louisiana. Pinchback was a major figure. Designated "a Negro," or "colored," in the newsprint diction of the time, he was a free black, a Civil War veteran in the Union army, and the first governor of African-American descent. He was later elected to the U.S. Senate but was prevented from taking his seat by a spurious reelection.

Language like Louisiana's was adopted by Mississippi. Combining the protections of the older and newer binomials is particularly clear in Reconstruction laws from Mississippi. The 1873 edition of the *Laws of the State of Mississippi* demonstrates the connections. Along with dealing with social ills such as habitual drunkards, the insane, and defaulting insurance companies, Reconstruction legislators in Mississippi passed an emphatic law on May 13, 1871.[138] "Be it enacted," it began,

> That all citizens of this State, without distinction of race, color or previous condition of servitude, are entitled to the equal and impartial enjoyment of any accommodation, advantage, facility or privilege furnished by common carriers running in or through, or plying within this State, whether upon land or upon waters, by any keeper, owners or lessee of any hotel, inn or restaurant, by any owner, managers or lessees of any theater or other place of public amusement, or of public entertainment or accommodation, and the equal and impartial enjoyment of any such accommodation, facility, privilege or advantage is hereby declared to have always been, is now, and shall forever remain a right inherent in every citizen or person, and which right shall not be denied, abridged, or infringed on account of any distinction of race, color or previous condition of servitude.[139]

Loophole-closing language appears throughout, and the binomials are part of the picture; the piling up of protections indicates the urgent motivation behind the law. Legislators knew what they were dealing with. The language of the new fifteenth amendment is explicitly included; so is the older language of infringement.

> The Act continued in the same vein;
>
> any person who shall violate any of the foregoing provisions, or who shall deny to, or withhold from any person the enjoyment of any of the foregoing accommodations, facilities, privileges or advantages, equally and impartially on any such account, or for any such reason, or who shall abridge or infringe the same, or who shall incite thereto, shall be guilty of a misdemeanor.

Further trying to close loopholes, it continued,

> And any corporation, association or individual violating the aforesaid provisions, or any of them, or denying, withholding, abridging or infringing, in any manner, any of the aforesaid rights, privileges, accomodations, facilities or advantages of any citizen or person, shall, upon conviction thereof, forfeit their, his or her charter or license, or other authority or power.
>
> Section 2 enacted
>
> That the Circuit Courts of this State shall have appellate jurisdiction in all causes arising under or by virtue of this Act, and it shall only be necessary for the plaintiff or plaintiffs [. . .] to show that he, or she, or they, as the case may be, were refused, denied or withheld equal and impartial accommodation [. . .] or that theirs, his or her right or rights as declared by this Act were

> abridged or infringed, and no sufficient cause was assigned, given
> or made known to the plaintiff, then and there, at the time of
> such refusal, denial, or withholding, or abridging, or infringing of
> such accommodation, facility, privilege or advantage applied for;
> and the burden of proof shall be upon the defendant to show
> that such refusal, denial or withholding of such accommodation,
> facility, privilege or advantage, or abridging or infringing of the
> same was not on account of race, color or previous condition of
> servitude.

The clear intent of the laws was to uphold protections for civil rights. As we know, neither the law nor the safeguards stood. Instead, irrational, hyper-intense segregation—whether *de facto* or *de jure*—became the law in Mississippi, despite its effects on education, employment, and the economy as well as on justice, in a misbegotten self-deprivation that has entrenched the state among the poorest in the union for generations.

On the other side of the line, the safeguarding binomial also continued to be used against the Constitution. In 1876, some prominent citizens in South Carolina published a widely circulated open letter "To the People of the United States." Its message was obvious. The letter began on a note to warm bloodthirsty hearts. "For ten long weary years the white people of South Carolina have endured a condition of things which any Northern State would have been tempted to throw off in two years at the point of a bayonet, if it could have been done in no other way."[140] It continued with a series of statements beginning, "It is not true";

> It is not true that the white people of the State are hostile to the
> colored people, or have any design or imposition to abridge or
> infringe their political or civil rights. On the contrary, in their
> conventions, and in the speeches of their candidates, for six years
> or more, the most public and solemn pledges have been given
> that all the rights of the colored people shall be respected and
> protected. The colored people should know that these pledges
> will be faithfully kept.

The connection with race was particularly destructive. As it happens, the letter was written partly to justify South Carolina "rifle-clubs":

> It is not true that the few 'rifle-clubs' in the State are 'combinations
> of men against the law,' or that they are engaged in 'murdering
> some peaceable citizens and intimidating others,' or that 'they
> cannot be controlled or suppressed by the ordinary course of
> justice.' The President has been deceived. These clubs existed
> with the knowledge and recognition of the governor. Not one
> of them ever acted in defiance of law, or against the government
> or constituted authorities. The hostility to them of Governor
> Chamberlain and his coadjutors is recent; it is political, and is
> designed to affect the coming election.

As an admirer pointed out, the letter was signed by "The entire body of the clergy of Charleston, of every denomination, together with the President's [*sic*] of the banks of that city." The twenty-one signers did in fact include seven local bank presidents, one bank vice president, the head of the Charleston Chamber of Commerce, and twelve men of the cloth—Baptist, Catholic, Episcopal, Jewish, Lutheran, Methodist, Presbyterian, and two military chaplains—all white.

Giving voice to the repressed financial and ecumenical elite of Charleston, the letter was entered into the congressional record in 1877, appeared in the *South-Atlantic* monthly magazine in 1878, and was printed again in a reference book titled *Representative Men of the South*, published in Philadelphia in 1880. It continued to be printed and praised until 1909. Whatever its impact on state or national politics, it accurately reflected the temper in some circles. Governor Daniel Chamberlain, the Reconstruction governor referred to, who supported civil rights, lost the upcoming gubernatorial election to former Confederate Wade Hampton III. Chamberlain left South Carolina in 1877, settled in New York City, and later became professor of constitutional law at Cornell. The "Letter" from Charleston, which now looks grotesque, is a valuable indicator of the period. It also reveals offhandedly that the supporters of Southern 'rifle-clubs' were familiar with the constitutional verbs *abridge* and *infringe*, and with the distinction between the two. They used the phrase "to abridge or infringe" themselves.

The binomials with such ample precedent continued to be used. The see-saw of shared tradition for opposing values kept moving. Writers pro-racial justice as well as anti- kept using the same lexicon. On October 18, 1877, the *Jackson Standard* in Ohio ran a long, eloquent speech by Senator John J. Ingalls of Kansas. Following some firsthand observation of combat and a touching defense of freedmen, Ingalls summarized the outcome of the Civil War.

> The United States were at last a nation, and not a mere aggregation of detached and incoherent communities. The nation existed, not at the pleasure of a State, nor of a majority of the States, nor of all the States, but by virtue of the will of a majority of all the people. Citizenship was made a National attribute. Behind every citizen, white or black, at home or abroad, stood the Nation, a beneficent, potential energy, pledged to protect him in the full, free and quiet enjoyment and exercise of all the rights of citizenship. No man could be so humble, so obscure, so remote, as to become an alien from its blessings. If his rights under the Constitution were infringed or abridged, and redress was refused by the localities, he could confidently apply to the Nation for restitution.[141]

In this optimistic and highly patriotic view, "The war was really a great convention to amend the Constitution, and 13th, 14th, and fifteenth amendments were the result."

Sadly, Ingalls went on, the War was followed by backlash. Service in the Union army was disparaged, Confederate sympathizers were taking control in Congress, and enfranchisement of former slaves was damaged or destroyed, partly from "the inexplicable blunders of reconstruction," which mistakenly in Ingalls' view took a top-down approach through the existing power apparatus of the South rather than by building from the ground up. The article conveyed a warning. "The gigantic revolution through which we have passed did not arise upon a point of etiquette, and it cannot be ended by a polite apology. It was a great struggle between two hostile and enduring forces, which must continue till one or the other shall become placed or expelled from our system of government." For Ingalls, the two hostile forces were not North and South; the struggle was between two mutually exclusive arrangements of rights and powers.

> It must go on, either till the right of one man, or class, by violence or force, to prescribe the opinions, control the acts and define the political relations of others is freely conceded, or until the right of every individual however humble, to think, act or vote, in accordance with the suggestions of his own judgment or conscience under the law shall be absolutely unquestioned. So long as this right is denied or abridged under any pretext, or in any locality, North, South, East, or West [. . .] so long the conflict must last.

On one side was the power of the few to control the many, "by violence or force." On the other side of the argument was the right of each individual to act and to vote "his own judgment or conscience under the law." Chaucer's Parson did not have the same vocabulary, but Ingalls' distinction aligns with values that centuries' worth of English binomials tried to protect.

After the Civil War

After the phrase "denied or abridged" had replaced it in a constitutional amendment, the binomial "infringed or abridged" continued to be used in the U.S., aside from North-South polarities and the contexts of race and Reconstruction. In 1872, Illinois' Superintendent of Public Instruction used it to satirize opponents of mandatory school attendance:

> But, let there be no compulsion in the matter of attendance. Any legislation on that subject would be un-American, anti-republican, arbitrary, despotic, odious. Every parent must be left

at perfect liberty to avail himself of these princely provisions or not, and to educate his child or leave it in ignorance, as he may elect; and where there is no parental control, the right of the child to go to school or stay away must on no account be infringed or abridged.[142]

The tone suggests that the phrase "infringed or abridged" had already suffered from over-exposure by 1872 and was ripe for satire. The National Educational Association convention offered a receptive audience; the speech was reprinted and published several times in several states.

Pennsylvania's state constitution of 1874 used "abridged" and "infringe," although not in the concise binomial, to rein in corporations. In the section on "Private Corporations,"

The exercise of the right of eminent domain shall never be abridged, or so construed, as to prevent the General Assembly from taking the property and franchises of incorporated companies, and subjecting them to public use, the same as the property of individuals; and the exercise of the police power of the State shall never be abridged or so construed as to permit corporations to conduct their business in such manner as to infringe the equal rights of individuals or the general well-being of the State.[143]

The 1874 constitution remained in use into the twentieth century. Pennsylvania's current constitution does not retain the section quoted, although it does specify that corporations are subject to changes in state law (Art. 10). No recent instances of Pennsylvania's exercising eminent domain against JP Morgan Chase or Bank of America come to mind. However, railroad companies often exercised eminent domain against landowners.

The protective language of the binomial must have been widely used to criticize corporations like the railroad companies. Examples can be found in old newspapers. On April 14, 1882, the *Omaha Daily Bee* scolded,

What private right have they [companies] not abridged and infringed? When the value and the purity of the greatest private right [. . .] the right of a free ballot—what need of naming any other invasion? This is the [. . .] final expression of all private rights in the United States. Destroy it or abridge it, and you destroy or abridge every right and every liberty which is builded upon it. That these corporations do systematically destroy or abridge it by injecting themselves illegally into our politics—by their interference with the machinery of our elections, and by the corruption of our officers after they are elected, no intelligent citizen will for a moment deny.[144]

A long piece in the *St. Paul Daily Globe*, October 6, 1887, taking an anti-corporate stance on the management of railway corporations and the effect of railroads on land use, stated that "These rights cannot be abridged without infringing on the rights of the people."

The infringed-or-abridged binomial also continued to be used in education and government. Even while usage of *infringed* was softening, the binomial continued to define policy. In 1892, New York's State Superintendent of Public Instruction provided guidelines on using schools for other lessons like music lessons.

> If no one objects and if the use does no injury to the property, the trustee is justified in permitting it. If objection is made by anyone who is not pestiferous by nature, the safe course is to heed it. In any event, he is bound to see that no injury is done to the property, and that the common rights which all have in it are in no wise infringed or abridged.[145]

The binomial explicitly protected common rights.

On the opposite coast, a similarly lofty note was sounded in 1893. When Washington State Governor Elisha P. Ferry retired, he reminded the state legislature that "A fundamental principle in all legislation should be, that the rights of all should be protected and the rights of none destroyed, infringed or abridged."[146] Usage was sometimes looser by 1893, needing a triple threat (trinomial) to reinforce the principles.

Admittedly the phrase could sometimes fail to clarify policy. In 1898, the Official Gazette of the U.S. Patent Office pronounced that

> The Office is not bound to declare an interference between a patent and an application in order to give the patentee the opportunity of contesting the grant of a patent to the applicant because in its judgment the patentee's rights would be infringed or abridged by granting a patent on a pending application.[147]

The idea here seems to be that a patent can neither be granted nor contested until it is approved, but the language is not crystal-clear.

In 1899, the "infringed or abridged" binomial arose again in *Brown v. New Jersey*. For the state, James S. Erwin argued,

> No privilege or immunity of plaintiff in error as a citizen of the United States is infringed or abridged by a trial by an impartial jury of twelve men in the state and county where the crime was committed.[148]

The case was important and is included in the *Encyclopedia of Capital Punishment in the United States* (2008). The Supreme Court ruled in *Brown* that a jury empaneled from a limited jury pool, in a capital case, did not deprive the defendant of due process of law. In the trial, the jury pool was reduced from ninety-six to forty-eight, from which defense and prosecution could each strike twenty-four names. Defense lawyers argued unsuccessfully that the five peremptory challenges allowed in the capital trial were fewer than Brown would have had in an ordinary jury trial. (This argument does not appear in the *Encyclopedia* entry.)

Brown also chalked up another minus. Following *Barron v. Baltimore* (1833), the court also held that the Bill of Rights did not apply to the state of New Jersey anyway. Delivering the opinion for the court, Mr. Justice Brewer said,

> The first ten Amendments to the Federal Constitution contain no restrictions on the powers of the state, but were intended to operate solely on the Federal government [. . .] The state has full control over the procedure in its courts, both in civil and criminal cases, subject only to the qualification that such procedure must not work a denial of fundamental rights, or conflict with specific and applicable provisions of the Federal Constitution [. . .] The state is not tied down by any provision of the Federal Constitution to the practice and procedure which existed at the common law. Subject to the limitations heretofore named it may avail itself of the wisdom gathered by the experience of the century to make such changes as may be necessary. For instance, while at the common law an indictment by the grand jury was an essential preliminary to trial for felony, it is within the power of a state to abolish the grand jury entirely and proceed by information.[149]

Brown v. New Jersey came thirty years after the fourteenth amendment. Only after another twenty-five years would the courts apply fourteenth amendment principles of due process of law and equal protection by law to the states, bringing the privileges and immunities clause of the Constitution—and the Bill of Rights—to bear on state governments. However, Mr. Justice Brewer's writing may have contained the seeds of change. Brewer's flatfooted statement that "the first ten Amendments" contain no restrictions on the states indicates that other amendments do contain some restrictions on the states, from which it follows that there are qualitatively different kinds of constitutional amendments. The logical inference would be that some constitutional amendments are more constitutional than others. Such an argument carries the seeds of its own demise.

In summary, the infringe-or-abridge phrasing often turned up in print in the U.S. as it had in Britain—before and after the Bill of Rights, before and after the Civil War, before and after the Fourteenth Amendment, and before and after U.S. expansion into western territories. In the nineteenth century, the phrasing went from communiqué to cliché. It appeared both as shorthand for principles of justice, as in Reconstruction laws, and as ridicule against highfalutin accusations. It still lasted into the twentieth century. "Any law passed by the legislature infringing or abridging this right is unconstitutional and void," argued a Texas appellant unsuccessfully in 1909, convicted of selling game out of season. The right in question was the constitutional right of selling (alienating) property, in this case dead ducks. The Texas Court of Criminal Appeals upheld the game laws and the conviction.[150]

Binomials as protection: government, law, and policy

The infringe-abridge binomial is used to protect rights throughout the English-speaking world. It continues to be used in former British colonies, sometimes expanded into a trinomial. The Canadian Bill of Rights, assented to in 1960, contains a provision that

> Every law of Canada shall, unless it is expressly declared by an Act of the Parliament of Canada that it shall operate notwithstanding the Canadian Bill of Rights, be so construed and applied as not to abrogate, abridge or infringe or to authorize the abrogation, abridgment or infringement of any of the rights or freedoms herein recognized and declared.[151]

New Zealand's Parliament acknowledges that

> the existence of other interests that may be infringed or abridged by the operation of parliamentary privilege justifies restricting the privileges to activities having a real connection with the operation of the legislature, and confining their scope in respect of such activities so as not to trespass on other rights unnecessarily.[152]

In 2001, India's National Commission on Labour stated that the rights expressed in the U.N. Universal Declaration of Human Rights "have so much become part of the human conscience that nations and groups are embarrassed and humbled when infringement or abridgement of these rights within their territories is exposed, and brought under public gaze within their country and outside."[153] Jamaica's new Charter of Fundamental Rights and Freedoms, passed in 2010, states that "Parliament shall pass no law and no organ of the State shall take any action which abrogates, abridges or infringes those rights."[154]

On this global English platform rests the language of American law; binomials, which have featured in the language of civil affairs for centuries, also feature in the language of governance. Obviously, lawyers as well as linguists are familiar with binomials. Legal writing and legal documents are replete with them. Many are terms of art, alliterative ("drunk and disorderly") or not ("null and void"). Many traditional English binomials convey familiar things—"hearth and home," "forgive and forget," "read and write," but the full spectrum of color and meaning extends well into the realm of law. There is not necessarily a hard line between familiar and official. Some very old, homespun, alliterative binomials had legal heft, such as "life and limb," "bed and board," "to have and to hold," and still have legal heft.

In government, law, and policy, many of the strongest binomials are action phrases—verb binomials. Acts and omissions matter for governance of self or others. For centuries, verb binomials have represented positive and negative actions—acts or omissions by individuals, governments, and other entities. They still represent things to do or not to do: "aid and abet," "cease and desist," "drink and drive." Examples include phrases dating from the early Patristic "use or abuse," in late antiquity and through the Medieval period; to "deny or delay," in the eighteenth and nineteenth centuries; to "abuse or neglect," in child protective services today.

In one familiar legal category, wills, binomial phrases are traditionally rife. In English wills, binomials go back to the Anglo-Saxons (410-1066). The oldest wills in English are a set of 62 extant wills in Old English (Anglo-Saxon), approximately 250 years before the Norman invasion.[155] Like wills today—"will and testament"—they contained frequent binomials including verb binomials. A will from the years 871 to 888 opened, "I, Ealdorman Alfred command to be *written and make known*," addressing "whatsoever man will rightly *observe and perform* these *benefactions and gifts* and these *written and verbal* [oral] statements."[156] The Anglo-Saxon wills consistently used phrases like "my estates and my possessions," "declare and order," "declare and command," "consent and write," "confirm and consent," "with cattle and with men," etc.[157]

This feature should not be downplayed. The wills averaged only 300 to 350 words apiece, yet they contained an average of four binomials.[158] If each binomial contained three or four words, then the binomials carried three percent to five percent of the total word count in the wills. Furthermore, a comprehensive study of the wills has found more than 100 binomials, and "Only about a quarter of these expressions occurred more than once. In other words, what is common is not any given expression but the general phenomenon of binomials." To clarify, again, these wills date from before the Norman Conquest; they were not using binomials to translate Old French into English. The binomials are pairs of Old English words. The styling provided by the binomials strengthened the performance of the wills. More than a thousand years ago, wills in English used binomials for economic, political, administrative, and legal purposes. Their function was not to translate separate languages but to reinforce, to protect—a function still performed in wills by binomials today.

Another familiar, long-lasting category for binomials in law language is oaths of office. Swearing-in ceremonies and oaths of office have used binomials for centuries. When James I took the coronation oath in 1603, he used language like that of every British monarch since 1308. James vowed to "protect and defend" bishops and others, and "to hold and keep" and to "defend and uphold" the laws and customs of Britain, intoning, "I grant and promise to keep them."[159] Three and a half centuries later, Queen Elizabeth II vowed to "perform and keep" and to "maintain and preserve inviolably" the Church of England and the laws and customs of British dominions.[160]

The sonorous phrases may be dismissed as boilerplate, but oaths of office are not mere formality. Like charters including Magna Carta, and like American police mottos such as "To serve and protect," they have been invoked as standard when a monarch or governor fell short on the job. Like laws, they are lesson and reminder of the objectives of governance, including self-governance. They are also shorthand references to the limits on power.

Descending to more ordinary law, verb binomials can represent crimes ("break and enter," "hit and run"), white-collar crimes ("to defame or defraud"), abuses of authority, and other abuses. "Deny or delay" is a famous example from legal maxim; "denied or abridged" figures in the 15th, 19th, 24th, and 26th amendments to the Constitution; and "to deny or disparage" is part of the Ninth Amendment: "The enumeration in the Constitution, of certain rights, shall not be construed to deny or disparage others retained by the people." The category of verb binomials is part of the focus of this book—the crisp English phrases used over millennia to ward off arbitrary exercises of power, to close loopholes under whatever name, to prevent affronts against rights and freedom, in whole or in part.

The umbrella concept is protection. Most people would prefer that injustice and abuses of power be identifiable, and the cultural heritage of the United States includes a long, proud history of English phrases that identify and limit arbitrary power. In a long-running game of constitutional Whack-a-Mole, the phrases have surfaced throughout the centuries when abuses have popped up. Geoffrey Chaucer (1343-1400) used them in the fourteenth century. A government official under kings Edward III and Richard II as well as a wellspring of English poetry, Chaucer closed out the *Canterbury Tales* with his Parson, who used the binomial "holdynge or abregynge" (withholding or abridging).[161] The "Parson's Tale" uses "holdynge or abregynge" to denounce "crewel lordschepes" (cruel lords) who withhold or dock the "wagis of servantes" (their servants' pay). Chaucer's fourteenth-century parson does not use the word "self-governance," but the concept informs and explicates his long prose sermon, including the criticism of "lordschepes" who behave in an unlordly way.

Self-governance and protection have continued to be joined to the concepts of humanity and governance for the seven centuries since Chaucer. In English public documents, the principles have always been reinforced by verb binomials. As the centuries unscrolled, the fourteenth-century binomial used by Chaucer's Parson was joined by "abbrege or abate" in the fifteenth century, as when a 1450 law neither abridges nor abates a patent granted earlier; by "refreyne & abregge," meaning that God restrains and limits evil, from an early Wycliffite piece; and by "defalcacion or abreggement," as in a law of 1475 mandating that officers ("Capetains") be paid their wages, "bethout any rewarde of curtesyie of colour gyven, bribe, defalcacion or abreggement, or undew assignacion"—without pretext, bribe, misappropriation or abridgement, or favoritism.[162] These in turn were joined in the sixteenth century by "alter or infringe," "reduce or annul," "take or destroy," and "take or hold"; and in the seventeenth century by "denied or delayed," "denied or detained," "to deprive or abridge," and "contradicted or infringed."

The over-all pattern is consistent from Magna Carta to the Bill of Rights. The phrase "infringed or weakened" appears in seventeenth-century translations of Magna Carta.[163] James I assured Parliament in 1621 that he had no intent to "derogate or infringe" the traditional privileges and liberties of Parliament.[164] James' exact degree of sincerity at the moment of speaking is beside the point; he used the right language to say what he needed to say. The 1641 Massachusetts Body of Liberties used "without impeachment and infringement."[165] Following and adding to the other traditional binomials came "deprived or abridged" in the seventeenth and eighteenth centuries, and "abridged and infringed" in the eighteenth century. New York State's preamble ratifying the U.S. Constitution in 1788 declared "that the rights aforesaid cannot be abridged or violated."[166] Additionally, the eighteenth century employed the phrase "deny or disparage," incorporated into the U.S. Bill of Rights in 1789 despite some Congress members' concern that the word "disparage" might not be widely understood. Elbridge Gerry of Massachusetts (1844-1814), a future Vice President, wanted to substitute "deny or impair."[167]

Beyond style to protection

The binomials in law and governance are not just stylistic effect. While they have been used and are used to highlight significance, they are not just highlighting. They might seem to invite parody, but they do not merely add sonorousness or make legal language sound more intimidating, imposing, or lawyer-like. They are not just 'poetic' or 'oratorical' flourishes; they are substantive. Furthermore, each term in the phrase is substantive. Therefore, most binomials are not just doublets, two words with the same origin but descended etymologically through different channels (such as "channel" and "canal").

And despite their utility, they do not necessarily come from translating Latin into Old English, or from translating at all. Contradicting an older theory, they did not just clarify Anglo-Norman law for Anglo-Saxons or provide dual Germanic and Latinate translations for the same concepts. With all due respect to World History classes and Sir Walter Scott's *Ivanhoe*, to pair two words like "will and testament" does more than just join Anglo and Norman dialects, transmitting the conquerors' law to the flaxen Saxon Rowena and the dusky biblical import Rebecca. Incidentally, Scott used "infringe" and "abridge" correctly, but he did not join them in a binomial. Scott was more likely to assign high-flown, sonorous language to Saxon courage and defiance than to Norman authority in the person of the evil Prince John and Brian de Bois-Guilbert.

In a document of public significance like constitutional amendments, the paired words are more than just appositives. The second term does not just paraphrase the first; it fills in gaps left by the first. In government and public policy, the pairs of action words identify two related acts or omissions. While earlier writers in Britain and America sometimes used quasi-synonymous phrases like "infringed or violated" in public documents, redundancy for emphasis largely passed out of fashion over time. As constitutional principles crystallized, the phrasing crystallized too, progressively refining pairings such as "infringed or abridged."

The relations between the words paired in binomials are a large topic in linguistics. Even simple, traditional, concise binomials display various internal relationships. At their simplest, they may be opposites like "night and day" or "work and play." But for the phrasing to be pointed, even opposing terms must be related. As in "acts and omissions," opposing terms are part of the same picture. "Sink or swim," both are in the water; "fast and loose" were an Elizabethan handkerchief game, a sixteenth-century version of spin-the-bottle. Paired words that overlap are more closely related, as in "rest and recreation," "pain and suffering," "rights and liberties." Overlapping words are joined not only to relate them but also to distinguish them. Although less adept writers may have used them as quasi-synonyms, they are not actually synonyms or alternative ways of saying the same thing. Rest in "rest and recreation" is part of recreation, if your brand of recreation is strenuous sports, or rest may be your brand of recreation, if not; but each term differently protects respite. Suffering in "pain and suffering" comes with pain, but not only from pain, while pain leads to more long-term effects suffered; both protect redress for the wrong done. Protection is the underlying rationale, the common denominator, in the pairings, as it is the underlying rationale of law and order in human society, and protection is linguistically accomplished by aligning related concepts in twos (or in threes, in trinomials).

In seventeenth-century binomials describing someone's manner as "warlike and threatening" or "hostile and threatening," the descriptors had distinct meanings. "Warlike" alone could mean appearance, costume, not necessarily threatening, and "hostile" alone might not convey force or threat. Both terms were necessary to identify and to protect against assault or harm. We use similar phrases today. In "laws and regulations" and "rules and regulations," laws and rules are different from regulations, but both must be upheld to work; both protect law and order, another familiar binomial. For a will to have "force or effect," one must be of "sound mind and body." A will may also bequeath "goods and chattels," protecting property both indoors and outdoors from loophole-seekers. In a contract, the phrase "express or implied" guards against underhanded indirection as well as direct wrong; it upholds both letter and spirit in an agreement. Britons in their country and in America had many such phrases, some surviving today, as in ordinary deeds, wills, and Powers of Attorney, which still use them abundantly.

The words in binomials are often paired by degree. The words relate, but one is greater than the other. In mathematical terms, they look like (A>B), as in "sewing and alterations" or "tailoring and alterations." Often the larger term comes first— "alive and well," "peace and quiet," "all or nothing," "more or less." This rule is not airtight; "day and age" works differently, as do arguably "law and order" and "letter and spirit."[168] In "force and fraud," force comes first because force presents the more immediate and urgent harm; with fraud, you may have time to deal with it; with a sufficient degree of force, not. A difference in degree can become a difference in kind.

Throughout the history of Anglo-American governing, the words paired in binomials have reinforced each other. The two words may be ordered in a way to refine their thrust or to intensify it, but either way they work together. Even ordinary examples like "goods and services" or "pain and suffering" or "express or implied" show the work. In phrases creating the Bill of Rights, the greater the precision, the greater the reinforcement. Reinforcement was particularly pointed in protection of just rights and liberties—"oath or affirmation," "life or limb," "cruel and unusual," to mention three progressively refined, internally tightened pairs in the Bill of Rights. The preamble to the Bill of Rights itself calls the first ten amendments "declaratory and restrictive," language "in addition to, and amendment of" the Constitution. Members of the Constitutional Convention and the first federal Congress may have had an ongoing temptation to fall into aphorism, drafting respectively the Constitution and the Bill of Rights, but both bodies largely abstained. Any binomials remaining in each document carry significant legal heft.

Eighteenth-century English binomials in America had precedent, but they did not necessarily come verbatim from hallowed constitutional documents. While many came to America from English history, some came from English *historians*. Binomial phrasing was an authorial fashion in eighteenth-century histories. If readers wanted to learn British history from contemporaneous books written in English, they would run across binomials, framing the central issue, the take-away, in every major episode of English history. From 1650 to 1789, any British historian would deal with the major chapters of constitutional history going at least back to Magna Carta, and the authors handled key episodes using traditional binomials and parallelism that sounded traditional and suggested tradition. That the original speeches, laws, commentaries, or promulgations might have been in Latin or French is beside the point. They were translated into the English of the seventeenth and eighteenth centuries—when English history was a hot topic—and the translations universally involved the kinds of pairings discussed here. Again, the pairings were not just style. In chapter after chapter of British constitutional history, they were used to convey the gravamen—the fundamental point, the main issue, the landmark.

A Londoner in 1745 wanting to learn about the Constitutions of Clarendon, for example—the famous clash in 1164 involving Thomas à Becket—would read that Clarendon, signed off on under Henry II, separated criminal and ecclesiastical cases. "These were sworn to by all the peers, spiritual and temporal, and even by Thomas à Becket, archbishop of Canterbury: but he afterwards refused to subscribe them with the rest; and appealing to the pope, was adjudged and declared a traitor."[169] "Spiritual and temporal" echoed Magna Carta. The binomials which transmitted the principles in the Clarendon Constitutions, in histories published between 1739 and 1767, are still understandable today—"duty and allegiance," "goods and chattels," "(loss of) life or limb," "law and custom." Clarendon is cited as a landmark in British jurisprudence. Historians' handling of Clarendon contributed to the lexicon of constitutional thought. Johnson's dictionary cites the Constitutions of Clarendon repeatedly.

The other major episodes of British constitutional history received similar handling—especially Magna Carta, the landmark of the thirteenth century, so famous that people around the globe recognize the name, even if they do not know what it represents. Every historian, lawyer, and judge writing on Magna Carta seems to have felt obligated to use dualities including binomials, both in translations of the charter itself and in commentary on it. From Lord Edward Coke in the seventeenth century to Daines Barrington in 1766 to Oliver Goldsmith in 1771 to Frederic Hervey in 1779, crisp parallelism and sonorous binomials come into play.[170] Samuel Johnson, writing the *History and Defence of Magna Charta* in 1772, kept up the reverent, symmetrical tradition, repeatedly using the phrase "laws and liberties."[171] Many of Johnson's references to "liberties" appear in binomials, and Johnson's *Defence* often paired concepts such as "liberties and free customs" and "rights and liberties."

Magna Carta was cited over and over in the seventeenth and eighteenth centuries. In 1670, a sympathetic history of William Penn's trial in England relied heavily on Magna Carta.[172] A passionate treatise against libel prosecutions, dedicated to the voters of Middlesex in 1769, did the same.[173] John Adams cited the great charter in the 1765 Braintree Instructions. Among the favored citations were those that "No freeman shall be taken or imprisoned" without due process; and that accusations must be vouched by oaths "by good and lawful men of that vicinage." The terms in these binomials are not synonyms or quasi-synonyms. "Taken" and "imprisoned" are different actions, and "good" and "lawful" are different characteristics. In the first binomial, without the protections, a defendant could be imprisoned after coming in, without being 'taken.' In the second, a witness could have ethical character but might not be a lawful resident with accurate knowledge of the circumstances.

Partly the parallel framing in later writing came from reverence; partly it came from citing the constitutional precedents. Magna Carta itself opens with phrases (in translation) such as "for us and for our heirs," "rights and franchises," "entirely and fully," "of our mere and free will." It affirms the "very great and very necessary privilege" of the churches.[174] It allows the right of property to all freemen, "to have and to hold," "to them and their heirs," "of us and our heirs." The "ancient customs and liberties" of the city of London are affirmed "by land and water"; merchants are to be allowed to move "with safety and security" "by land and water." "Life or member" are not to be endangered; officials are not to be influenced by gifts or offers "given or taken." "We will sell to none, we will deny nor delay to none right or justice." King John's colorful reign (1199-1216) overflowed with significance for British readers—it produced more history than it could consume—and the history was often transmitted in manageable as well as symmetrical binomials. However, in the eighteenth century, British history, Irish history, and Scots history were matter not of mere brilliant aphorisms but of constitutional distinctions.

The framers of the U.S. Constitution had two millennia of European political philosophy to draw on, from classical antiquity onward, and the more learned founders, like Adams, evoked classical forebears in their writing as buildings in the new U.S. capitol evoked classical architecture. Now, less revered but more recent books joined the older works on political philosophy and British history. The oldest concepts were transmitted in phrasing established, yet fresh. Recorded in contemporaneous histories and dictionaries along with more official sources, eighteenth-century language created the Declaration of Independence, the Constitution, and the Bill of Rights.

English binomials in America

For anyone interested in English history or English literature, major caches of English binomials can be found in three large sources among others—the works of printer William Caxton in the fifteenth century, versions of the Book of Common Prayer in the sixteenth and seventeenth centuries, and the writing of William Blackstone in the eighteenth century. The main difficulty in the research is the sheer number of examples.

British colonists carried the use of binomials with them to North America and elsewhere. Eighteenth-century America had a high literacy rate.[175] It also had a foreordained penchant for wheat-and-chaffing in the fertile fields of British constitutional history. Inevitably, Americans in the eighteenth century used a full complement of constitutional and legal binomials. Some remain recognizable, even familiar. The Pennsylvania Constitution of 1776 used the binomial "deprived or abridged," saying that any man professing belief in God could not be deprived or abridged of any civil rights because of his religion.[176] This (limited) phrasing was swiftly transmitted to Europe, was retained by successive versions of the Pennsylvania constitution, and was pointedly quoted back at the 1787 Constitutional Convention by Philadelphia Jewish citizen Jonas Phillips.[177] It was adapted by James Madison in his draft Bill of Rights for Congress in 1789 for what became the first amendment.

The U.S. Constitution in 1787 employed several binomials, none for mere flourish. The first opened the famous Preamble in which we the people "ordain and establish" the Constitution. The concise phrasing was a deliberate choice; similar language in the 1686 Dongan Charter used longer phrases to establish the city of Albany, New York.[178] The precise binomial "ordain and establish" had also been used in British public documents; examples date from Henry V onward. In 1642, Charles I ordained and established October 23 as a day of thanksgiving for deliverance from "malignant and devilish Papists" and other conspirators in Dublin.[179] In 1644, the House of Commons used the same phrase to set up a Court Martial for London.[180] The "ordain and establish" binomial crops up in British histories of monasteries, of the City of London, and of the Church of England.[181] With Yankee frugality, the thrifty American colonists kept using, re-used, and recycled English phrases, ransacking august English sources for their own lofty objectives of governance.

Binomials appear in the Constitution even though the framers wanted to avoid aphorism. Congress has power to make all laws "necessary and proper" to perform its duties, the phrase used earlier by Parliament.[182] In Article 4, the citizens of each state shall be entitled to all "privileges and immunities" of citizens in the several states. The deeply traditional phrase "privileges and immunities" was much used in eighteenth-century histories and other books, although like "ordain and establish" it also appeared as part of longer phrases like "rights, privileges, and immunities." "Privileges and immunities" were applied to the Church of England and to English universities.[183] In 1749 the phrase was applied to dissenters from the

Church of England; an author using the pseudonym "Machiavel" argued that dissenters should be admitted to all privileges and immunities of the state.[184]

As with other binomials, the phrase "privileges and immunities" became part of a pointed back-and-forth. In 1769, several British government officials authored an anti-independence pamphlet, the *Controversy between Great-Britain and Her Colonies Reviewed*, reminding Americans several times of their "privileges and immunities" as British subjects.[185] Of course, the pamphlet responded to the colonists' having claimed those same privileges and immunities.[186] London printer John Almon bound the Massachusetts and Virginia resolutions, declaring said rights, together in the same volume with the British reply. Clearly the reply failed to change hearts and minds, and the "privileges and immunities" phrase in the U.S. Constitution could be considered a final riposte. The exchange was another example of a binomial's featuring in dueling public documents.

Sometimes the binomials inherited by the Constitution were condensed from the earlier sources. Sometimes they were transferred from other fields. For the section of the Constitution laying out legislative powers (Article 1, Section 8), provenance is mixed. Congress's power "to lay and collect" taxes, duties, imposts, etc., seems to be an American coinage. The neat binomial was not used earlier by Parliament. (Precisionist Noah Webster found this clause in the Constitution possibly "ambiguous," although not because it was a binomial; Webster speculated that it could perhaps seem to refer to more than one part of the sentence.)[187] "To define and punish" piracies and felonies is not found verbatim in British law prior to 1787. Legitimate though the aim may be, the concise phrase calling on government to define as well as to punish the crime of piracy was more American than British in 1787. "To raise and support" is a phrase found in earlier British print, but mainly as to raise and support one's spirits, not as in America to raise and support troops. "To provide and maintain a navy" is another Constitutional binomial not found in earlier British sources. In Britain, "to provide and maintain" attached more to keeping a horse or establishing a library than to keeping ships, although a 1758 history of England did refer to a levy to provide and maintain "a certain number of ships to guard the seas," imposed under Charles I in 1634.[188]

That the framers re-used binomials, re-worded them, and coined them demonstrates that they took them seriously. The usage also further attests the longevity of the binomial form in public documents. The binomial form was deliberately adopted, even when individual words had to be adapted; the form itself outlasted individual words. In turn, the economically worded coinages of the framers echoed in the language of later U.S. documents.

Ratifying the Constitution in 1788, the New York state legislature declared as quoted that the rights in the Constitution could not be "abridged or violated." Earlier in the ratification process, on September 17, 1787, New York had declared

> That every person restrained of his liberty is entitled to an inquiry into the lawfulness of such restraint, and to a removal thereof if unlawful; and that such inquiry or removal ought not to be denied or delayed, except when, on account of public danger, the Congress shall suspend the privilege of the writ of habeas corpus."[189]

Sad to say, the phrasing underwent some damaging changes. On June 27, 1788, Virginia's ratifying convention adopted similar language—but replaced the word "person" with the word "freeman": "That every freeman restrained of his liberty is entitled to a remedy, to inquire into the lawfulness thereof, and to remove the same, if unlawful, and that such remedy ought not to be denied nor delayed."[190] North Carolina proposed the same wording for a tenth amendment.[191] North Carolina also proposed a twelfth,

> That every freeman ought to find a certain remedy by recourse to the laws for all injuries and wrongs he may receive in his person, property or character; he ought to obtain right and justice freely without sale, completely and without denial, promptly and without delay, and that all establishments or regulations contravening these rights, are oppressive and unjust.

Obviously, the proposals expressed the legal maxim "Justice delayed is justice denied." The maxim itself went back to Magna Carta, cited by Parliament in 1643, defending itself for having ordered a new Great Seal when the royal seal was "withdrawn and detained" from it. "Fourthly, the Parliament is bound to take care, That publike Justice (according to *Magna Charta*, (and other Acts) *be not delayed, nor denied to any Subjects that desire or neede it.*"[192] A similar reference dates to 1652; "To look downward *Magna Charta* has it: *We sell no man, nor deny, or delay no man justice and right.*"[193]

North Carolina's ratifying convention adopted Virginia's statement containing "denied nor delayed" with "freeman" rather than with "person." On September 8, 1789, North Carolina went farther. The North Carolina-Virginia version was proposed to the U.S. Senate as a Constitutional amendment: 'That every freeman restrained of his liberty, is entitled to a remedy, to inquire into the lawfulness thereof, and to remove the same, if unlawful, and that such remedy ought not to be denied nor delayed."[194] The proposal was rejected. Debating revisions of the Bill of Rights on September 8, the first federal Senate voted on the Virginia-North Carolina statement. The motion lost. Thus, the key action words of the famous legal maxim "Justice delayed is justice denied" could have been included in the U.S. Bill of Rights, reinforcing *habeas corpus*, but lost out in Congress, tainted by the expression "freeman," connected to slavery. While the "freeman" wording came close to the language of Magna Carta and of William Blackstone, its connection to slavery was not in the spirit of either. Rhode Island's constitutional convention adopted the "freeman" version in 1790.[195]

The biggest challenge in discussing eighteenth-century English binomials in America, as in Britain, is the number of examples. A quick overview of high-profile binomials from the eighteenth century is like a quick review of classroom U.S. history lessons. Representative writings come from John Adams, Thomas Jefferson, and James Madison among others. The binomials provided tradition and emphasis, longevity and highlighting. Some binomials countermanded practices that the authors opposed on principle. Others enshrined and elevated principles that the authors supported. When the framers of the Bill of Rights separated the two terms in the traditional infringed-or-abridged binomial, they threw the emphasis on protection against abridging core rights—the protection that became the first amendment.

American English separates from British

As discussed, binomials were used as constitutional protections in both Britain and America. However, American independence understandably sharpened a divide between public discourse in America and public discourse in Britain. Both nations continued to use English (notwithstanding British wisecracks), but at the end of the eighteenth century, the political English of the two nations diverged. The infringe-abridge binomial is an example. It virtually disappeared in Britain at the end of the eighteenth century, while it became entrenched in America for the next hundred years.

The extensive archive of seventeenth- and eighteenth-century newspapers in the Burney Collection confirms the change. The Burney Collection contains all major British newspapers of the eighteenth century, with more than 1,200 titles digitized. Searching it for forms of *abridge* and *infringe*, up to 1787, turns up more than 6,000 examples. Their frequency confirms that both words were used extensively in eighteenth-century British print. Binomials using forms of *infringe* and *abridge* appeared often in English, Irish, and Scots periodicals, pamphlets, parliamentary papers, books, and elsewhere in the eighteenth century, to 1787.

Yet a mere thirteen years later, they became drastically less frequent. The database for Nineteenth Century British Newspapers holds twice as many newspaper pages as the Burney Collection—around two million pages, with full runs of the most influential national and regional newspapers. There was more printing and publishing in the nineteenth century, and less loss of the more recent papers. Yet for the entire nineteenth century, the enormous archive yields only ten examples of the binomial containing both *infringe* and *abridge* in print. Of the ten examples, nine refer to the pro-slavery 1858 Lecompton Constitution in Kansas, with its "nothing in this act shall be construed to abridge or infringe any right of the people [. . .] to alter, reform, or abolish their form of Government." The one other example comes from a Belfast newspaper dated July 14, 1896. Thus, of a mere ten examples of the infringe-or-abridge binomial in nineteenth-century British newspapers, none come from England. Nine are American (duplicates), and one is Irish. The end of the eighteenth century had brought about a difference.

Like the language of American books, the language of American newspapers in the eighteenth century was inherited largely from Britain. But the two nations went onto separate tracks in the nineteenth century. What the archive reflects is that the binomial dropped out of use in Britain. In American newspapers, on the other hand, the use of infringing and abridging in a single binomial developed into near cliché in the nineteenth century, as discussed. To analyze nineteenth-century British reluctance to use the binomial would go outside the scope of this book, but there are a few hypotheses. One possibility is that British writers in the nineteenth century shied away from cliché more than Americans did—a difference sometimes satirized in Britain. Another is that the British political lexicon in the nineteenth century moved away from traditional binomials in general, while Americans continued to use them.

Perhaps the American Revolution was a factor in Britain's letting go the infringe-abridge binomial. Loss of appetite for the binomial may have been connected to the who-lost-America issue. As quoted above, the infringe-abridge binomial continued to be used elsewhere in the Commonwealth—in Canada, New Zealand, India, and Jamaica. But in Britain itself, the pain of the Revolution may have been addressed partly by some defensive distancing, relegating some American language of core freedoms to the realm of cliché. A tendency to distance the losses would be natural—especially when sensitivities continued in Britain over rights infringed closer to home.

Another factor may also have influenced the British—the association of the infringe-abridge binomial with slavery. A prominent example from 1803 respects Jamaica. British landowners in the late eighteenth century resisted limits on the slave trade. Robert Charles Dallas (1754-1824), a barrister and Jamaican landowner, shared their perspective.[196] In Dallas's *History of the Maroons*, the planters asserted that the colonists had the right to regulate all their internal affairs. This right, the slaveholders argued unsuccessfully, "though not publicly recognized by an act of parliament, had nevertheless been deemed, by all wise and just characters in Great Britain, to exist in full force, and that parliament had no right to infringe or abridge it, by enacting any law for their internal regulation."[197] Dallas's history included an extensive discussion of the slave trade and went through several reprints in the 1820s. Britain finally abolished slavery in 1833. The infringe-abridge binomial itself resurfaced in nineteenth-century Britain only in the Kansas Lecompton language, as mentioned.

Judging from Dallas's background, his use of the binomial was deliberate precision. The young Robert Charles Dallas and his brother Alexander were sent from Jamaica to London, to be tutored by a close friend of Dr. Johnson. According to biographies, the student brothers met Johnson and Ben Franklin at the house. Robert Charles' brother, Alexander James Dallas (1759-1817), moved to the States and went on to become a Secretary of the Commonwealth of Pennsylvania, U.S. District Attorney, and U.S. Secretary of the Treasury under President Madison from 1814 to 1816. Alexander Dallas' son George Mifflin Dallas (1792-1864) served with U.S. diplomats and went on to become a senator from Pennsylvania, state Attorney General, and from 1845-1849 Vice President of the United States. The city of Dallas, Texas, was named after him. The infringe-abridge binomial was still the language of communiqué; its use sometimes in rarefied circles did not mean that those networks were outliers.

"Denied or abridged"

[T]he Joint Reconstruction Committee of Congress intended that section 1 of the Fourteenth Amendment should have the broadest scope, and that it should constitute a universal rule applicable in all cases in which an attempt was made to deny, infringe, or abridge the fundamental rights and liberties of the individual, whatever his race.[198]

When Congress passed the fifteenth amendment in 1869, the securing verbs were simplified as much as possible.

The right of citizens of the United States to vote shall not be denied or abridged by the United States or by any State on account of race, color, or previous condition of servitude.

The protective binomial in the fifteenth amendment is "denied or abridged." To protect citizens' voting rights, the amendment abolished any uncertainty that could stem from vocabulary. The sentence is condensed, the word *infringed* is updated to *denied*, and the two key verbs are paired in a binomial.

Nineteenth-century writers like William Guthrie, quoted above, were clear that *deny* fulfilled the function earlier performed by *infringe*. The word *denied* declares unconstitutional the outright, overt withholding of elections or votes. The word *abridged* declares unconstitutional any roundabout, fractional attempts to keep formerly enslaved people from voting. As with earlier binomials, the effort is to cover all the bases. By 1869, however, the destruction of a protected right—voting—is no longer called infringement but denial. Unlike earlier public documents in America, the fifteenth amendment does not state "infringed or abridged." It states, "denied or abridged."

The newer binomial was evidently clear and definitive. It was adopted in 1919 for the nineteenth amendment, extending the vote to women,

The right of citizens of the United States to vote shall not be denied or abridged by the United States or by any State on account of sex;

in 1962 for the twenty-fourth amendment, prohibiting use of a poll tax to keep people from voting in federal elections,

The right of citizens of the United States to vote in any primary or other election for President or Vice President, for electors for President or Vice President, or for Senator or Representative in

Congress, shall not be denied or abridged by the United States
or any State by reason of failure to pay any poll tax or other tax;
and in 1971 for the twenty-sixth amendment, lowering the voting age to
eighteen;

The right of citizens of the United States, who are eighteen years
of age or older, to vote shall not be denied or abridged by the
United States or by any State on account of age.

In 1972 it was proposed for the Equal Rights Amendment, rewritten after
Alice Paul, that

Equality of rights under the law shall not be denied or abridged
by the United States or by any State on account of sex.[199]

There was a new sheriff in town. Four constitutional amendments in
America from 1870 to 1971 protected or extended the vote by using
"denied or abridged." The word *infringed* was never used in constitutional
amendments again after the Bill of Rights. The fifteenth amendment
crystallized the phrase adopted to protect voting for the next hundred
years.

Had debate in Congress gone differently, the phrase "denied or
abridged" could have appeared in the fourteenth amendment. On January
15, 1866, Rep. Roscoe Conkling of New York submitted a resolution for
an amendment:

Representatives and direct taxes shall be apportioned among the
several States which may be included within this Union according
to their respective numbers, counting the whole number of
citizens of the United States: Provided, That whenever, in any
State, civil or political rights or privileges shall be denied or
abridged on account of race or color, all persons of such race or
color shall be excluded from the basis of representation.[200]

The resolution was referred to the Joint Committee on Reconstruction.

A week later, Rep. Thaddeus Stevens of Pennsylvania repeated
Conklin's binomial in the resolution submitted by the Committee to
Congress:

Representatives and direct taxes shall be apportioned among the
several States which may be included within this Union according
to their respective numbers, counting the whole number of
persons in each State, excluding Indians not taxed: *Provided*, that
whenever the elective franchise shall be denied or abridged in
any State on account of race or color, all persons of such race or
color shall be excluded from the basis of such representation.[201]

The tug of war over the amendment in Congress was not just between
North and South. Members committed to protecting the vote were
fighting a two-front war, not only against southerners and southern
sympathizers but against some on their own side. Some members who

feared that extending the franchise to all freed slaves would increase the proportional representation of southern states, at the expense of other states, obstructed the more generous abolitionists.

Part of the battle involved the "denied or abridged" binomial, not yet adopted. On January 24, Rep. Thomas Eliot of Massachusetts proposed it again;

> striking out all after the word "Constitution," and inserting in lieu thereof, "providing that representatives and direct taxes shall be apportioned among the several Sates which may be included within this Union according to their respective numbers, counting the whole number of persons in each State, excluding Indians not taxed; and the elective franchise shall not be denied or abridged in any State on account of race or color.

A more consistent abolitionist was Rep. George Washington Julian of Indiana, the author of the future fifteenth amendment. On May 7, Julian proposed a law that would reinforce the constitutional amendment, using forms of the binomial twice.

> Resolved, That the Judiciary Committee be instructed to inquire into the expediency of reporting a bill providing that hereafter the elective franchise shall not be denied or abridged in any of the Territories of the United States on account of race or color, and providing further, and thereby giving notice of the fact, that henceforward no State which the people of any of said Territories may organize shall be admitted into the Union whose constitution shall sanction such denial or abridgement of the elective franchise.[202]

Like Eliot's proposed amendment, Julian's proposed law failed by a sizeable majority.

On June 8, the Senate followed the House in removing the crisp phrase "denied or abridged" from the fourteenth amendment. Sen. George H. Williams of Oregon moved a more cumbersome section which contained the words "denied" and "abridged" but separated them.

> Section 2. Representatives shall be apportioned among the several States according to their respective numbers, counting the whole number of persons in each State, excluding Indians not taxed. But when the right to vote at any election for the choice of electors for President and Vice-President of the United States, representatives in Congress, the executive and judicial officers of a State or the members of the legislature thereof, is denied to any of the male inhabitants of such State, being twenty-one years of age and citizens of the United States, or in any way abridged, except for participation in rebellion, or other crime, the basis of representation therein shall be reduced in the proportion which

the number of such male citizens shall bear to the whole number of male citizens twenty-one years of age in such State.[203]

The proposed language was adopted—after a motion to remove the phrase "or in any way abridged" was shot down. On June 13, the House passed Williams' language for the fourteenth amendment.

If the intent was to protect the vote of freed slaves, the amendment fell short. Its language was too squishy and loophole-prone. Section 1 also contained the terms "denied" and "abridged," but not effectively.

All persons born or naturalized in the United States, and subject to the jurisdiction thereof, are citizens of the United States and of the State wherein they reside. No State shall make or enforce any law which shall abridge the privileges or immunities of citizens of the United States; nor shall any State deprive any person of life, liberty, or property, without due process of law; nor deny to any person within its jurisdiction the equal protection of the laws.

In hindsight, trying to protect former slaves in the South by using congressional representation as the carrot and reducing representation as the stick did not work.

Some members of Congress recognized the problem beforehand. Rep. Julian had told the House in January 1866 that "Instead of restricting representation to actual suffrage, we can extend suffrage to actual representation, which will be far better."[204] Julian recommended,

Why not say, in the plain affirmative words of the amendment submitted by the gentleman from Massachusetts [Mr. Eliot], that—"The elective franchise shall *not* be denied or abridged in any State on account of race or color"?

As Julian told the House, "The shortest distance between two given points is a straight line."

Julian had forethought. Much earlier, in 1850, he had tried to warn Congress that free persons of color who were citizens of Northern states

cannot visit South Carolina, Louisiana and I believe some three or four other Southern States, without being thrown into prison; and if they are not removed from the State by the persons in whose care or employ they came, they are sold into slavery. This is a most palpable violation of the Constitution of the United States, which provides that "the citizens of each State shall be entitled to all the privileges and immunities of citizens of the several States."[205]

At the time, slaveholders and others were using the privileges and immunities clause to justify returning escaped slaves to slaveholders. Julian was one of few public figures to state the logical converse: free persons of color were equally entitled to the privileges and immunities of *their* home state, including their freedom. Congress passed the shorter, crisper, and clearer fifteenth amendment in 1869, and it was ratified three years later:

"The right of citizens of the United States to vote shall not be denied or abridged by the United States or by any State on account of race, color, or previous condition of servitude."

To understand the intent of Congress, it helps to compare the fifteenth amendment to the fourteenth. The intention behind the fourteenth amendment was laudable—to protect people formerly enslaved, by protecting their civil rights. To do so, the amendment deliberately drew upon principles and phrases from the Constitution. Section 1 of the amendment explicitly included what has been called the "antislavery trilogy"—the constitutional clauses on privileges and immunities, due process, and equal protection. As described in 1898 by Supreme Court attorney and constitutional law professor William Guthrie, "This great amendment to the Federal Constitution has done more than any other cause to protect our civil rights from invasion, to strengthen the bonds of the Union, to make us truly a nation, and to assure the perpetuity of our institutions."[206] Unfortunately, the long-winded language of the fourteenth amendment left the door open to states to erect barriers to voting, eagerly passed, which resulted in continuing race-based abuses in education, employment, and the justice system. By shortening and strengthening the language in the fifteenth amendment to "denied or abridged," Congress clarified its intent in the fourteenth amendment. The contrasting fifteenth amendment was meant to correct the weaknesses and supply the deficiencies of the fourteenth.

The change in the amendments reflected not only changes in U.S. society but also changes in American English. That the word "infringed," as in the second amendment, was now replaced by a clearer word strongly suggests that it needed to be replaced. As in Britain, the association of the infringe-abridge binomial with slavery may have been one factor. But also, understanding of the English word *infringed* was shifting.

Changing usage in nineteenth-century English

Again, the fifteenth amendment does not say, "The right of citizens to vote shall not be infringed or abridged." By mid-nineteenth century, the English verbs of the first and second amendments had undergone changes. Earlier, the problematic word had been "abridge." Locke in the seventeenth century had ranted about people who misunderstood it. Ainsworth in the eighteenth century had discussed the difficulties translating it into Latin. Yet Congress retained "abridged" in the fourteenth and fifteenth amendments, used as in the first amendment. Since lawmakers took care to retain it in 1866 and 1869, it must have been considered clear enough. It continues to be thus regarded; as noted, it was further retained in the amendments of 1919 (votes for women), 1962 (abolishing the poll tax), 1971 (lowering the voting age to eighteen), and 1972 (the Equal Rights Amendment).

In contrast, *infringed* as in the second amendment makes no further appearance in amendments. When did the meaning or understanding of *infringe* change, so that it was no longer workable for the Constitution? Clearly the usage shifted between 1789 and 1869.

The timeline of language use is continuous, but not every movement in it is immediately perceptible. Global English usage is a big river, with ripples and eddies—slang, educational changes, new inventions, historical events—that affect each other and affect the larger current. Within the full stream, individual variation and regional variation have their own movements. Developments in English between 1789 and 1869 did not happen overnight or uniformly across the United States.

However, in the shift from eighteenth-century phrasing to nineteenth-century phrasing in U.S. constitutional amendments, some broad patterns can be seen. First, "denied or abridged," as in the fifteenth and later amendments, came into wide use only in the nineteenth century. The eighteenth century did not use it widely. Second, nineteenth-century America still used the related "infringed or abridged," as discussed, but the use overlapped with other binomials as protection. The "infringe or abridge" phrasing remained frequent but became less prevalent, gradually displaced by newer phrasing. Third, in nineteenth-century America, "denied" performed the function previously performed by "infringed." Sometimes the newer phrasing was coupled with the older, as in the headnote to this chapter and in some Reconstruction laws.

The short background of "denied or abridged"

The exact English phrase "denied or abridged" appears in public documents only after 1800. The earlier absence of the phrase "denied or abridged" is indicated by American archives. One of the best resources is the American Memory collection in the Library of Congress, which includes the George Washington Papers (1741-1799), the Thomas Jefferson Papers (1606-1827), and the documents of Congress from 1774 to 1875—thousands of pages of original documents, many transcribed. A search of the collection turns up no example of "denied or abridged" before 1800. Furthermore, the exact phrase "denied or abridged," or its different forms, is not found in U.S. Congressional documents and debates until 1866. Nor did it appear in charters, declarations, resolutions, state constitutions, or state or federal legislation before 1800. Nor does it appear in transcribed private letters from and to the founders, congressional correspondence from the Continental Congress on, congressional debates, state ratifying conventions, or in the Federalist (and anti-Federalist) papers, before 1800. Nor did it occur in statute or case law before that date. Even Rep. Julian did not use it in his anti-slavery speeches before January 1866. Simple though the phrase "denied or abridged" is, the exact phrase is not found in American government, at any level, before the nineteenth century, although similar language was used to convey related concepts.

The exact wording "denied or abridged" was also rare in Britain before 1800. No examples turn up in the electronic archive Eighteenth Century Collections Online (ECCO). Further search turns up only four similar examples in English writing before 1800. The first two examples were religious. The first appeared in 1658; "Sometimes the same hypocrite runs into both extremes [binging or starving]. But usually he begins with the last, abridging or denying himself the due use of the liberty purchased by Christ."[207] Another appeared in a 1701 theological treatise. Explaining the eighth commandment (against stealing), the author clarifies that it forbids not only outright theft but also the indirect ways of "invading our Neighbours Property,"

> all unjust gains, Usury, Vexatious Suits, over-reaching in point of Trade, breach of Trust, tho' unknown to him by whom we are Trusted, Immoderate Bills of Lawyers, Physicians and Inn-keepers, Fraudulent Bankrupts, denying or abridging Ministers of their dues, refusing to Servants their Salaries, and innumerable other tricks known to his Conscience, who will seriously examine them.[208]

The thinking is traditional, though by no means 'traditional' as merely *pro forma*. Like Chaucer's Parson, who three hundred years earlier had criticized cruel lords for "withholdynge or abreggynge" wages or jobs for servants and alms for the poor, the vicar condemns "denying or abridging" pay to ministers. The binomials proscribe fraud and exploitation.

A third example dates from 1716, in an anonymous paper titled "The Excellence of Virtue Appearing in a Publick Character." The author recommends (while scoring a point for Protestants) that public figures should keep their word; "On which account the present Parliament of Ireland cou'd not be provok'd by all past Injuries receiv'd, nor present and future justly dreaded, from their sworn Enemies the Papists, to deny or abridge them of any Privilege granted them by the Articles of Limerick."[209]

The exact wording of "to deny or abridge them of any Privilege" edits a broader idea that had previously appeared mainly in the language of charters. An Act of Parliament in 1702, for example, protecting the charter for North Carolina in typical language, provided "that nothing herein contained shall be construed to extend any ways to alter, take away, diminish or abridge" previously granted rights.[210] The later binomial neatened and tightened the loophole-closing.

A fourth example dates from 1736. As protection, this example may be the most interesting.

> Again, as it was denied in respect of some offenses, so this *privilegium clericale* [clerical privilege] was by the common law abridged in respect of the person; for certainly by the canon laws nuns had the exemption from temporal jurisdiction, but the privilege of clergy was never allowd them by our law.[211]

As the author observes, "privilege of clergy" did not include nuns; clearly, therefore, privilege of clergy could be and was abridged. The concepts and the key verbs of "denied or abridged" are used, but not condensed into the single phrase. The definition of clerical privilege lasted through multiple editions of law dictionaries in the eighteenth century.

American public documents reflect a shared understanding of the concepts. Well before the nineteenth-century "denied or abridged" came into use, the underlying idea was upheld with similar language. In June 1788, ratifying the U.S. Constitution, Virginia's convention led off with cold-dead-hands language on freedom of conscience and freedom of the press:

> no right, of any denomination, can be cancelled, abridged, restrained, or modified, by the Congress, by the Senate or House of Representatives, acting in any capacity, by the President, or any department or officer of the United States, except in those instances in which power is given by the Constitution for those purposes; and that, among other essential rights, the liberty of conscience, and of the press, cannot be cancelled, abridged, restrained, or modified, by any authority of the United States.[212]

The phrasing of "cancelled, abridged, restrained, or modified" echoes the language of royal charters and proclamations.

The contrast between this prohibitive language and the second amendment is clear and apparent. The second amendment to the U.S. Constitution does not circle the wagons this way. It does not say, "The right to bear arms shall not be cancelled, abridged, restrained, or modified." It does not say, "The right to bear arms shall not be infringed or abridged, using the older binomial." Nor does it say, "The right to bear arms shall not be denied or abridged," using the newer binomial. All these phrases, all these forms of expression, and more along the same lines, were available to the framers. The second amendment uses none of them.

With so many similar passages, so emphatic, from U.S. history, the omission should be conspicuous. But weapons absolutists and the gun lobby do not mention it. "Congress shall make no law" is not part of the second amendment as it is part of the first amendment. The public does not hear about the omission. The differences between the second amendment and the first amendment are under-discussed; the changed language of U.S. amendments in the nineteenth century have been under-discussed; and changes in American English into the twentieth century have been under-discussed.

The effect is to veil American history from Americans. The flame-throwing founders of the new United States were well capable of using fiery and unequivocal language when they wanted to. The delegates to state ratifying conventions in the late 1780s, like the delegates to the Continental Congress in the 1770s, often used fiery prose. But they reserved the strongest language for the "great rights"—especially freedom of religion and freedom of the press. When their intent was to cover all the bases, as in the Virginia ratifying convention, they used every verb or participle applicable; and from colonial times to their own century, they used them preeminently to protect the rights of conscience and of expression. They did not depreciate them to protect an absolutist or fanatical attachment to weapons—which they did not hold, in the first place. They no more reverenced weapons than Aaron Burr garnered widespread admiration for fatally shooting Alexander Hamilton in a duel.

The newer safeguard: changing phrasing

The infringe-abridge binomial did continue in use in the United States in the nineteenth century. The new century did not bring about an abrupt dismissal of the phrase in America as it did in Britain. Language on infringing and abridging continued to appear in U.S. public documents, newspapers, and books including textbooks. But while the older infringed-abridged phrasing continued to be used, the phrasing of "denied" was coming in. The parallelism in "infringed or abridged" is retained in the newer phrase. The progressively intensified loophole-closing of the paired verbs is retained. The over-all protection is retained. But the first verb in the inherited binomial changes, from *infringed* to *denied*.

Forms of "denied or abridged" appeared in government sources from early in the century. In 1810, the Supreme Court of New York heard dueling arguments on the power of the Court of Errors. One side was represented by Thomas Addis Emmett, who argued "That a writ of right, issuing by law, as matter of course, should be under the control of the Court of Chancery, who may abridge or deny this right, cannot be law."[213] Emmett, older brother of martyred Irish revolutionary Robert Emmett, became New York State Attorney General two years later. The case, *John van Ness Yates v. the People of New York*, was a high-profile legal battle over jurisdiction between New York's Supreme Court and the

Court of Chancery. The landmark ruling established that a judge in a civil action may not be sued for an error of judgment in a matter within his jurisdiction.

In 1839, the *National Magazine and Republican Review*, in Washington, D.C., ran a vehement anti-Democrat polemic criticizing President Andrew Jackson. This was the year the New York court cases were published, including *Yates v. New York* with its "abridge or deny." Editor Henry Brent used the same phrase in the *National Magazine*.

> There never was any administration so profuse in the *profession* of States Right and Democratic principles. But, if the acts of the Administration be carefully examined, it will be seen that the United States powers, which it sought to abridge or deny, were *such of those powers as pertain to Congress or the Judiciary*—while it was the never ceasing practice of the Administration to exert, to the utmost, all such powers, express or implied, as are of *Executive* resort.[214]

In 1841, the Concord Railroad Corporation published a remarkable pamphlet using the phrase. The purpose was to justify the corporation's seizing private land for railroads. The pamphlet displayed a striking affirmation of buccaneering.

> In the early history of man, his right of way over the earth was free. There was nothing then to interrupt it; and, with the aid of the government to secure him in its reasonable enjoyment, there is nothing now. It is a right essential to and paramount to the improvement of the soil. Man is not confined by his nature to any one spot. It is a part of his destiny that he should go forward and possess the earth. This he cannot do without a right of way [. . .] For the land-holder to set up a right of soil against a right of way, is to set up a secondary against a primary right; is to assert a claim which is in fact subversive of all title to real estate; is to *abridge or deny* our means of intercourse and exchange of commodities with our fellow men, to which we are entitled.[215]

Some lobbyists are good writers. The anonymous pamphlet author, undoubtedly commissioned by the company, did the best he could with what he had, romantically invoking the frontier to uphold "right of way" as a primary right. In this perspective, the "right of soil"—farming, or you might call it property—is a secondary right. No case law is cited; the argument rests on assertion and an aura of timelessness. Interestingly, the word "property" is not used, although the old commonplace that all wealth was once commonwealth is suggested; "In the early history of man, his right of way over the earth was free."

Disregarding the whizzing noise from old Gower and Hobbes spinning in their graves, the company had already argued this position in the Superior Court of New Hampshire. The case was *Concord Railroad v. Greeley*.[216] A jury had awarded Greeley, the landowner, more compensation for his farmland taken by Concord Railroad than the company wanted to pay. Concord Railroad appealed the verdict to the Superior Court and won on a split decision. One winning argument was that on matters such as ordinary, understandable damage to farmland, expert testimony should not be allowed. "Upon subjects of general knowledge," such as whether horses would likely be frightened by an approaching train, "which are understood by men in general," specialized testimony by an expert who had not himself witnessed the horse being frightened was ruled not admissible.[217] *Concord Railroad v. Greeley* helped to define building a railroad as a public use of land, justifying appropriation.

"Denied or abridged" and the slave trade

In public documents, meanwhile, the denied-abridged binomial could be and was applied to the slave trade. Like the infringed-abridged binomial, it could be used and was used both pro- and anti-slavery. Monday, February 17, 1840, was a lively day in the state senate of New York. On that day, the senate accepted at least twenty petitions and memorials on issues ranging from usury to road commissioners to health quarantine, which were referred to the appropriate committees. More than one pertained to escaped slaves, including one from the Genesee Yearly Meeting of Friends, "praying for an extension of the right of trial by jury to persons claimed as fugitive slaves."[218] On the same day, the senate passed two resolutions supporting petitions to Congress, "the common right of any and every citizen of this country to be heard by their representatives," and expressing disappointment that the New York house had refused to receive "any petition relating to slavery in the United States."[219] The New York senate actions took place in the context of the U.S. Congress actions known as the Gag Rule, in which pro-slavery members tried to prevent petitions on slavery from reaching the Capitol.

In passing the resolutions, the senate voted down an amendment proposed by Daniel S. Dickinson which stated that "it is the right of every citizen of this Republic to petition Congress upon any and every subject [. . .] and that such right of petition cannot be denied or abridged without violating the Constitution of the United States."[220] Dickinson's ostensible support may have sounded acceptable in the first paragraph, but the next paragraph conveyed a poison pill; "by the Constitution of the United States, Congress has no power to legislate upon the institution of slavery in the several States of the Confederacy; that the Territory of the District of Columbia having been ceded for the use of the General Government by States in which slavery existed at the time of such cession and still exists, any attempt to abolish slavery in said district" would violate "the true meaning and spirit of the Constitution." Dickinson further wanted the resolution to read

> That the right to petition does not necessarily carry with it the
> right to have the prayer of the petition granted, and that it is no
> violation of either the letter or the spirit of the Constitution, for
> Congress to decline action upon petitions relating to the abolition
> of slavery, a domestic institution of the States, within the control
> of the several State Legislatures, and over which Congress has no
> jurisdiction.

Each paragraph of Dickinson's amendment, voted on separately at his motion, lost decisively.

Having won the battle, however, the senate lost the war over fugitives. Escaped slaves were more than familiar to the state and the city of New York. In July 1839, a fugitive slave called Isaac claimed by John Colbey of Norfolk, Virginia, was found on board a ship in New York City and was returned to Virginia. The governor of Virginia demanded that Governor Seward extradite three African-American sailors on the ship, accused of aiding Isaac's escape. Seward refused, and the bitter dispute between New York and Virginia continued for the rest of his term. On May 6, 1840, a law was signed into effect designed to provide jury trials for anyone claimed as a fugitive slave in New York. A jury would determine the facts of the case, and the District Attorney or a Supreme Court attorney would be appointed to defend the alleged fugitive at the state's expense. "Thus the State of New York tried to grant to fugitive slaves protection, legal assistance, and a fair trial."[221] The bill had the governor's full support; in his annual speech to the state legislature in January 1841, Seward stated among other things that the "acts charged upon the persons demanded," i.e. helping a slave to escape, "were not recognized as criminal by the laws of all civilized countries."[222] But the U.S. Supreme Court ruling in *Prigg v. Commonwealth of Pennsylvania* in 1842 rendered the New York law unconstitutional.

Naturally, Seward's words infuriated slaveholders. In January 1841, a new magazine appeared in Virginia, titled the *Southern Magazine and Monthly Review*. It was created by Edmund Ruffin and Julian C. Ruffin, two Virginia relatives of North Carolina Supreme Court Judge Thomas C. Ruffin, who had issued the infamous decision in *North Carolina v. Mann* (1829) that a master had absolute power over an enslaved person. The new *Southern Magazine* unambiguously championed slavery. The first issue devoted several pages to escaped slaves, claiming mandatory return of fugitive slaves as "the law of nations."

> No other than the nation itself can be competent to decide
> what is dangerous to its safety, or injurious to its interests; and

in proportion as its power in this respect is abridged or denied, it ceases to be either independent or free. This is directly asserted by the law of nations, as that law is interpreted in the practice of "all civilized countries."[223]

Obviously, the phrase "abridged or denied" is not the only phrase appropriated in the passage. The quotation marks around the phrase "all civilized countries" were a pointed reference to Governor William Seward of New York.

In all, the Ruffin relatives who printed the magazine quoted Seward's "all civilized countries" back at him some forty-seven times, in pages of diatribe against "slave-stealing," sympathy for slaves, and impertinent meddling in other men's affairs. "And if Virginia should witness this, where is she to find redress, if she now submit to the pretensions of New York? Such a state of things, between independent nations, would, at once, lead to open war; and the law of nations, on which Governor Seward is so fond of relying, would justify it."[224]

In the words of its preface, the magazine was founded to boost "the rule of strict limitation of federal powers" and "the principles, of free trade, in which the interests of the southern states, especially, are so deeply involved."[225] Obviously, promoting free trade and limited federal powers supported the slave trade. But the magazine sweetened the pill by serving literary fare including articles on the ancient world translated from German (primarily focused on trade), boosting claims to literary culture; unpublished letters by George Washington and some historical family papers, beefing up Virginia's colonial heritage; and an essay on Joan of Arc and a sympathetic, indignant criticism of the French occupation of Algeria, boosting rebellious spirit.

Undoubtedly, the *Southern Magazine* was spurred by New York Governor William H. Seward's efforts to protect escaped slaves; it appeared in print in reaction to New York's actions. Publication seems to have ceased after two issues. Clearly the venture involved family connections as well as pro-slavery views, although members of the extended family went on to very different ends. Judge Thomas Ruffin in North Carolina lived to a hale old age, admired for much of his legal work aside from *Mann*. Fervent secessionist Edmund Ruffin was troubled by alcohol, although he did some genuinely valid work on soil quality and soil nurturing as a farmer. He killed himself on June 18, 1865, bereaved of his wife and several children and infuriated when the Confederacy lost the Civil War.

Judge Ruffin's *Mann* ruling had a coda in literature. Harriet Beecher Stowe, author of *Uncle Tom's Cabin*, took the entire transcript of Ruffin's decision and used it verbatim in her follow-up novel, *Dred, a Tale of the Great Dismal Swamp*.[226] "The power of the master must be absolute, to render the submission of the slave perfect." Stowe puts the speech into the mouth of a fictional judge, the father of the male romantic lead in the novel. The consequence in the fiction is to convert the judge's son into an ardent abolitionist; "Never had Clayton so forcibly realized the horrors of slavery as when he heard them thus so calmly defined." The fictional result was, of course, an idealized upcycling of the real-life ruling, which established that a master could not be held liable for battering an enslaved person—reversing the decision of an all-white jury and judge in a lower court, which had convicted and fined an abusive slaveholder. The title of Stowe's novel was not literary accident. The case of Dred Scott had been making its way through the courts for years; the decision in the case came a year after the novel. Stowe herself drew attention to her use of the *Mann* decision; "The author has placed in the mouth of one of her leading characters a judicial decision of Judge Ruffin, of North Carolina."[227] The actual swamps were in fact a destination for escaped slaves.

In December 1844, Congress finally restored the right of petition and rescinded the Gag Rule. Passionately opposing the Rule, Rep. Samuel Beardsley of New York made a speech now using the abridged-denied binomial on the abolitionists' side. Beardsley told Congress that the right of petition went back to the English bill of rights after the Glorious Revolution of 1688, that it was "the right of the subject to petition the King," and that "Nothing could be more explicit than this recognition of the rights of Englishmen. It was their *true*, their *ancient*, and their *indubitable* right; and no King should be permitted to deny or abridge it."[228] Moving on to American history, Beardsley further reminded Congress that language safeguarding the right of petition was part of the first amendment and that it had been included in the Constitution at the behest of Virginia. The clincher; "No one, then, believed that either House of Congress alone would venture to deny or abridge this right."[229] Beardsley won the argument. He resigned from congress in 1844 to become Associate Justice in the New York Supreme Court, later becoming Chief Justice.

The binomial had also been used in religion, and it continued to be, alongside the use in politics. In an 1846 *Quarterly Review*, Orestes Brownson was provoked to defend the Catholic Church, heatedly, against criticisms previously printed in the *Methodist Quarterly*. Insisting that the Catholic Church and the Pope did not oppose freedom of speech, the press, and conscience, Brownson used concepts familiar from Locke. "Liberty is violated only when one's rights are denied or abridged. But in forbidding a man to do what the law of God gives him no right to do, we do not deny or abridge any one of his rights; Therefore, do not violate his liberty."[230]

The phrase continued to be used in courts, as in 1853 by the Supreme Court of Vermont in *Peck v. Crane*. The question before the Vermont high court was the power of Chancery Court to issue a writ—somewhat like the 1810 case in the New York high court, except that the writ in Vermont was an injunction. The high court ruled in favor of Chancery, ending,

> We merely intend to hold, here that this injunction, coming fairly
> within the powers ordinarily exercised by the English Courts of
> Chancery, and the Courts of Chancery in many of the American
> States, we do not deem it expedient to deny or abridge their
> power, in this preliminary proceeding, and without opportunity
> for more examination than we could here bestow.[231]

By the middle of the century, coupling *deny* and *abridge* had become
customary—to obviate, to disavow, to oppose, or to prevent either or both
actions in the two verbs. Hence the words in the fourteenth amendment
of 1868, somewhat spread apart; in the fifteenth amendment, together in
a concise phrase; in congressional debate over the amendments; and in
combination with *infringe* in Reconstruction laws.

As in the Ruffin magazine, some writers re-ordered "deny or abridge"
to "abridge or deny." The meaning of the phrase is not destroyed by
reversing the order of the two verbs, which was typical but not hard and
fast. Still, the "deny or abridge" sequence works better. For one thing, it
progressively strengthens the protections in the two words. For another,
it aligns with other linguistic rules for binomial word-order. *Deny* is the
stronger word, and the stronger or more important word often precedes
the softer.[232] *Deny* is total, and the principal word precedes the subsidiary;
the greater the smaller. *Deny* is slightly shorter, and the shorter word
usually precedes the longer. *Deny* is a word used more frequently than
abridge, and the more frequently used or familiar word usually precedes
the other. In contrast, *abridge* is the word more subtle, or difficult, or
unusual (marked); and the more marked term usually follows the less
marked term.

George Washington Julian and others who amended the Constitution
with "denied or abridged" did so with good reason. The two terms are
not interchangeable. *Denied* means wholesale destruction of the right
to vote, completely withholding it; *abridged* means partial damage. The
first term covers a unitary act of denying the vote *in toto* to one or more
people; the second covers multiple smaller acts. The two terms progress
toward more fine-tuned and careful loophole-closing; the binomial works
like closing the hatch first, in a ship taking on water, then plugging up
each separate leak. As in other developments in legal history, the ordering
of the binomial made for additional protection; the newer version of the
binomial added precision, having improved over the course of time.[233]
Progressive fine-tuning might have been less important in earlier religious
writing, where either self-denial or self-abridgement might be called for.
But in public policy, the ordering mattered. Reversing the order in the
binomial weakens it. A side-slip into "abridge or deny" can telegraph
thoughtlessness or ulterior motive.

The changing meaning of *infringe*: "infringe upon"

Since "infringe" was still being used in nineteenth-century America, and still coupled with "abridge," one question is how the word changed so that it was no longer workable, or adequate, as a constitutional safeguard. If the question *why* the phrase changed is hard to answer, the plain fact *that* it changed can be shown. One specific change is that in the nineteenth century, "infringe" more often became "infringe upon," and the phrase softens the verb.

Simple as the phrase "infringe upon" sounds, its existence was scant in the 1600s. No Briton accused Charles I, James II, or Charles II of 'infringing upon' his rights, nor did James I assure Parliament that he was not 'infringing upon' the ancient rights, liberties, and privileges of Englishmen. The word was *infringe*. An action either was an (alleged) infringement, or it was not; there was little 'infringing upon.' Government, law, justice, and political philosophy did not for the most part use the phrase "infringement upon" (or "infringement on") before 1700. The expression in use was "infringement *of*." In keeping with usage, there were also no dictionary entries with forms of "infringe upon," before the eighteenth century. The seventeenth-century dictionary definitions were clear, public documents and political philosophy were clear, and English speakers before 1700 were clear on what they meant by infringement—so clear that, as mentioned, the word itself seldom needed defining.

Infringement was breaking something. Today we still say that to break or violate a law, treaty, contract, or copyright is to infringe it. In the fifteenth through seventeenth centuries, the clarity of the concept was shored up by clarity of diction. Infringement was not a mere overlapping the boundaries of the acceptable; it was violation, and English speakers before 1700 were no more likely to write "infringe upon" than they were to write "expound upon" or "expand upon" rather than just "expound" or "expand."

The shift took place between 1700 and 1900. Before 1700, the phrase "infringe upon" was seldom used. A rare example in America dates from December 1672, when eight Quakers of Oyster Bay wrote to the governor of New York to plead exemption from taxes to repair "ye fforte of new Yorke." The group reminded the governor that its members have willingly paid all other taxes, and have lived "peaceably and quietly" among their neighbors, "& are readie to bee serviceable in any:thing wch doth not infringe upon or [our] tender consciences."[234] But on grounds of conscience, "being Jn measure Redeemed out of warres, & strifes," they request relief from the tax in question.

The "upon" usage increased over the decades, very gradually at first, then more with each decade, more in the second half of the eighteenth century than in the first half, more toward the end of the century, and far more in the nineteenth century. One interesting example from 1789 appeared in the *American Museum* magazine. In a report on congressional debate over a national bill of rights, the author paraphrases James Madison, introducing his draft bill of rights on June 8. "It has been observed, that the constitution does not repeal the state bills of rights; to this it may be replied, that some of the states are without any—and that some articles contained in those that have them, are very improper, and infringe upon the rights of human nature, in several respects."[235] The reference is fascinatingly cryptic; the article does not clarify which state bills of rights and provisions are being referred to. Given that there are some early examples of "infringe upon," or "least infringement," etc., it is significant that the second amendment is not one of them. The amendment does not say "infringe upon," let alone "cannot even infringe upon."

By 1887, "infringes upon," "infringe upon," and "infringe on" were in common use, and by 1900, they were ordinary. Part of the increase of the phrase in print must be due to increased publishing, but only part. The change is not just a growth in numbers but a shift in meaning. In a related trend, few expressions like "in the slightest degree infringes upon" appear early in the eighteenth century, compared to the use of "infringe"; more appear toward mid-century, and yet more late in the century—about five times as many, increasing decade by decade. If no examples of "infringe in the slightest degree" come to light before 1700, or of "slightest infringement," it is because the *concept* of slight infringement was not current in the sixteenth and seventeenth centuries. The idea of infringing "in the slightest degree" seldom if ever appeared in print before the Revolutionary War ended. The same pattern holds for the simpler phrase "least infringement," found only a few times in the late seventeenth century, somewhat more in the eighteenth century, and widely only in the nineteenth century.

Meanwhile, eighteenth-century dictionaries did not change. Dictionaries defining *infringe* in the eighteenth century, as in the seventeenth century, did not include the phrase "infringe upon," which does not appear as an entry or in a quotation. Neither Dr. Johnson nor other dictionary authors used the expression. The sole exception was ironic. In 1795, Charles Pigott defined *prerogative* in his satirical *Political Dictionary*, "Prerogative (a regard for the royal),—a worn out pretence to infringe upon the laws, and a glaring design upon the privileges of the People."[236] (John Cowell might have viewed this license with horror, if not envy.) No reference works of any kind use "infringe upon" in definitions before the 1790s, and no general English dictionaries even then.

Nor was the phrase "infringe upon" used by America's most famous dictionary author, "forgotten founding father" Noah Webster (1758-1843).[237] None of Webster's works, either in the eighteenth century or in the nineteenth century, contained "infringe upon"; Webster used *infringe*. In 1817, Webster's school dictionary defined *infringe* briefly,

Infringe, *v.t.* to violate, break, transgress

Infringement, *n.* violation, transgression.[238]

Webster's large *American Dictionary of the English Language* in 1828 carried a fuller entry:

1. To break, as contracts; to violate, either positively by contravention, or negatively by non-fulfillment or neglect of performance. A prince or a private person *infringes* an agreement or covenant by neglecting to perform its conditions, as well as by doing what is stipulated not to be done. 2. To break; to violate; to transgress; to neglect to fulfill or obey; as, to *infringe* a law. 3. To destroy or hinder; as, to *infringe* efficacy [*little used.*][239]

Thus, Webster's dictionary of 1828 reflects some partial shifting from earlier definitions; the third definition of *infringe* is characterized as "little used," though the primary definition remains "to break, as contracts; to violate; to transgress." There is still no "infringe upon." Webster held the line.

Only after Webster had been dead five years did a 'Webster's' dictionary include "infringe upon" to define *infringe*, in 1848. (So-called Webster's dictionaries continued to appear to 1999. Editions now are called Merriam-Webster.) Later 'Webster's' in 1854, 1856, and 1857, co-edited, reflect the change. The big new one-volume 'Webster's' *American Dictionary of the English Language* of 1854, revised by Chauncey Goodrich, canonized it. Below the definition for *infringe* as in Webster's in 1828, it added, "This word is very frequently followed by *on* or *upon*; as, to *infringe upon* one's rights."[240] The newer 'Webster's' usage then continued to appear in other general dictionaries.

As late as 1842, a dictionary of synonyms showed *infringe* as a synonym only for harsh verbs:

To Break—rend, rack; violate, infringe; demolish, destroy.

To Encroach—intrude, infringe, invade.

To Intrench—encroach, infringe, invade, intrude.

To Intrude—obtrude, encroach, intrench, infringe, invade.

To Violate—infringe, transgress; injure; hurt; ravish, deflower.[241]

The synonyms for *infringe* itself were equivalent: "To Infringe—encroach, infract, invade, intrude; transgress, violate."[242] Just three years later, however, there were signs of lexical change. A different dictionary of synonyms in 1845 again provided *invade, violate, transgress*, etc., as the synonyms for *infringe*. However, the definition also used the phrase "infringe upon."[243]

Speaking of synonyms, the history of dictionaries includes reference books that selectively deal with words often confused, or words "esteemed synonymous," as Dr. John Trusler (1735-1820) put it. In 1766, Trusler published the first edition of the *Difference Between Words, Esteemed Synonymous, in the English Language*. A second edition came out in 1783 and a third in 1794. None of Trusler's lists of words commonly mistaken includes "abridge" with "infringe." The two words were not esteemed synonymous.

However, Trusler's third edition does signal a change by adding an entry for the word "infringe." Presumably none had been considered necessary in the previous editions. Unlike Dr. Johnson and previous centuries, Trusler delicately distinguishes between "infringe" and "violate." "To *Infringe, Transgress, Violate*. All these words imply an acting contrary to law, but the proper idea of *infringe*, is to break; of *transgress*, to go beyond the bounds of, and of *violate*, to use violence, or commit an outrage." Infringing is still breaking. "If we break those public or private laws, which we have sworn, or engaged ourselves to obey, we may be said to *infringe* them."[244] Trusler does not discuss infringing rights.

In connection with rights, the 1794 edition added a single reference to abridging, not found in the first two editions. Under the entry "*Liberty, Freedom*," Trusler spelled out,

> *Liberty* rather supposes a right; *freedom*, a privilege. The liberty of exercising all sorts of honest professions, is, or ought to be common to every nation; but, for the benefit of trade, government has abridged this *liberty*, and confined it to those who have served an apprenticeship to particular branches of manufacture; in which case they have the *freedom* of following their professions.[245]

The entry on liberty and freedom was another addition; the first and second editions did not contain an entry on liberty or on freedom, separately or together, although both editions used the words to discuss other terms.

No dictionary of synonyms in the eighteenth century or the nineteenth century offers *abridge* and *infringe* as synonyms. It is difficult to prove a negative, but another example of a dictionary of synonyms, early in the nineteenth century, will help to illustrate the trend line. In 1816, George Crabb's *English Synonymes Explained* clarified the similar words *encroach, intrench, intrude,* and *infringe*. Spelling out the difference, Crabb explains that "All these terms denote an unauthorized procedure; but the two former designate gentle or silent actions, the latter violent if not noisy actions."[246] Separately, Crabb devotes a page to *abridge* and *abridgement*, distinguishing them from similar terms *curtail* and *contract*, and *debar* and *deprive*, partly in the editorial sense, partly as a Lockean abridgement of rights.[247] Two years later, Crabb's second edition, "expanded and enlarged," added the entry "To infringe, violate, transgress," closely based on Trusler's discussion of the terms in 1794.[248] The word *infringe* still meant to break something. While Noah Webster was clear on *infringe*, Crabb's books suggest that by 1818, the word was beginning to need clarifying.

The suggestion is borne out by casual usage in the nineteenth century. The dictionary definition of *infringe* stayed solid; casual usage did not. If careless writing comes from careless thinking, as Orwell said, then the phrase "infringe upon" helps in evaluating some nineteenth-century authors. In a few pairings—not chosen at random—Charlotte Bronte and Emily Bronte did not use "infringe upon," but William Wordsworth and Robert Southey did; Henry Makepeace Thackeray did not use it, but James Russell Lowell did; Mark Twain did not use "infringe on," but James Fenimore Cooper did. Since most of the authors using the later "upon" phrasing were born somewhat earlier, the difference is not between earlier and later authors but between some of the best and the next best. When "infringe upon" came into use, it must have felt to some writers the way "based off of," instead of "based on," feels now. The strongest nineteenth-century writers, vibrant with Noah Webster's feel for language if not Webster's vocabulary, did not slide into "infringe upon" or "infringe on."

The pattern holds true for fields beyond literature. In law, William Blackstone did not use forms of "infringe upon" anywhere, amid frequent references to the concept of infringement. In history and political philosophy, David Hume did not use the expression "infringe upon" or "infringe on." In general, public documents in the eighteenth century in America did not use the phrase "infringe upon." John Adams and James Madison did not use it. George Washington and Thomas Jefferson did, but only rarely. A rare example from Jefferson is cited by the *Oxford English Dictionary*—"Let no act be passed by any one legislature which may infringe on the rights and liberties of another," from Jefferson's letter to the Virginia delegates in the Continental Congress.[249] Washington's papers in the Library of Congress turn up just one example from Washington, from 1789: "It will also appear by the Papers that the States of North Carolina and Georgia protested against said Treaties as infringing upon their legislative rights and being contrary to the Confederation."[250]

Modern corpus research confirms that forms of "infringe upon" increased after 1800, further increasing in each decade of the nineteenth century, increasing more and faster in the second half of the century. The Brigham Young University-Google Books database for American English includes more than 1.5 billion words, searchable with companion words (collocates). The database turns up more than 10,000 examples for *infringement* with *upon* in American English, with usage heaviest after 1870. But no examples of "infringement upon" turn up in the database for 1810 or 1820; few for 1830 or 1840. The usage develops in the following decades. Searching *infringes* with *on* turns up 4,323 examples, the overwhelming majority dating since 1880. Searching *infringes* with *upon* turns up 3,530 examples, again most dating since 1880.

By the end of the nineteenth century, forms of "infringe upon" had become so standard that they showed up in law books. In John Bouvier's *Law Dictionary* of 1879, the phrase appears in an entry for "insolvency."

> From a desire of avoiding what might seem to be an infringement upon an exclusive right of congress, the laws passed by the various states—with the exception of Texas—upon the subject, whether properly insolvent or bankrupt laws, have been termed insolvent laws. In Texas there is a "bankrupt law."[251]

Bouvier's dictionary reflects the nineteenth-century transition from "infringe" to "infringe upon." Previous editions from 1855 to 1859 had used the verb *infringe* without "upon."

Bouvier's "exception of Texas" and "In Texas there is a bankrupt law" refer to the Texas of the time, a debtors' haven. In the late nineteenth and early twentieth century, states close to the Mexican border, like Texas, had populist legislation. One effect was to boost the state's population; if fugitive debtors and others had not found refuge in Texas or nearby states, they would have kept running across the border. The Great State had no alimony, did not garnish wages, and capped interest rates including mortgage rates; well into the twentieth century, Texas was the only state in the union where a householder could lose the home only for failing to pay the mortgage—not for arrears on a lien or taxes. By the late twentieth century these provisions were dismantled, with little attention from large media outlets. Regrettably, most debtor protections stemmed from the Texas constitution of 1876, written in reaction to Reconstruction laws of the 1860s; provisions that made it harder for a government to abuse a poor white man revoked some protections for freedmen. But while the provisions lasted, they did serve to bolster some stability for the working class.

Even in the nineteenth century, most uses of "infringe upon" or "least infringement" did not occur in the context of law or an official document. A phrase like "not in the slightest degree infringed" was more often emphasis or defensiveness. Saying "not the slightest infringement" in the nineteenth century was rather like saying "literally" nowadays, used the way "literally" is used for emphasis now—a verbal token of sincerity, a voucher, rather than (literally) meaning "literally."

The end of the nineteenth century and beginning of the twentieth

Searching the enormous twenty-first-century repositories that Beowulf would have called word-hoards also sheds light on the infringe-abridge binomial. From 1810 to 1919, forms of *infringe* appeared in print thousands of times in America. Most of the time, it appeared alone (with or without "upon"), rather than as half of a binomial. When it appeared in a binomial in the nineteenth century, it was often paired redundantly with a quasi-synonym; less clarity resulted in less precision. Forms of "infringed" thus come first with forms of "violated" more than 2,000 times in the database, most heavily from 1890 to 1919. The imprecision increased as the word moved farther away in time from its earlier strong meaning. The word "violated" comes first, in turn, paired with "infringed," another 1,387 times. From 1810 to 2000, the quasi-synonym "infringed" ranks 32nd on the list of collocates most likely to appear with "violated." As the protections conveyed in each word diminish or soften, ordinary usage tends to pile on quasi-synonyms. The result is more verbiage but less reinforcement. (For perspective, the collocate "Microsoft" appears 157 times with "violated," almost all in the year 2000. "Microsoft" ranks 100th on the list of collocates most likely to appear with "violated.")

Forms of *infringe* also appear in binomials with the quasi-synonym "broken," mostly up to 1870; "breach," 245 times from 1820 on; and "denial," mostly from 1900 on. Less often, but consistently, *infringe* also appears in the 155-billion-word database paired with other verbs that refine, intensify, and reinforce the protections. Forms of "diminished" were one such refinement, as in "infringed or diminished." "Dilution" and "misconstruction" have also been paired with forms of *infringe*, to forestall indirect or partial damage as well as destruction.

Setting aside binomials, the top two collocates for the word "infringed" are two short and simple English words: "infringed" is preceded by the word *be* 22,916 times; and by the word *not* 19,184 times. In contrast, *infringe* is preceded by forms of "serious" only 1,021 times—almost all from 1870 on. Only one combination of "serious" and "infringe" appears in the decade beginning 1810, one in the decade beginning 1820, and three apiece in the decades beginning 1830, 1840, and 1860. Before 1870, "serious" was seldom used with "infringement," because there was no such thing as un-serious infringement.

Beyond any doubt, the BYU-Google database reflects the influence of the fifteenth amendment and later amendments. The effects of "denied or abridged" in the constitutional amendments can be traced in the usage of the late nineteenth century like reverberations of sound or force through a medium. Searching the word "denied" with collocates yields a pairing with "abridged" 13,849 times, tenth among words most likely to be paired with "denied." The overwhelming majority come after 1870—after ratification of the fifteenth amendment. The database yields one appearance in the 1830s, one in the 1850s, 37 in the 1860s. Then, in 1870, the floodgates opened for the remaining 13,810 or so examples. The constitutional amendment swayed the American lexicon and the entire body of American print.

Reversing the order of "abridged" and "denied" yields another 647 examples, all from 1850 on. Searching "denial" with collocates yields the same pattern; the noun appears with the noun "abridgment" 453 times, 70th on the list of probable pair words. Only five of these appeared before 1870. "Denial" appears with "abridgement" another 289 times, all from 1870 on. English usage changed the wording of the amendments; the amendments also changed English usage, at least in the United States.

What a difference a hundred years can make. Less than a century after Webster published his first dictionary, the expressions "infringe" and "infringe upon" were being used interchangeably, sometimes even in dictionaries. By 1895, identification of *infringe* with *infringe upon* had increased to such an extent that one dictionary took pains to spell out that *infringe* had force: "*Infringe* or *infringe upon* means a breaking into; hence it is a much stronger word than those that precede it [trespass upon, encroach upon]."[252] The reference book was the authoritative *Century Dictionary and Cyclopedia*, the most comprehensive American dictionary yet published, a multi-volume set produced by the Century Company (based ultimately on Webster's 1841 *American Dictionary of the English Language*). The careful definition in *Century* was a reminder that the word *infringe*, even with upon, should not be mistaken for a weaker term. Since the reminder was considered needful, presumably it addressed a common misconstruction; less than thirty years after the fourteenth and fifteenth amendments, the word *infringe* was being used too loosely or too lightly. The change supports the probability that ordinary use of "infringe upon" had already affected "infringe" when Congress composed the amendments.

Change, Misunderstanding, and Loss; How Did We Get to this Point?

> Madison found this interpretation of the free exercise clause so absurd that to state it was to refute it. Despite its plausibility as a textual matter, the narrow interpretation of "prohibiting" should therefore, be rejected, and the term should be read as meaning approximately the same as "infringing" or "abridging."[253]

Times changed in the twentieth century. In 1990, the *Harvard Law Review* ran an article using "infringing" and "abridging" as synonyms. As the headnote quotation indicates, understanding of two key verbs in the first and second amendments has gone downhill. Forms of the words can be presented as synonyms, even in law review articles and in published court rulings. This chapter will deal with the relevant changes in modern English usage, emphasizing changes since World War II.

In a broad and variable way, *infringed* has moved downward a place, has lost gravitas, since 1789. It has shrunk, shriveled, lightened up. Even when dictionary definitions follow the earlier definitions, ordinary use of *infringe* often suggests something more trivial or superficial than infringement of essential rights as in the eighteenth century—an 'infraction' rather than a break. In fact, use of *infraction* often displays the same error. The word "infraction" comes from the same Latin root as the word "infringe" and may be defined as violation or infringement. But somehow it *sounds* like a crack instead of a break, like a "minor infraction"—a term used often, even in writing about law, and often in contrast to something like a "serious felony." The lightening up of "infraction" may stem from the internal rhyme with "crack." Or it may stem from the similarity of "infraction" to "fractures" in medicine, as the word is used by non-physicians. (In medicine, a fracture is a break in bone or cartilage.)

The study of meaning (semantics) could benefit from examining the history of *infringe*. That American English has mostly misplaced the 1789 meaning of *infringed* is an example of what linguistics calls semantic change.

Semantic change in the context of words describes the gradual shift in the conventional meaning of words, as people use them in new types of contexts and these usages become normal. Often in the course of semantic change, a word shifts its meaning to the point that the modern meaning is radically different from the original usage.[254]

Semantic change has various causes. One is the sound of the word or its resemblance to other words that sound like it (phonetically similar). The word *infringe* has been unlucky in its phonetic neighbors. Words that sound like *infringe* include its rhymes—binge, cringe, fringe, hinge, singe, tinge, twinge, impinge. Most of them signify something temporary, or slight, or both. A tinge is a slight tint; a twinge is a slight pain; to cringe is to shrink slightly; to singe something differs from setting it on fire. Each of these rhyming words is more akin to an abridged version of its full condition than to a law broken or rights violated. If one question is why the original strength of the verb *to infringe* seems lost to view now, part of the answer is the linguistic seepage from other words including rhyming words.

Another partial answer is that we have not totally lost the original meaning. Dictionaries still define *infringe* as "(v.t.) to commit a breach or infraction of; violate or transgress."[255] But for public usage, dictionary definitions have not been enough to keep the 1789 meaning of the word intact. After publishing the longer version of this book, I still got reactions like, "What part of 'Shall not be infringed' do you not get?" So, how did we come to this point?

Infringement and "fringe"

For a non-linguistics professor, the suspiciously similar-sounding words *fringe* and *impinge* look like the main culprits. Before reviewing the etymology of "fringe," let's start with an easier approach and look at some obvious political associations. Phrases like "fringe group" have been used to mean irrational, marginal, or politically disfavored for so long now that the word "fringe" is routinely applied in politics without definition. 'Everyone knows what it means,' but the meaning tends to shift with the perceived status of the individual or group characterized.

For anyone concerned about original intent in the Bill of Rights, an unconscious association of *infringe* with "fringe" is regrettable. Until the twentieth century, "fringe" meant a form of ornament, thus something superficial or frivolous. During the twentieth century, "fringe" began to mean 'outlier.' With the civil rights movement in the 1960s, the assassination of President John F. Kennedy in 1963, and the high tensions animating the Goldwater-LBJ presidential election in 1964, the phrase 'fringe groups' entered the political lexicon, understood across the board to mean the same thing as the more recent 'whack job.' Ironically or not, much of the "fringe" tinge has been applied to gun groups including the National Rifle Association (NRA), self-described 'militias,' and white-supremacy groups or hate groups, some of whom self-identify as "fringe." (When this author was growing up in Texas, the similar phrase 'gun nuts' was ordinary use.) Unfortunately, being called "fringe," by self or others, reinforces the misuse of "shall not be infringed" in the second amendment to mean 'untouchable.'

Thus, "fringe group" showed up in mass periodicals. The phrase was big in the newsmagazine *Time*, for example. From 1946 to 2011, some two hundred articles in *Time* referred to "fringe groups" or a "fringe group." In 1946, a *Time* magazine article accused a retired Brigadier General of being "an apostle of Communistic causes and Communist-fringe groups," part of the who-lost-China dispute.[256] Another example was quoted though not authored by *Time* in 1948, when the then-governor of Virginia railed against President Harry Truman; "The people of the Southern states have been placed upon the sacrificial altar to appease racial and other minority fringe groups."[257]

By mid-twentieth century, the term "fringe group" was effectively launched, along with 'Danish modern' furniture, Sputnik, Atomic Age design, Pier 1 Imports, Rachel Carson's *Silent Spring*, the environmental movement, and a new JFK-inspired emphasis on fitness. Most of the trends might have been criticized earlier as 'fringe' themselves, but they quickly became prevalent.

Oddly, even while the term 'fringe group' appeared as a loaded term in magazines, it retained a more neutral meaning in sociology. Most 1950s periodical articles referring to a "fringe group" applied to statistics in labor, health, or science. In labor and management, the sociological term meant statistical exceptions or small numbers of workers. The phrase "fringe group" in labor resembled the phrase "fringe benefits"—hospitalization insurance, etc., aside from wages. A quick search of a periodicals database turns up thousands of examples of "fringe benefits" after about 1950. Generally, the same provisions are now called just "benefits"—where they exist. "Fringe benefits" may not have become as loaded a term as "fringe group," but association with the word "fringe" did not strengthen benefits.

As the 1950s continued, the political intensity of "fringe groups" picked up. So did frequency of use. *Time* magazine faithfully reflected the trends and reinforced them. Later in the decade, nearer to 1960, the pendulum swung back and forth. *Time*, which had referred to "left-wing fringe groups" in 1956, reversed direction in 1957.

> In Montgomery, where Negroes and whites rode together peacefully in the first days after integration, Christmas week brought the first big kickbacks from lunatic-fringe groups. In three nights snipers fired on and struck four buses, wounding a 22-year-old Negro laundry worker in both legs. The city commission, declaring that "an emergency exists," ordered all nighttime bus operations suspended through New Year's Day. None of the snipers was arrested. Said a city detective: "We have no leads—nothing to work on."[258]

Moving from civil rights in Montgomery, Alabama, that year to New York the next, *Time* reversed direction again. In 1959, the magazine applied the phrase "fringe groups" in New York to "black supremacists."[259]

By 1960, in a sign of tense times, the lurid, highly charged connotations of "fringe group" were established. Again, *Time* held up the mirror, writing during the election of 1960,

> Long the rising Senate spokesman of Republican conservatives— and, to his irritation, of wild-eyed fringe groups as well—Barry Goldwater found himself in the national eye as he spoke out in wrath against the Nixon-Rockefeller platform agreement ("Governor Rockefeller," he told the Arizona delegation, "is out to destroy the Republican Party"). By convention's end, Goldwater, in some imperceptible investiture, had been crowned king of the nation's conservatives just as surely as Dick Nixon won the nomination.[260]

The shift was mostly complete after the 1960 election, and the phrase "fringe group" settled into the political lexicon—mostly to mean the extreme right wing—as Kennedy moved into the White House. On the issue of fluoridating the water supply, *Time* wrote in 1961,

> Yet fluoridation fails to get approval in most referendums, whether in Boston suburbs or anywhere else in the U.S. (places that fluoridate generally do so as the result of decisions by city managers or councils). The reason is that psychologically the issue lends itself to the purposes of otherwise insignificant political fringe groups. Playing on the populace's anxieties, they can get on a winning side and look more influential than they are.[261]

Anyone who grew up in Houston, Texas, during those years might remember the proposal to fluoridate the water supply. It eventually won, but it was opposed with virulent intensity as government mind control or a communist plot. The debate could hardly have gotten more intense had the fluoride been LSD.

References to fringe groups continued to appear in periodicals throughout the sixties, and of course after the sixties, mostly with the same slant. Many "fringe group" references show up in vintage university alumni magazines or letters to the editor, so many that their use may have been a marker of going to college. If so, it is less a marker now, whether because the use of "fringe group" has expanded or because going to college has.

Over time, the use of "fringe" and "fringe group" increased so much that it sometimes became self-parody, a self-deprecating voucher of self-awareness like "politically correct." This trend developed more in Britain, with the famous self-identified Edinburgh "Fringe" theater and the 1960s comedy production "Beyond the Fringe." On a somber note, the fact that *Time* in 1961 called fringe groups politically insignificant looks blind in hindsight. President Kennedy, Martin Luther King, and Robert F. Kennedy were all killed by marginalized individuals who compensated for their deprivations through loose, shadowy social and political networks that reinforced their motivation. Like the phonetic networks of *binge, cringe, syringe*, etc., such political networks can sound like jokes and can be ridiculed. They always were. But they still had, and have, genuine negatives.

Unfortunately, some kinds of opposition intensify defiant self-identification. It is a mistake to drive a human being beyond the pale. The hysterical parochialism of self-identified insiders is not less destructive than the hysteria of 'fringe groups,' though it may be one or two steps removed from the ultimate harm.

Etymology and phonetic neighbors

The primary definition of *fringe* in the *Oxford English Dictionary* is the decoration everyone knows—"An ornamental bordering, consisting of a narrow band to which are attached threads of silk, cotton, etc., either loose or formed into tassels, twists, etc." In English literature, the word dates from at least *Sir Gawain and the Green Knight* (c. 1390); when Gawain rides up to the lords and ladies of the court, his horse's saddle has "golden frenges." With the popularity of fringe, beads, lavish colors, vintage clothes, and American Indian artifacts in the sixties, fringe probably became associated with hippies in more than one way. The phonetic nearness of "fringe" and *infringe* has affected politics and history.

However, the similarity between the two words does not stem from etymology. Freakishly, the two very similar words do not share the same origin or word history. The word *fringe* does not derive from *infringe*, or vice versa; *fringe* comes from a different Latin word entirely (*fimbria*). Since *fringe* and *infringe* are so alike in look, sound, and spelling, the disconnect is confusing—and ordinary usage has compensated for it, by drawing the two words together. The word 'fringe' invariably means something marginal, and the word 'infringe' is misunderstood to mean some borderline or gray-area transgression.

Infringe and impinge

Word association can be powerful. A famous example arose in World War II. On April 19, 1940, the *Times* of London explained why Vidkun Quisling became infamous overnight. Quisling was the Norwegian traitor who turned Norway over to Nazi Germany. As described in the expert run-down by the *Times*,

> Major Quisling has added a new word to the English language. To writers, the word Quisling is a gift from the gods. If they had been ordered to invent a new word for traitor they could hardly have hit upon a more brilliant combination of letters. Aurally it contrives to suggest something at once slippery and tortuous. Visually it has the supreme merit of beginning with a Q, which (with one august exception) has long seemed to the British mind to be a crooked, uncertain and slightly disreputable letter, suggestive of the questionable, the querulous, the quavering of quaking quagmires and quivering quicksands, of quibbles and quarrels, of queasiness, quackery, qualms and quilp.

The "august exception" meant, of course, the queen. The *Times* editorial board did a masterful job on the aural associations of "Quisling" as the new synonym for "turncoat," more up-to-date, more potent, and more brown-shirt-like than "turncoat." Probably, for the British, "Quisling" was also a more fitting name for a traitor than "Benedict Arnold." *Life Magazine* reprinted the Quisling passage (May 6, 1940).

Returning from 1940 to 2020 and from World War II to the carnage now, the word *infringe* has also been affected by phonetic seepage from another word that sounds like it—the verb "impinge." Judging from law dictionaries, *impinge* is a particularly relevant and unfortunate phonetic associate for *infringe*. In 1968, the fourth edition of *Black's Law Dictionary* did not define *impinge*. The 1968 edition contained no entry for it. In 1999, the seventh edition of *Black's* defined "Impinge, *vb.*" as "To encroach or infringe (on or upon) <impinge on the defendant's rights>." In a major law dictionary, over a period of thirty-one years, the word *impinge* went from being omitted to being a synonym for *infringe*. The result is a loss of force for both terms.

Undoubtedly the newer and weaker definition in widely used law dictionaries reflected changing usage in legal cases—in trials and judges' rulings. It did not come from etymology. Like *fringe*, the word *impinge* is unrelated etymologically to *infringe*. The two simple words both came from Latin, but not from the same origin. From the *Oxford English Dictionary*,

> Latin *impingĕre* (only transitive) to push, strike, drive (at or into), thrust, strike, or dash (against), < *im-* (IM- *prefix¹*) + *pangĕre* to fix, drive in.

The two words had no shared history—until both their meanings started to change, when both *infringe* and *impinge* underwent analogous shifts. Ironically, in Latin *impinge* was another word for a strong, forceful action.

Over the same thirty years, *Black's Law Dictionary* also reflects change in *infringement*. In 1968, *Black's* defined *infringement* as "A breaking into; a trespass or encroachment upon; a violation of law, regulation, contract, or right. Used especially of invasions of the rights secured by patents, copyrights, and trademarks." Thus, in 1968, *Black's* said that infringement meant violation of law and violation of right. Infringement of copyright or trademark was a main example, with two columns for "Infringement of patent," "Infringement of copyright," etc., and an entry for "Infringer," as "One who appropriates another's patented invention." But the 1968 *Black's* did not restrict the definition of *infringe* to copyright and patent. Furthermore, just before "Infringement," Black's also defined "Infraction" as violation: "A breach, violation, or infringement; as of a law, a contract, a right or duty. In French law, this term is used as a general designation of all punishable actions."

By the time 1999 rolled around, *Black's* applied the word *infringe only* to intellectual property. The seventh edition defined "Infringement" as "Intellectual property. An Act that interferes with one of the exclusive rights of a patent, copyright, or trademark owner.—infringe, *vb*. See INTELLECTUAL PROPERTY. Cf. PLAGIARISM." Two pages defined and discussed infringement in intellectual property. As in 1968, the next entry was "Infringer," defined more fully as "A person who interferes with one of the exclusive rights of a patent, copyright, or trademark owner. See INFRINGEMENT."

The later *Black's* shows at least two significant changes: the definition of infringement applied to intellectual property is much more extensive, and more importantly the definition of infringement applies only to intellectual property. Furthermore, the 1999 edition contains no entry for "infraction." So, there is no definition for either of the etymologically related *infraction* and *infringement* as breach or violation; there is no explanation that they are etymologically related; no indication that they are synonyms; and French law is jettisoned, omitting early French and law-French etymology. Without context or etymology, the relevant synonym for *infringement* became *impingement*.

During the election cycle of 1968, at least one public figure employed a form of "infringe upon" to project gravitas if not gentility.

In April 1967, former Alabama Governor George Wallace explained on NBC's *Meet the Press* that he opposed the Civil Rights Act of 1964 as "an infringement upon the property-right system."[262] Wallace's third-party candidacy threatened to attract longtime constituencies of both major parties in 1968. Ironically or not, Wallace himself was a main avatar for the "fringe" characterization in politics. As discussed in the excellent book *American Melodrama*, which reported Wallace's comment,

> The Wallace movement, like any other national political movement in America—or, for that matter, in any country—was a coalition. At the risk of oversimplifaction, it can be said that after the Democratic Convention Wallace could count on two elements: the Deep South and the right-wing lunatic fringe.[263]

Not that the potential coalition included only these two voting blocs. Wallace

> could hope to get at least a good share of the vote of a third element: the traditional conservatives. The absolutely critical question, now squarely posed, was how many votes he could draw from a fourth and much larger group: the white working class and lower-middle class in the urban and industrial areas of the North and Middle West.

Similar dynamics played out in the 2016 election. The semantic change of *infringe* had already been felt in 1968; it had developed farther by 1999; by 2016, many voters probably took for granted that the second amendment means that weaponry cannot be touched by law. No major news media outlet set them straight. One consequence of the semantic change in "infringed" has been less understanding of law under the U.S. Constitution. When a widely used law dictionary defines a word differently from the way it was used in 1789—especially a word that appears in the Bill of Rights, and especially without acknowledging the earlier definition—the outcome for understanding is not good.

Again, one question is how the change came about. Since *infringe* and *impinge* ended up in *Black's* as quasi-synonyms, it is reasonable to hypothesize that the semantic changes in the two words are connected. To rule out the possibility would be illogical. The history of *impinge* parallels that of *infringe*. In early use, *impinge* meant a forceful clash. Over time, it has become less forceful in law—except in medical lawsuits—and in ordinary use. Both verbs have come to signify lighter or softer actions, and as they have lightened, they have drawn together in law English.

Whatever caused the changes, the changes themselves are not conjecture. To try to explain *why* a word shifts in meaning over decades or centuries may involve hypothesis, but to show *that* a word has shifted in meaning can be done with evidence. The shift in meaning can be tracked, even if not every cause can be pinpointed. The clear change in *impinge* is easy to track. In 1789, it was virtually nonexistent in political philosophy or law; by now, it has appeared in many published court rulings. In 1789, it had no connection with *infringe*; by now, some law writing and even law dictionaries have virtually equated the two words.

Taking the first point first, *impinge* may seem to have an eighteenth-century sound, a harpsichord ring to it, but the eighteenth century seldom used it. In 1789, *impinge* was much rarer, more specialized, and more obscure than *infringe*. It was used mainly in mathematics and science, in a sense later used in industry in Britain and America. In 1789, the second edition of Thomas Sheridan's *Complete Dictionary of the English Language* defined it, "To fall against, to strike against, to clash with." Before Noah Webster came along with his game-changing work, Sheridan's was the dictionary most widely used in America.[264] Sheridan defined *infringe*, "To violate, to break laws or contracts; to destroy, to hinder," and like other dictionary authors, used *infringe* to define the words *break* and *violate*. The words *impinge* and *infringe* were not synonyms, but both words were more forceful in 1789 than they are today.

That the verbs *impinge* and *infringe* were not synonyms when the Bill of Rights was produced is confirmed by contemporaneous books besides dictionaries. One especially on-point example was a book about weaponry, translated from Italian into English by Captain Henry T. Thomson of the Royal Regiment of Artillery and published in 1789. The work itself was the *Treatise on Gun-Powder*, firearms, and artillery by Alessandro d'Antoni (1714-1786), director of artillery and fortifications in Turin. Thomson used forms of *impinge* more than two dozen times, always to mean striking, landing on, or hitting something, as in, "a shot impinging on a thin wall with great force, makes a hole without shaking the contiguous parts."[265] Incidentally, Thomson criticized Samuel Johnson for his relative lack of artillery terms and expressed a wish that future lexicographers at Oxford fill in the gap.[266] Thomson's critique suggests that he used Johnson's dictionary in translating d'Antoni's treatises. Closing the circle, Johnson's dictionary defined *impinge* exactly as Sheridan and Thomson later used it: "To fall against; to strike against; to clash with." The same sense is included in *Oxford English Dictionary* definitions since 1605.

During the eighteenth century, use of *impinge* began to change. Most often, the term referred to physical objects or physical collision, as in mechanics—as in gun-making. But a more abstract sense of "To encroach or infringe *on* or *upon*" (*OED*) also came into use. As early as 1818, the Supreme Court of Virginia ruled in an inheritance case that the late Richard Adams' debts would not only have wiped out his money, "but [would] have impinged on the lands."[267] Other state and federal published cases from the 1820s, 1830s, and 1840s contain similar examples, more abstract than mechanical, to mean that something affects or does not affect a right, a principle, a jurisdiction, or an obligation.

By 1850, at least thirty-five published rulings contained forms of *impinge* to mean encroaching on something—a principle, a right, the legislature, the Constitution, etc. Following up unpublished cases citing these would yield more examples. But even the shorter list shows that nineteenth-century courts in the U.S. used the word *impinge* in varying senses. The examples include a couple of Supreme Court cases—*Thurlow v. Massachusetts* in 1847 and *Smith v. Turner* in 1849—in which jurisdictions or governments were said to 'impinge on' one another. The shifting usage of *impinge* would be one more reason to remove *infringe*, the word for which it was confused, from the later constitutional amendments. The verb "deny" was harder to misunderstand.

For the rest of the nineteenth century, the older physical sense of *impinge*—to strike against—continued to be used in the U.S. alongside the more abstract meanings. This was the mechanical-industrial sense, still used in medical lawsuits today. Forms of *impinge* in the more abstract sense of encroachment, usually non-physical except where they involved land, also continued to show up in nineteenth-century cases. Published court rulings in the LexisNexis database catalogue both senses. Published federal and state cases used the mechanical, chemical, or scientific sense of *impinge* almost every year from 1865 through 1899, and in cases from 1900 through 1929, in some years more than once. The heyday of pre-World War I American industrial invention is reflected in the database. Courts seem to have made no effort to standardize usage; the more physical and the more abstract senses of the word can be found in cases from the same year. Moving into the twentieth century, the more abstract sense also continued to appear. In these cases, the action of impinging applies to powers, laws, rights, etc. In some new cases the word appeared in the briefs or in the judge's comments; in some it appeared in citation of precedent. Later, naturally, the precedent became overwhelming.

Summing up: the meaning of *impinge*, like that of *infringe*, has changed over two centuries. Its mechanical-industrial sense as defined by Samuel Johnson and the *OED*—"to fall against; to strike against"—has not disappeared and continues to be used in optics, orthopedics, and ballistics, among other fields. As mentioned, it continues to be used in legal cases. However, this sense is not used exclusively, or even consistently, in law. To the contrary, legal cases now use the more abstract senses of *impinge* more widely, as shown in hundreds of published rulings.

In this evolution, *impinging* and *infringing* have come to seem interchangeable, especially in law; and both have lost their earlier forcefulness, even in law. The mutual influence of the semantic neighbors has been detrimental. When *impinge* moved next door, parking its rusting conveyances around the yard to harvest for spare parts, *infringe* suffered collateral property damage. Internalizing the damage, it began putting some of its own wheel-less vehicles up on blocks. Fortunately, the internal corrosion of *infringed* over time led to its being replaced in later amendments by the shorter and straightforward *denied*. But regarding the amendments, there has been too little checking under the hood.

The language in recent years

Today, there is no question that the two words *infringe* and *impinge* are often interchanged, often with the words "on" or "upon" added. Many people have lost sight of the 1789 meaning of the word *infringe*, and even more have lost sight of the 1789 meaning of *impinge*—even though the 1789 usage for each persists today. Remember the "reading comprehension" section of your high-school SAT? A well-known test-prep product, Sparknotes, defines *impinge*,

> **1.** *(v.)* to impact, affect, make an impression (The hail *impinged* the roof, leaving large dents.)
>
> **2.** *(v.)* to encroach, infringe (I apologize for *impinging* upon you like this, but I really need to use your bathroom. Now.)[268]

Some recent authorities have tried to disentangle the two words. In *Artful Nuance: A Refined Guide to Imperfectly Understood Words in the English Language*, Professor Rod Evans sets the record straight on *infringe* and *impinge*.

> IMPINGE/INFRINGE (V.)
>
> To *impinge* is to hit, strike, or collide, whether literally or figuratively: "The bright light *impinged* on our eyes." *Impinge* can also mean "encroach" (trespass or intrude) when its meaning is close to *infringe*.
>
> *Infringe* means "to intrude or trespass": "We didn't want them to infringe on our privacy." *Infringe* can also mean "violate" (as a law or agreement): "The US government often *infringed* treaties with Native Americans."[269]

The Penguin *Writer's Manual* also includes a rare explicit entry for both terms:

> **impinge or infringe?** *Impinge* is a formal word meaning 'to affect' (often adversely) and is always followed by the preposition *on* or *upon*: *impinge upon someone's private life*. *Infringe* is often used in the same way and with the same meaning: *infringe on the rights of others*. *Infringe* is also and, according to some traditionalists, more properly used with a direct object meaning 'to violate': *to infringe the regulations/a patent/someone's rights*.[270]

Among other online sources, the *Grammarist* website deals with *impinge* and *infringe*, but still garbles them together.[271] The Oxford *Dictionary of Modern English Usage* straightens out *infringe* and *impinge*, but only by providing a long explanation for *infringe*. The dictionary gives examples of "infringe upon" from the public discourse and explains the confusion, in the Oxbridge version of a nutshell—half a page. The shorter and more recent Oxford *Pocket Fowler's Modern English Usage* defines *infringe* correctly, concisely includes transitive and intransitive uses, and briefly connects *infringe upon* or *on* with threat or encroachment.[272] Other recent Oxford reference books provide similar information.

"Impinge" and "infringe" in recent law language

If one searches—even quickly—the thousands of legal cases electronically archived in the LexisNexis database, a widespread mingling of the verbs *infringe* and *impinge* shows up. Current law uses them almost interchangeably. Legal writing in the twenty-first century has forgotten that the words were ever different, let alone that they were different for centuries. To begin with, the word *impinge* is used vastly more often now than in the years before and after the Constitutional Convention. Published rulings in federal and state cases from August 2005 to August 2015 contain thousands of results for forms of *impinge*. Of these, most recent uses of *impinge* apply to rights, freedom, obligation, liberty, etc.—some principle or jurisdiction, said to be "impinged on" or not. Only in medical lawsuits is the industrial sense used widely; when a legal case involves medical equipment, prosthetics, surgery, eyesight, or the spine, one part (mechanical or human) is often said to "impinge on" another.

A LexisNexis search for cases using *both impinge* and *infringe* also turns up thousands of results. That is, the same published case contains both *impinge* and *infringe* (with or without a preposition); thousands of federal and state cases each mingle the two terms together. Thus, a search does not bring to light any wide-scale effort in law writing to distinguish between the two, let alone to rescue the sense of *infringed* used in the second amendment.

To the contrary, mingling the two terms has accelerated. Of the thousands of cases using both words, only forty-three took place before 1900. And of those nineteenth-century cases, only ten used "impinge" to mean "infringe." The other thirty-three cases, all dating from 1865 through 1899, used "impinge" in a mechanical or scientific context; most involved patents. From 1900 through 1949, only 156 published rulings used both terms, and many of those cases applied "impinge" in industry. Legal cases over one physical thing impinging on another involved player pianos, turbines, stoves, furnaces, collar-ironing machinery, and acetylene burners, among other products. Widespread use of both words in the same case did not occur until the late twentieth century.

Since 1950, however, interchanging "infringe" and "impinge" in courts has increased every decade and has accelerated in the recent decades. For 1950 through 1959, forty-six published cases contained both words, most using "impinge" in an industrial context. From 1960 through 1969, seventy-four published cases contained both "impinge" and "infringe," again with most "impinge" industrial. The year 1968 was a turning point. There were twenty-four such published cases in 1968 and 1969 alone, out of which only six used "impinge" in the industrial sense. Three-fourths of the cases from 1968 and 1969 used "impinge" (on) to mean "infringe," as in infringing rights.

In the seventies, 312 published cases used both "impinge" and "infringe," increasingly as loose synonyms. In the eighties, 607 cases used both words, again with large and growing use of "impinge" to mean "infringe." By this time, therefore, precedents came to establish the trend. The number of case citations using the words as synonyms was large enough to dominate the lexicon. By now, in case citation, "impinge" more likely means "infringe" than refers to machine parts or mechanical or chemical actions; the industrial meaning shows up more in briefs or in case histories than in a judge's ruling.

Moving forward, published rulings in the nineties show 824 cases using both "impinge" and "infringe," from *NAACP v. Hunt* in 1990 to *Women's Medical Center v. Archer* in 1999. Published rulings from 2000 through 2009 show 1,079 cases each using both words. From 2010 to 2015, there were 776 published cases using both. The muddling of the two words accelerated in the twentieth century and is accelerating more in the twenty-first.

Not to undo the labor of the previous search, the same over-all pattern can also be spotted in a shorter and easier way. When "impinge" is used with *on* or *upon*, it is generally as synonym for "infringe." Legal cases involving patents or industrial applications seldom use "impinge on." From 1844 through 2015, the LexisNexis database turns up 913 federal and state cases using "impinge on." Of these, nineteen came before 1900, the next seventy-two from 1900 through 1949, and the next fifty from 1950 through 1968. Thus, 772 of the 913 examples of "impinge on" usage date from 1968 to 2015.

Naturally, the same pattern holds for the equivalent "impinge upon." From 1860 through 2015, 905 published cases used forms of "impinge upon." Of these, eighteen date from before 1900, the next eighty-six from the first half of the twentieth century, the next seventy-six from 1950 to 1968. So, 725 of the examples come from 1968 through 2015. Along with the substitution of "impinge" for "infringe," the softening of "impinge" into "impinge upon" accelerated after 1968.

By now, the changed usage has made its way into thousands of law review articles. A LexisNexis search of articles using forms of "impinge on" from 1972 to 2015, either directly or in citation, turns up thousands of examples. Of the thousands, 2,803 were published after 2010. A database search for law review articles using both *impinge* and *infringe* turns up 995 articles from 1985 to 2015. Obviously, the law reviews also reflect the semantic change of "infringe" into "impinge." There were 2,694 articles using forms of "impinge upon" from 2000 to 2015. The law reviews further demonstrate the loss of force for both "infringe" and "impinge."

By the way, association with copyright or patent has not strengthened either verb. Copyright infringement is a major issue in intellectual property. It matters very much to writers and other creators. But in politics it is not an issue equal to the second amendment. It is not considered life-and-death. Intellectual property disputes in recent decades have not lent greater force, or weight, to the legal term *infringement*. And quite possibly the dilution of the word has had a reciprocal effect to dilute enforcement of copyright law.

Recent federal rulings: *Heller I*

Now comes the grimmest part of this book. The semantic changes that have cost us our understanding of the first two amendments have now surfaced in U.S. courts including the Supreme Court. The difference between abridging a right, as necessary for joining together in human society, and infringing a right has been muddied, diluted, or undermined, and some federal courts have been sucked into the mistake. This is the most disheartening aspect of the gun-control discussion aside from the terrible gun violence itself. It is disheartening to read the writing of men steeped in U.S. law and promoted in our judicial system, and to find English mistakes that could be avoided by a sharp eighth-grader.

This chapter will take up three recent federal cases involving gun laws in the nation's capital. The first is the 2008 Supreme Court ruling in *District of Columbia v. Heller*. The next is "Heller II," the 2011 ruling in the Court of Appeals for the D.C. Circuit, in *Heller v. District of Columbia*. The third is a 2015 ruling in *Wrenn v. District of Columbia*. There had already been linguistic slips and slides before these cases. The three cases taken in chronological order show the linguistic slips getting worse.

The published Supreme Court decision in *District of Columbia v. Heller* runs 157 pages. In some ways it is a model of precision. Refreshingly, in 157 pages of legal writing, no form of the word *impinge* is used. Nothing is said to "impinge on" anything. No form of "infringe on" is used, either, and the phrase "infringe upon" occurs only once, in a dissent. Closer to eighteenth-century understanding of the word, something is either infringed, or not. Forms of *infringe* are used in *Heller*, reasonably enough, twenty-two times. Of these, twenty are the word "infringed" itself, mostly quoting or paraphrasing the second amendment or public documents citing it. With laudable purity of diction, the Supreme Court in *Heller* thus sidestepped two hundred years' worth of gradual linguistic corruption of *infringe*.

Regrettably, the Court did not use *abridge* with equal precision. And the error goes beyond imprecision. Like Judge Catron in 1861, the 2008 Court *inserted* "abridge" into discussion of bearing arms. In fact, the high court went beyond Catron and inserted "abridge" twice. The first insertion of *abridge* comes in the Court's summary on the first page:

> (b) The prefatory clause comports with the Court's interpretation of the operative clause. The "militia" comprised all males physically capable of acting in concert for the common defense. The Antifederalists feared that the Federal Government would disarm the people in order to disable this citizens' militia, enabling a politicized standing army or a select militia to rule. The response was to deny Congress power *to abridge the ancient right of individuals to keep and bear arms*, so that the ideal of a citizens' militia would be preserved. Pp. 22–28. [emphasis added]
>
> (c) The Court's interpretation is confirmed by analogous arms-bearing rights in state constitutions that preceded and immediately followed the Second Amendment. Pp. 28–30.
>
> (d) The Second Amendment's drafting history, while of dubious interpretive worth, reveals three state Second Amendment proposals that unequivocally referred to an individual right to bear arms. Pp. 30–32."[273]

The second comes in the expanded reference to the Federalist period:

> Federalists responded that because Congress was given no power to *abridge* the ancient right of individuals to keep and bear arms, such a force could never oppress the people. See, *e.g.*, A Pennsylvanian III (Feb. 20, 1788), in The Origin of the Second Amendment 275, 276 (D. Young ed., 2d ed. 2001) (hereinafter Young); White, To the Citizens of Virginia, Feb. 22, 1788, in *id.*, at 280, 281; A Citizen of America, (Oct. 10, 1787) in *id.*, at 38, 40; Remarks on the Amendments to the federal Constitution, Nov. 7, 1788, in *id.*, at 556. It was understood across the political spectrum that the right helped to secure the ideal of a citizen militia, which might be necessary to oppose an oppressive military force if the constitutional order broke down.[274] [emphasis added]

Again, the Supreme Court in *Heller* went beyond Judge Catron in 1861. Catron at least retained *infringed* in revising the second amendment, while adding *abridged*. In 2008, in the second passage quoted above, the high court *substituted* "abridge" for wording in the second amendment.

This word choice is astonishing in its degree of error. The second amendment specifically did *not* deny Congress power to "abridge" the right to bear arms. Putting that same point another way—in 1789, Congress, creating the Bill of Rights, did *not* deny itself the power to regulate arms. The "abridge" wording was available, but the framers and the first federal Congress did not choose to use it. Inserting first amendment language into the second amendment happened only later, and only with figures like Catron. The entire history of English usage and public documents in the United States up to 1789 contradicts any notion that when the second amendment said "infringed," it really meant "abridged."

Furthermore, some of the Court's references to historical documents in *Heller* were also distorted. In substituting "abridge" for "infringe," the Court referred to history, but the sources mentioned by the *Heller* court do not in fact support the *Heller* opinion. In the first insertion of "abridged" quoted above, the Court refers to "analogous arms bearing rights in state constitutions that preceded and immediately followed the second amendment." But the state constitutions of 1776 and 1777 did not bar "abridging" the right to bear arms. Nor did state declarations of rights, nor did the state conventions on the eve of the Revolutionary War. To the contrary, even states declaring a right to bear arms—something not all of them did—joined it to conditions protecting conscientious objectors or the common defense. They shored up defense of Americans by linking the right to bear arms with provisions against a standing army and against quartering troops. The same concerns carried over into state constitutions during and after ratification of the federal Constitution. But no state constitution or declaration of rights in the late eighteenth century used the word "abridge" in connection with bearing arms.

In the summary, the Court also referred to "the second amendment's drafting history," although dismissing it as "of dubious interpretive worth." The Court then went on to mention "three state second amendment proposals that unequivocally referred to an individual right to bear arms." However, the *Heller* ruling does not quote them. That lacuna may be because drafts of the second amendment and the Bill of Rights did not include any that prevented "abridging" a right to bear arms. At no time did the first federal Congress treat bearing arms as untouchable by law or constitution. And as said, the "three state second amendment proposals" each limited a right to bear arms.

In the second insertion of "abridged," the *Heller* Court named sources including "A Pennsylvanian," 1788; and Noah Webster's "A Citizen of America," October 1787. Each source is worth looking at.

"A Pennsylvanian" was written by Tench Coxe, a Federalist. The context was ratifying the U.S. Constitution, which Coxe supported. Although *Heller* did not quote Coxe verbatim or provide his name, presumably the writing referred to in *Heller* is Coxe's fiery and much-quoted support for civilian militia:

> The powers of the sword are in the hands of the yeomanry of America from sixteen to sixty. The militia of these free commonwealths, entitled and accustomed to their arms, when compared with any possible army, must be tremendous and irresistible. Who are the militia? Are they not ourselves?[275]

Coxe went on,

> Congress have no power to disarm the militia. Their swords, and every other terrible implement of the soldier, are the birthright of an American [. . .] the unlimited power of the sword is not in the hands of either the federal or state governments, but, where I trust in God it will ever remain, in the hands of the people.

In marshaling support for the federal Constitution, Coxe argued, in the sentences quoted, that the new federal government would not have unlimited power.

However, in between the sentences quoted, Coxe also posed a rhetorical question: "Is it feared, then, that we shall turn our arms each man against his own bosom[?]" Perhaps Coxe's question explains why *Heller* did not quote Coxe verbatim or name him directly. In 1788, Coxe did not envision a time in which "every terrible implement of the soldier" can be marshaled by private individuals against other citizens. The patriotic Coxe had been a militia member himself and a member of the Continental Congress. He did not envision that army powers, in the hands of an individual, can be abused as an army might collectively abuse its powers. Faced with our arms indeed turned against us by ourselves—in schools, churches, universities, movie theaters, shopping malls, workplaces, and courtrooms, as well as on the street; against children, wives, partners, and elderly relatives as well as against perceived enemies; against self as well as others—in my view, Coxe would have recommended taking steps.

This view is borne out by Coxe's career after the new nation was formed. In 1788, Coxe was writing before the second amendment was composed, let alone ratified. He did not repeat his rhetoric afterward. When Congress created a less than absolute right to bear arms, there is no indication that Coxe opposed or criticized it. In the new nation, he played an active part—Assistant Treasury Secretary under Hamilton, revenue commissioner under Washington, supporter of industry. Nor did he re-publish the statements presumably referred to in *Heller*. When Coxe later published a collection of his writings, he did not include "A Pennsylvanian" in its 513 pages.[276]

In the self-edited collection of his works, Coxe in 1794 chose to boost the United States, its form of government, and the American economy. He noted arms, with satisfaction, as products of American manufacturing.[277] As revenue commissioner, he expressed no opposition whatsoever to taxing and tabulating weaponry in his home country. He listed tariffs on "arms, fire and side," and on other weapons, matter-of-factly, with other tariffs in a table at the back of the book.[278] In 1788, he had written about arms as a check on power, together with other checks on power. In 1794, he wrote about arms as production, together with hoops, stoves, plough irons, "hoes, and other farming utensils," carriages, shipbuilding, axes, and other tools. The uses are civilian, and the tools, including weapons, are ordinary. The powers of a military unit in the hands of an individual are not in the picture. Neither are mass shootings of civilians by other civilians.[279]

In his second book a decade later, Coxe again boosted the nation, this time supporting the U.S. Census. Several pages in it relate to arms and weaponry.

> The improvements in the manufactory of steel and the experience in the general manufacture of arms, with the exigencies of the times, and above all the evidences, from the operations, that the expense and trouble of a judicious and rigorous inspection are required to be surely and effectually provided for, have made favorable changes in the condition of this important branch of our manufactures.[280]

Coxe supported good inspecting, and he supported good weapons inspecting. He favored whatever boosted U.S. manufacturing and industry, including tariff protection and sound inspection. As he said, "it appears highly worthy of consideration, whether, after a proper notice, military guns or pistols should be allowed to be sold, without the evidences of the inspection of a sworn and responsible officer." If Tench Coxe is to be quoted on bearing arms, it is only fair to quote him on taxing arms and on inspecting arms.

In *Heller*, the Supreme Court also briefly referenced Noah Webster from 1787. Like Coxe, Webster was writing before the second amendment was written. Like Coxe, Webster viewed a citizen militia as a check against a standing army.[281] In common with the other public figures of his time, he viewed a militia as by far the lesser of two evils. Like Coxe, he wrote to support a federal government, and one way to boost the new government was to reassure readers that there would be ways to keep a government or an army in check.

Like Coxe again, Webster did not envision military capabilities, in riotous private hands, turned against other Americans. He focused on the order and productivity of a unified nation.

> Congress likewise are to have power to provide for organizing, arming, and disciplining the militia, but have no other command of them, except when in actual service. Nor are they at liberty to

call out the militia at pleasure—but only, to execute the laws of the union, suppress insurrections, and repel invasions. For these purposes, government must always be armed with a military force, if the occasion should require it; otherwise laws are nugatory, and life and property insecure.[282]

Webster never proposed an unlimited private right to an unlimited quantity of weapons and ammunition, or to weapons of virtually limitless capability. He wanted to limit governmental power to use force, not to advocate an unlimited right to use force on private individuals. In fact, he included "insurrections," along with crime and invasion, among hypothetical ills to be faced. Noah Webster did not propose an unlimited right to force in 1787, Tench Coxe did not in 1788, and Congress did not in 1789. Granted, the take-away from these writings is not simply militia over individuals. But it is simply legitimacy over the illegitimate. Regrettably, a half-sentence of misattribution can require several pages to refute a mistake that should not have been made in the first place.

The important fact about *Heller* is that the ruling twice re-worded the second amendment to the U.S. Constitution. *Heller* in effect substituted "abridge" for "infringed" in the second amendment, in defiance of ten centuries of dictionaries in English and more than a century of public documents in the U.S. To support the re-wording, the Court referred to "state constitutions," "the second amendment's drafting history," and some open letters from the Federalist period including Coxe and Webster's. But the historical documents adduced by the Court in 2008 do not support the re-wording. The original documents did not apply forms of the word *abridge* to bearing arms, nor did they substitute it for forms of *infringe*.

Recent federal rulings, continued: *Heller II*

In the next ruling, use of the relevant English words deteriorated even more. This was *Heller v. District of Columbia*, 2011, known as "*Heller II*." Where the Supreme Court in 2008 did not use *impinge*, the appeals court in *Heller II* in 2011 used it at least fifteen times (counting the table of contents). Almost all uses of "impinge" in *Heller II* are followed by "upon"; something is said to "impinge upon" something else. Thus, the language views askance even a possibility of 'impinging upon.' Any law that touches upon the second amendment is already placed on the defensive.

The opinion in *Heller II* also uses forms of *infringe on*, sometimes in quotation, once in a dissent, out of fifteen uses of forms of *infringe*. Most uses of *infringe* are quotation; two quote the second amendment. There are several direct, transitive instances of *infringe* in the traditional use, and at least one *infringement of*.

Maybe one question is why *Heller II* or any other case would use *impinge* side-by-side with *infringe*. Logically, one verb should preclude the other. If "infringe" and "impinge" meant the same thing, why use both? For that matter, why add "impinge" to the English in the Bill of Rights at all? The 2011 ruling is not unique in this regard; as discussed, thousands of court cases have used forms of both *impinge* and *infringe*. But in an appeal involving the second amendment, why not just stick to the constitutional language?

It is interesting that *Heller II* uses *abridgment* only once. The single example quotes a dissent by Mr. Justice Black on 'balancing,' from 1957. Evidently, the line between abridging and infringing was so thoroughly blurred by 2011 that the term for abridging had dropped out of the court's lexicon.

At least the appeals court did hand down some good news. It held that a minimal requirement to register guns did not 'impinge upon' rights.

> To apply this analytical framework, we first consider whether each of the challenged registration requirements impinges upon the right protected by the second amendment. We uphold the requirement of mere registration because it is longstanding, hence "presumptively lawful," and the presumption stands unrebutted.[283]

Using the same language, the court pointed out that automobiles and other products, services, and activities require licensing and registration, and that much of the nation requires handgun registration.

> In sum, the basic requirement to register a handgun is longstanding in American law, accepted for a century in diverse states and cities and now applicable to more than one fourth of the Nation by population. Therefore, we presume the District's basic registration requirement, D.C.Code § 7-2502.01(a), including the submission of certain information, § 7-2502.03(b), does not impinge upon the right protected by the second amendment.[284]

Even so, applying "impinge upon" to expansive possession and use of weapons stacks the deck. The phrase is defensive. Merely a tinge of sniffing around in the vicinity of the second amendment makes common-sense safety measures suspect.

> Our dissenting colleague asserts [. . .] heightened scrutiny is also "a form of interest balancing" and maintains that strict and intermediate scrutiny "always involve at least some assessment of whether the law in question is sufficiently important to justify infringement on an individual constitutional right."[285]

With the meaning of "shall not be infringed" so undermined, almost dismantled, and reconstituted as 'shall be un-tinged,' or 'shall be untouched,' public health and public safety fall by the wayside. An inch of a pinch of a misconstrued second amendment can prevent arms safety. Instead of safety measures, the public gets attorneys and judges tiptoeing around, "interest balancing" in a minefield of "heightened scrutiny" or "intermediate scrutiny." Public danger and the public stake in having fewer untimely violent deaths and fewer illegal killings are not pointed out. Neither is the fact that the public comprises millions of individuals, each with an equal right not to be shot, endangered, or threatened by deadly weapons. Nor is the Orwellian situation of gun-control laws subjected to more "heightened scrutiny" than are caches of deadly weapons. This is a very un-1789 view.

As must be clear to any reader, the author is a non-lawyer. As I have written elsewhere, the only law course I ever took was one in constitutional law, years ago. To a non-lawyer, it is mystifying that our Constitution and our laws on commerce can be argued not to apply to deadly weapons. For comparison, see how an American law book of 1830 explains the commerce clause in the Constitution:

> "Art. 1. s. 8.3. Congress shall have power to regulate commerce with foreign nations, and among the several states, and with the Indian tribes."
>
> Under the power to regulate commerce, Congress may adopt measures that abridge commerce, if they deem them proper and necessary for the advancement of great national purposes of policy, and may apply such means in enforcing the law, as the exigency of the case requires.[286]

Thomas Sergeant (1782-1860), who wrote this admirably clear comment, was a Pennsylvania Secretary of State and Attorney General who became a judge on Pennsylvania's Supreme Court. The difference between Sergeant's accurate and appropriate use of "abridge" in 1830, and the confusion now with infringing, impinging, or a "narrow" interpretation of prohibiting, is like day and night.

Recent federal rulings, continued: *Wrenn v. District of Columbia*

In *Wrenn v. District of Columbia*, 2015, things got worse. Ruling against part of a Washington, D.C., gun law, the judge halted enforcement of a provision requiring gun permits. The *Wrenn* ruling did not use *infringe* or *abridge*, in any form. The court did not state that anything was infringed, including a right. By May 2015, the action words of the first and second amendments were so thoroughly displaced that *Wrenn* omitted both.

However, the court did use forms of *impinge* three times. The three paragraphs in May 2015 show the semantic change taking hold. The first cites *Heller*: "The first step in this analysis requires that the court determine whether a particular statutory provision impinges on a right that the second amendment protects."[287] The "right that the second amendment protects" is not analyzed. Remarkably, the *Wrenn* ruling did not even quote the second amendment. The baseline is that even longstanding gun regulations can be knocked down if plaintiff shows more than a minimal (de minimis) effect on his right. As a result, an individual could amass an enormous cache of deadly weapons and thus argue more than a minimal effect on his right, if regulations compelled him to spend on storing them in a safe place, or building a safe place to store them, or protecting them from theft or explosions, etc. In another context, this might seem like killing your parents and throwing yourself on the court's mercy as an orphan. But in the context of gun control, it is the right to weapons that is treated as a given, rather than your parents' right to live. Weapons have the high ground, and law and regulation are represented like an insurrectionary attack, burdened with the uphill climb.

The outcome in *Wrenn* was predictable. The decision favored plaintiffs including the Second Amendment Foundation, which in other actions had successfully sued the New Orleans mayor for confiscating weapons during looting after Hurricane Katrina.

> In any event, as Plaintiffs point out, "the 'longstanding' inquiry is irrelevant" because the District of Columbia's "good reason"/"proper reason" requirement "has far more than a 'de minimis' effect on [their] rights it completely bars the right from being exercised, at all times and places and in any manner, without exception." [. . .] Plaintiffs, as well as the vast majority of law-abiding citizens, who fail to satisfy the District of Columbia's "good reason"/"proper reason" requirement because they cannot "show a special need for self-protection distinguishable from the general community" or that they are engaged in a "type[ ] of employment that require[s] the handling of cash or other valuable objects that may be transported upon [their] person," are unable to exercise their fundamental right to bear arms for self-defense under the second amendment. Thus, the Court concludes that the District of Columbia's "good reason"/"proper reason" requirement impinges on Plaintiffs' second amendment right to bear arms.[288]

The *Wrenn* ruling did not define the term "self-defense." If a gun is present, apparently, self-defense is a given. No accounting for error, no accounting for mental illness. The right to arms is a right to be "exercised, at all times and places and in any manner, without exception."

In *Wrenn*, no question is raised even as to whether self-defense was possible. Is the weapons holder mentally ill? Can s/he use guns? Get to them? See behind him or around corners or in the dark? Use more than one? Would the purchaser shoot a mentally ill family member? Again, the mere presence of a weapon is apparently an *a priori* claim of self-defense—a claim that need not be established and cannot be questioned. Contravening the language of 1789, even a massive cache of deadly weapons is "self-protection" until someone proves otherwise. Stockpiling deadly weapons has the high ground; questioning it is like some disorderly sniping.

The next step is to determine how far such "impingement" goes: "The Court must next determine whether that impingement unlawfully burdens that right." Given the language, the result is predictable. Notwithstanding the weakened or softened suggestion of the word *impingement*, it is still too much for an absolutist version of the second amendment. Relying further on the plaintiffs' argument, the judge ruled that

> The District of Columbia's arbitrary "good 13 reason"/"proper reason" requirement, however, goes far beyond establishing such reasonable restrictions. Rather, for all intents and purposes, this requirement makes it impossible for the overwhelming majority of law-abiding citizens to obtain licenses to carry handguns in public for self-defense, thereby depriving them of their second amendment right to bear arms.[289]

Wrenn mentions the second amendment twenty-five times—but does not quote it once. Small wonder. This was no place for quoting "the security of a free state" or a "well-regulated militia." If carrying weapons is assumed to be self-defense, "without exception," raising a question about whether it is "well-regulated" is basically out of order.

In this view, not only are laws restricting guns tossed aside, so is a rationale for law itself. In *Wrenn*, the re-worded second amendment trumps every rational criterion for human law. Over the side go the "reasonable man" and the "necessary and proper," including Thomas Jefferson's "Laws of necessary and pressing importance." However bleak this proposition may be, *Wrenn* sets it out clearly.

> There is no dispute that the Committee Report sets forth in detail the reasons that the District of Columbia implemented the current licensing mechanism. However, the issue here is not whether the District of Columbia's "good reason"/"proper reason" requirement is a reasonable or wise policy choice. Rather, the issue is whether this requirement, no matter how well intended, violates the second amendment.[290]

The question of whether a policy or law is "reasonable or wise" is ruled out. The only criterion to be applied is an erroneous re-wording of the second amendment, asking whether a law 'impinges on' a right to bear arms.

In *Wrenn*, furthermore, scrutiny is applied only to the second amendment, isolated as though it were the only right in the Bill of Rights. That deadly force has recently jeopardized freedom of assembly, freedom of religion, freedom of speech, and freedom of the press—and property, commerce, education, and the lawful and proper operation of government in the shooting of Congresswoman Gabrielle Giffords—is not mentioned. Forgetting the meaning of the words has borne deadly fruit.

Recent federal rulings, continued: *Grace v. District of Columbia*

In *Grace v. District of Columbia* in May 2016, plaintiffs won a preliminary injunction.[291] The *Grace* decision quotes uses of *impinge* from previous decisions and contains one new use: in Step One, the court found that "The 'Good Reason' Requirement Likely Impinges Upon A Right Protected by the Second Amendment." Unlike *Wrenn*, *Grace* uses forms of *infringe* eight times. Two quote the second amendment. One is "rights are being infringed." The other five are forms of 'infringe on' or 'infringe upon'—again, a nuancing that makes any law touching on guns an infringement.

Like *Wrenn*, the *Grace* decision does not define "infringed." Instead, when the court quotes the second amendment, it defines the word "bear" and the phrase "bear arms":

> The second amendment states, a well regulated Militia, being necessary to the security of a free State, the right of the people to keep and bear arms, shall not be infringed. To "bear" means to carry. One does not typically think of carrying as an activity exclusively done within the home. Thus, reading the second amendment right to bear arms as applying only in the home is forced or awkward at best, and more likely is counter-textual. Moreover, when "bear" is used with "arms" the term has a meaning that refers to carrying for a particular purpose, confrontation. As used in the second amendment, the phrase to "bear arms" means to wear, bear, or carry arms upon the person or in the clothing or in a pocket, for the purpose of being armed and ready for offensive or defensive action in a case of conflict with another person.

At least *Grace* acknowledged that bearing arms could have an "offensive" as well as a "defensive" purpose. And the court rightly observed that bearing arms inside and outside the home is still bearing arms. But giving free rein to "carrying for a particular purpose, confrontation," is troubling.

When someone goes around armed, the potential danger is general, not particular; even when the shooter has a specific target in mind, supposing that were acceptable, there can be collateral damage. And obviously, calling "confrontation" a "particular purpose" shows a blind spot about mass shootings.

There is no sentence in *Grace* beginning, "'Infringed' means…" As in dictionaries of the seventeenth, eighteenth, and nineteenth centuries where *infringe* was used to define other words without being defined itself, the meaning is taken as self-evident. The difference is that previous centuries did know what it meant.

Changing language, lost logic

For a non-lawyer, to prioritize deadly weapons is an upside-down reading of the Constitution itself as well as of the Bill of Rights. Constitutions constitute. They build something. The United States Constitution can be differentiated from the British Constitution in exactly this way. They are both written in English, but the British constitution is a series of roadblocks over time; the U.S. constitution is a blueprint. As people have pointed out, the word "freedom" is not in the Constitution. The Constitution does not argue for freedom. It builds in support of it. Setting up the framework for reasonable, wise, and lasting policy choice is exactly what the Constitution does. In the words of the famous Preamble,

> We the People of the United States, in Order to form a more perfect Union, establish Justice, insure domestic Tranquility, provide for the common defence, promote the general Welfare, and secure the Blessings of Liberty to ourselves and our Posterity, do ordain and establish this Constitution for the United States of America.

People with a vested interest in military-grade hardware have a first amendment right to argue their interest. However, the rest of us have a first amendment right to say that short-term or individual financial gains are outweighed by an irrevocable human cost. Aside from life and limb, we have first amendment rights of assembly, religion, and speech. All are currently and demonstrably jeopardized by gun violence; none are protected by an all-or-nothing application of the second amendment. Yet nothing in the raft of materials left from the eighteenth century, public or private, indicates that the second amendment outweighed the first amendment for either the framers of the Constitution or the Congress that created the Bill of Rights. Quite the contrary.

As shown, some language used even in courts today reflects loss of understanding. The phrase "slight infringement" provides an additional example. Today, "slight infringement" can be found expressed in several published rulings; in 1789, it would have been oxymoron. It was not used when the Constitution and the Bill of Rights were written; infringement was, by definition, serious. Rewriting 1789 to insert a concept of 'slight infringement' would be analogous to retroactively inserting 'slight treason'—historical fantasy, not history. Or to take an analogy from 2019, the phrase "slight infringement" resembles the phrase "more unique." Something either is unique, or is not; uniqueness means single, standing alone as one. There is no such thing as "more unique," "very unique," or "almost as unique." The misunderstanding of language and the slip in logic go together.

Today's English lesson: with all due respect, some imprecise uses of "slight infringement," "insignificant infringement," or "minor infringement" in courts could have been easily corrected. "Minor infringements of procedural rules" should read 'infringements of minor procedural rules,' or at worst 'temporary and quickly corrected infringements.' If "trivial infringement" or "slight infringement" means breaking an unenforced rule, or causing little harm, the record could be set straight by saying so. Sometimes stating the facts rather than characterizing them would help. Sometimes correcting English grammar would help. To write "merely infringed" rather than "infringed merely" some small thing is a misplaced modifier.

Condense the language and convey facts and law with precision, concision, and clarity where possible. Surely law would do better if courts avoided suggesting that infringement is trifling, that breaking something is a trifling offense. In English, something either is infringement, or it is not. The goal should be to determine whether something does infringe rights (or a contract, patent, or copyright, etc.), not to redefine 'infringement' hysterically as 'touching on.'

The change in logic

Here is where the changes in language seem to have affected logic. In American textbooks, it was a given that a law, any proposed law, would be weighed in the balance. The scale was not tipped to one side by an artificial weight of absolutism.

> Every law should be considered in two points of view: first, how far it abridges natural liberty, and how far, therefore, it is an evil; and secondly, the good it will do by prevention of evil, or by direct procurement of benefit to society.[292]

Reasoned discussion was about how to weigh the law realistically. After all, it is a given that *every* law in some sense abridges absolute liberty.

> Every law is a restraint and an abridgment of absolute or natural liberty. A law against murder, imposes the restraint of not killing a fellow man. Thus laws against stealing, wounding, maiming, cheating, swindling, setting houses on fire, defaming a man's character, breaking into a man's house with intent to steal, robbing on the highway or the high seas—all these impose restraints on natural liberty.[293]

This common-sense recognition was not considered an argument for abolishing law. Nor was it an argument for abolishing 'regulation.' Laws in America as well as in Britain often carried the title "An Act to regulate" such-and-such, or "An Act for the better regulation of" such-and-such.

Failing to remember that every law abridges absolute liberty, the failure to understand the concept of abridgement, is a failure of logic. It is a lapse of memory about U.S. history. "The rights of man in a state of nature, and the power of society to abridge those rights," were staple political philosophy in America.[294] Nor were they just 'abstract,' although political philosophy was read and discussed. The principles were preserved and transmitted in court and at home and in school. They were explained in textbooks on the U.S. Constitution. Thinking about government in a democracy, as in the 1857 law book just quoted, meant joining the concept of rights abridged in a nation to that of rights in a state of nature.

Closer to the issue of gun violence, a few points stand out. First, to abridge a right to bear arms is not to destroy it. Weapons are not conscience, inalienable from the person. Bearing arms is an alienable right. Laws in early America abridged it. I am aware that poking through centuries of English dictionaries is not everyone's cup of tea. But anyone who looks at them will be exposed to the difference between abridging a right, power, or privilege and destroying it. This difference is part of the difference between the first amendment and the second amendment. Abridgement of power or privilege was favored by the framers. Voluntary abridgement of natural right was part of the social bargain; infringement of rights or laws, not.

Second, Americans in 1789 differentiated between firearms—carried by individuals singly, in militia, or in infantry—and artillery. No individual right to artillery, no individual right to arsenals, is enunciated in the first three-hundred-plus years of American settlement, from Jamestown in 1607 to mid-twentieth century. Americans in 1789 did not have today's semi-automatic weapons, flash bombs, or grenades. They did not carry high-capacity magazines or clips. To claim that their weapons were equivalent to today's portable artillery and one-man arsenals would be as anachronistic as to claim that they had shoulder-to-air missiles.

Third, since the late 1960s, a giant misconstruction has developed in English. Changing use of "infringe," "impinge," and related words has contributed to a vague but deadly notion that the individual right to keep and bear arms is limitless, absolute, and untouchable by law. The gun lobby has contributed to the notion. It may deny holding such a position, but while simultaneously opposing every common-sense measure to reduce gun violence. The result is that ordinary people fear that any law limiting arms is unconstitutional. Using LexisNexis and skimming hundreds of published federal and state rulings to track changes in their use of English is not an option for everyone. But it is important to recognize that some of the English in the Bill of Rights has undergone semantic change. Over the last 230 years, understanding of some of the words has changed. This is not theory but fact. The changes can be seen in language used by judges in U.S. courts, over the decades from the late nineteenth century to 2019.

Fourth, a claim of 'self-defense' is applied in ways that jeopardize all the other rights in the Bill of Rights, even where the claim is unexamined, and even where it is unstated. The framers supported three material rights—life, liberty, and property. The unlimited-weapons avatar of a right to bear arms jeopardizes all three. Letting any or every individual store an arsenal of guns, a few blocks from your home, is not self-defense. Letting any or every individual carry military-grade weaponry on crowded streets, in schools, or in airports, theaters, or shopping malls, is not self-defense. Refusing to license gun sales, opposing background checks, leaving street sales of weapons unchecked, and preventing the tracking of crime guns are not self-defense.

Equal justice means equal protection: where we go from here

To reduce gun violence, the nation and the states must pursue *equal* justice. Some measures are indicated above. All have been proposed; some have been implemented in some places or in some ways; none have been applied consistently. The nation and every state should have gun licensing, and the laws behind the licensing should have teeth. Street sales of weapons—which often do not even pretend to be lawful—should be prosecuted effectively. More to the point, they should be prevented, and law enforcement supported in the prevention. Background checks and other safety requirements should apply to all weapons transactions, including sales in stores, at gun shows, and online. The requirements should apply to all transactions involving weapons—not just official 'sales'—including purported gifts, bequests, and swaps. Gathering information on crime guns should be supported at all levels of law enforcement, in all regions. The information should remain accessible to law enforcement and the justice system across jurisdictions.

Speaking of language, opponents tend to characterize these proposals as 'expanding' gun laws. They are more precisely efforts to apply the law equally to all. No special exemptions for successful sneaking. No special exemptions for weapons trafficking across the border, in extra large shipments, or by multi-national companies. No special exemptions for gun shows or for the Internet. The features of semi-automatic weapons do not change in different venues or in different kinds of transactions.

As to guns that *do* have different characteristics—hunting rifles, for example—where they are carried makes a difference. Population density makes a difference. What is safe in the country is not equally safe in the city. No one is elk hunting on a city street. The law need not take a fictive stance that circumstances in Baltimore, Maryland, are the same as in Essex County, Vermont, or Niobrara County, Wyoming. The laws need to recognize differences between open-air hunting on one hand and going to school, riding in an airplane, or going to the theater or a place of worship on the other.

Equal justice means an effort toward equal protection, headed toward an ideal of equal safety. Danger to schoolchildren is a failure of equal protection. A judicially expanded threat for women and children trying to escape volatile domestic situations is a failure of equal protection. Heightened danger for those already liable to harm themselves irrationally—the mentally ill, the addicted, the depressed—and for those around them, some of whom are trying to take care of them, is a failure of equal protection. More danger for returning veterans with PTSD, and their families, is a failure of equal protection. Danger to law enforcement personnel and others, in neighborhoods already identified as 'hot spots,' is a failure of equal protection. More danger in poorer neighborhoods where pawn shops sell weapons, and in zip codes where automobile insurance companies already demand higher premiums, is a failure of equal protection.

In this kind of discussion, this is the place where someone may point out (scripturally) that we have always had poor people. Quite so, and the streets of early Philadelphia in 1787 and 1789 were dirty and contaminated places, not 'safe' from a public health perspective. Some delegates to the Constitutional Convention had to return home for health reasons. But early America prided itself in not treating poor people as vilely as in the old country. And poor citizens in eighteenth-century Philadelphia were not forced to rub elbows with people carrying semi-automatics or carrying handguns that could shoot through an automobile engine block. How did those one-person portable caches of artillery become lawful in the first place?

The answer to this rhetorical question is that what is lawful depends on what is constitutional, and the constitution is being misconstrued.

Hence this book. However, the book does not address people who want to throw away the constitution or go around it, who want revolution regardless of law or constitution or who believe a revolution must be unconstitutional to be authentic. American revolutionaries in the eighteenth century considered their rebellion to be constitutional.[295]

This book addresses people who want to understand constitutional gun control, or who would prefer sensible gun laws but sincerely fear that they would violate the second amendment, or who mistakenly believe that the second amendment is anachronistic and needs to be repealed. The Bill of Rights is created from English words. Understanding the rights requires understanding the words.

November 2019

Notes

1 Alexander Hamilton, *History of French Influence in the United States* (Philadelphia, 1812), 3.

2 *U.S. Const. amend. I.* Italics added. Any further citations from the Constitution will be noted in text.

3 "From Thomas Jefferson to Madame de Bréhan, 14 March 1789," *Founders Online, National Archives*. http://founders.archives.gov/documents/Jefferson/01-14-02-0406.

4 "Pennsylvania Assembly: Proposed Reply to the Governor, 25 November 1755," *Founders Online, National Archives*. http://founders.archives.gov/documents/Franklin/01-06-02-0115.

5 "X. Draft Preamble of Committee Report on Inducing Foreign Officers to Desert, 27 August 1776," *Founders Online, National Archives*. http://founders.archives.gov/documents/Adams/06-04-02-0001-0011.

6 "From Thomas Jefferson to John Randolph, 25 August 1775," *Founders Online, National Archives*. http://founders.archives.gov/documents/Jefferson/01-01-02-0121.

7 "Draft of a Declaration on the British Treatment of Ethan Allen, [2 January 1776]," *Founders Online, National Archives*, http://founders.archives.gov/documents/Jefferson/01-01-02-0146.

8 For example, John Dickinson, *Essay on the Constitutional Power of Great Britain over the Colonies in America* (Philadelphia, 1774), 374; *Proceedings of the Convention for the Province of Pennsylvania* (Philadelphia, 1775), 5.

9 John Perceval, *Full and Fair Discussion of the Pretensions of the Dissenters* (Oxford, 1740), 10.

10 Michael W. McConnell, "Origins and Historical Understanding of Free Exercise of Religion," *Harvard Law Review*, 103 (1990), 1409-1517.

11 *A Dictionary of the English Language: A Digital Edition of the 1755 Classic by Samuel Johnson*. Edited by Brandi Besalke. https://johnsonsdictionaryonline.com/. Quotations from Johnson's Dictionary refer to this online edition. See alphabetical entries (I and J alphabetized as the same letter).

12 Joshua Kendall, *The Forgotten Founding Father* (New York, 2010), 271-276.

13 Gwin Kolb and James Sledd, "Johnson's 'Dictionary' and Lexicographical Tradition," *Modern Philology*, 50 (1953), 175-176.

14 *Corpus Glossary*, eds Wallace Lindsay and Helen Buckhurst (Cambridge, 1921), 95. Early dictionaries do not usually have page numbers; dictionary entries discussed are found under the headings for the words defined, usually in alphabetical order.

15 *Eighth-Century Latin-Anglo-Saxon Glossary*, ed Jan Hendrick Hessels (Cambridge, 1890), 67.

16 As in definitions given by the Centre National de Ressources Textuelles et Lexicales: "1283 « diminuer les services attachés à un fief » terme de dr. médiév. (Beaumanoir, éd. Beugnot, XLV, 25 ds GDF.: s'aucuns abrege le fief qui est tenu de li)." At http://www.cnrtl.fr.

17 At http://quod.lib.umich.edu/m/med. The Middle English Dictionary is the most comprehensive accessible source for Middle English vocabulary. Subsequent citations from ME will refer to it.

18 "Confessio Amantis," in *English Works of John Gower* (Oxford, 1969), 287, sect. 1990.

19 "Confessio Amantis," in *English Works of John Gower* (Oxford, 1969), 313, sect. 2920.

20 English translation of Gower's Latin from U. Rochester. At www.lib.rochester.edu/camelot/cav3b7nts.htm.

21 "John Adams to Abigail Adams, 2 June 1777," *Founders Online, National Archives* (http://founders.archives.gov/documents/Adams/04-02-02-0198) Source: *The Adams Papers, Adams Family Correspondence*, vol. 2, June 1776–March 1778, ed. L. H. Butterfield. Cambridge, MA: Harvard University Press, 1963, pp. 253–254.

22 *Promptorium Parvulorum: The First English-Latin Dictionary* (London, 1908).

23 *Ortus vocabulorum alphabetico ordine* (London, 1532).

24 John Palsgrave, *L'esclarcissement de la langue francoyse* (London, 1969).

25 John Rastell, *Exposition of certaine difficult and obscure wordes and termes of the lawes of this realme* (New Jersey, 2003).

26 John Rastell, *Exposition of certaine difficult and obscure wordes and termes of the lawes of this realme* (New Jersey, 2003), Introduction.

27 John Rastell, *Exposition of certaine difficult and obscure wordes and termes of the lawes of this realme* (New Jersey, 2003), Rastell's preface.

28 "V. Notes on Acts of Parliament and of the Virginia Assembly concerning Religion, 11 October – 9 December 1776," *Founders Online, National Archives*. http://founders.archives.gov/documents/Jefferson/01-01-02-0222-0006.

29 Giles Du Wes, *Introductory for to Learn to Read, to Pronounce, and to Speak French Trewly* (Menston, 1972).

30 William Salesbury, *Dictionary in Englyshe and Welshe* (Menston, 1969). Citations refer to this edition, not paginated; see individual entries.

31 Peter R. Roberts, "Welsh Language, English Law and Tudor Legislation," *Transactions of the Honourable Society of Cymmrodorion* (1989): 19-75.

32 Guillaume la Pichonnaye, *Playne Treatise to Learne the Frenche Tongue* (Menston, 1968); Jacques Bellot, *French Grammer* (London, 1578).

33 Richard Perceval, *Bibliothecae Hispanicae* (London, 1591).

34 John Minsheu, *Dictionarie in Spanish and English*, Ian Lancashire, ed. At http://leme.library.utoronto.ca.

35 Richard Mulcaster, *First Part of the Elementarie*. At http://quod.lib.umich.edu/e/eebogroup.

36 John Rider, *Bibliotheca Scholastica* [1589] (Menston, 1970).

37 John Florio, *World of Words* (London, 1598). At http://www.pbm.com/~lindahl/florio1598.

38 Robert Estienne and John Veron, *Dictionariolum Puerorum Tribus Linguis* (New York, 1971).

39 Richard Huloet and John Higgins, *Hvloets Dictionarie, Newelye Corrected* (London, 1572).

40 Peter Levens, *Manipulos Vocabulorum* (Menston, 1969); Thomas Thomas, *Dictionarium Linguae Latinae et Anglicanae* (Menston, 1972); *Thomae*

Thomasii Dictionarium (London, 1596).

41 William West, *Symbolaeographia* (Norwood, New Jersey, 1975).

42 John Cowell, *Interpreter* (Menston, 1972). Citations from the text will refer to this edition; see alphabetical entries.

43 S. B. Chrimes, "Constitutional Ideas of Dr. John Cowell," *English Historical Review*, 64 (1949), 461-464; and Jocelyn Simon, "Dr. Cowell," *Cambridge Law Journal*, 26 (1968), 260-272.

44 *Select Statutes and Other Constitutional Documents*, ed. George W. Protheroe. (Oxford, 1894), 409n.

45 *Royal proclamations of King James I, 1603-1625*, ed. James F. Larkin and Paul L. Hughes (Oxford, 1973), v-vi.

46 *Royal proclamations of King James I, 1603-1625*, ed. James F. Larkin and Paul L. Hughes (Oxford, 1973), 243.

47 *Royal proclamations of King James I, 1603-1625*, ed. James F. Larkin and Paul L. Hughes (Oxford, 1973), 244.

48 Jocelyn Simon, "Dr. Cowell," *Cambridge Law Journal*, 26 (1968), 270.

49 Jocelyn Simon, "Dr. Cowell," *Cambridge Law Journal*, 26 (1968), 270-271.

50 Jocelyn Simon, "Dr. Cowell," *Cambridge Law Journal*, 26 (1968), 271.

51 On the early spread of Machiavelli's works to England, see Allessandra Petrina, *Machiavelli in the British Isles* (Burlington, Vermont, 2009), 1-45, esp. 15-25.

52 *Parl. Debates*, 81 (1862), 19.

53 *Royal proclamations of King James I, 1603-1625*, ed. James F. Larkin and Paul L. Hughes (Oxford, 1973), 244.

54 "Preface," *A Law Dictionary, or, The Interpreter of Words and Terms* (London, 1708), not paginated.

55 "Preface," *A Law Dictionary, or, The Interpreter of Words and Terms* (London, 1708), not paginated.

56 Robert Cawdrey, *A Table Alphabeticall of Hard Usual English Words* (Gainesville, Florida, 1966).

57 DeWitt Starnes and Gertrude Noyes, *English Dictionary from Cawdrey to Johnson* (Chapel Hill, North Carolina, 1946), 13-19.

58 Edward Coote, 'Table', in *English School-Maister* (London, 1596).

59 Thomas Blount, *Glossographia, or a Dictionary* (Menston, 1969).

60 Thomas Blount, *Nomo-Lexikon* (Clark, New Jersey, 2004).

61 John D. Cowley, *Bibliography of Abridgments, Digests, Dictionaries and Indexes of English Law to the Year 1800* (Holmes Beach, Florida, 1979), lxxxix.

62 Edward Phillips, *New World of English Words* (Menston, 1969).

63 Gwin Kolb and James Sledd, "Johnson's 'Dictionary' and Lexicographical Tradition," *Modern Philology*, 50 (1953), 172-173.

64 John Locke, *Works* (London, 1751), Vol. 3, 727.

65 *Glossographia Anglicana Nova, or a Dictionary, Interpreting such Hard Words of whatever Language, as Are at Present Used in the English Tongue* (London, 1707).

66 John Kersey, *Dictionarium Anglo-Britannicum* (London, 1708).

67 Nathan Bailey, *Dictionarium Britannicum* (New York, 1969).

68 Nathan Bailey, *Universal Etymological English Dictionary* (London, 1731).

69 Robert Ainsworth, *Thesaurus Linguae Latinae Compendiarius* (London, 1751), Preface.

70 Robert Ainsworth, *Thesaurus Linguae Latinae Compendiarius* (London, 1751), Preface, xiv.

71 John Adams, *Defence of the Constitutions of Government of the United States of America* (London, 1788), Vol. 3, 160.

72 Vera Smalley, *Sources of A Dictionarie of the French and English Tongues* (Baltimore, 1948), 14.

73 Vera Smalley, *Sources of A Dictionarie of the French and English Tongues* (Baltimore, 1948), 92-94.

74 Albert Montefiore Hyamson, *History of the Jews in England* (London, 2012), 145, 164-165.

75 Francis Gouldman and William Robertson, *Copious Dictionary in Three Parts* (Cambridge, 1678).

76 William Robertson, *Phraseologia Generalis* (Cambridge, 1693).

77 Elisha Coles, *A dictionary, English-Latin, and Latin-English* (London, 1699).

78 Abel Boyer, *Royal Dictionary Abridged*. Menston: Scolar Press, 1971.

79 Jeremiah Burroughs, *Moses His Choice* (London, 1650), 184.

80 Jacob Serenius and Eric Benzelius, *Dictionarium Anglo-Svethico-Latinum* (Hamburg, 1734).

81 Andreas Berthelson, *English and Danish Dictionary* (London, 1754), Vol. 1.

82 Gwin Kolb and James Sledd, "Johnson's 'Dictionary' and Lexicographical Tradition," *Modern Philology*, 50 (1953), especially 175-176.

83 "From Benjamin Franklin to Peter Collinson, 26 June 1755." *Founders Online, National Archives*. http://founders.archives.gov/documents/Franklin/01-06-02-0045.

84 "A Full Vindication of the Measures of the Congress, &c., [15 December] 1774." *Founders Online, National Archives*. http://founders.archives.gov/documents/Hamilton/01-01-02-0054; "The Farmer Refuted, &c., [23 February] 1775," *Founders Online, National Archives*. http://founders.archives.gov/documents/Hamilton/01-01-02-0057.

85 Claudia L. Johnson, "Samuel Johnson's Moral Psychology and Locke's "Of Power"," *Studies in English Literature* 24 (1984): 563-582.

86 Locke, *Works* (London, 1751), Vol. 1, 113.

87 Locke, *Essay Concerning Humane Understanding* (London, 1706), 168.

88 Locke, *Works* (London, 1751), Vol. 1, chapter heading, xxii.

89 "Poor Richard Improved, 1748," *Founders Online, National Archives*. http://founders.archives.gov/documents/Franklin/01-03-02-0103.

90 "Thomas Jefferson to John Minor, 30 August 1814, including Thomas Jefferson to Bernard Moore, [ca. 1773?]," *Founders Online, National Archives*. http://founders.archives.gov/documents/Jefferson/03-07-02-0455.

91 "From George Washington to William Stephens Smith, 20 June 1783," *Founders Online, National Archives*. http://founders.archives.gov/documents/Washington/99-01-02-11486.

92 Robert DeMaria and Gwin J. Kolb, "Johnson's 'Dictionary' and Dictionary Johnson," *Yearbook of English Studies* 28 (1998), 35-36.

93 Gwin Kolb and James Sledd, "Johnson's 'Dictionary' and Lexicographical Tradition," *Modern Philology*, 50 (1953).

94 "Exploring Binomials," 2012. At http://www.arts.kuleuven.be/ling/ICEHL18/workshops/exploring-binomials.

95 Sarah Benor and Roger Levy, "The Chicken or the Egg?" *Language*,

82 (2006), 233-278; Sandra Mollin, "Revisiting Binomial Order in English," *English Language and Linguistics*, 16 (2013), 81-103; Heiko Motschenbacher, "Gentlemen before Ladies?" *Journal of English Linguistics*, 41 (2013), 212-242.

96 "Exploring Binomials," 2012.

97 Ibid.

98 *Black's Law Dictionary*, 7th ed.

99 Sarah Benor and Roger Levy, "The Chicken or the Egg," *Language*, 82 (2006), 235, 250.

100 Sarah Benor and Roger Levy, "The Chicken or the Egg," *Language*, 82 (2006), 250-251, 254.

101 Sarah Benor and Roger Levy, "The Chicken or the Egg," *Language*, 82 (2006), 240.

102 Sarah Benor and Roger Levy, "The Chicken or the Egg," *Language*, 82 (2006), 239.

103 On "semantic-pragmatic constraints," see Sarah Benor and Roger Levy, "The Chicken or the Egg," *Language*, 82 (2006), 236.

104 Sarah Benor and Roger Levy, "The Chicken or the Egg," *Language*, 82 (2006), 239.

105 Heiko Motschenbacher, "Gentlemen before Ladies," *Journal of English Linguistics*, 41 (2013), 213-216.

106 Heiko Motschenbacher, "Gentlemen before Ladies," *Journal of English Linguistics*, 41 (2013), 223.

107 Heiko Motschenbacher, "Gentlemen before Ladies," *Journal of English Linguistics*, 41 (2013), 226, 227.

108 "Exploring Binomials," 18th International Conference on English Historical Linguistics, 2012.

109 Nashe, in *Miscellaneous Tracts* (Collier, ed.), 93.

110 Adam Winthrop, John Winthrop, Waitstill Winthrop, *Winthrop Papers* (Boston, 1889), 16.

111 Charles Lucas, *Political Constitutions of Great-Britain and Ireland* (London, 1751), 67.

112 *Gentleman's and London Magazine*, 24 (1767), 308-309.

113 *Scots Magazine*, 29, 160.

114 *Journal of the Votes and Proceedings of the General Assembly of the Colony of New-York* (Albany, 1820), 70; further versions of the statement on other dates, 5, 45, 51, 53.

115 Edward Long, *History of Jamaica* (London, 1774), 184.

116 Hugh Knox, *Select Sermons* (Glasgow, 1776), Vol. 2, 98.

117 *Collections of the Vermont Historical Society* (Montpelier, 1871), Vol. 2, 330.

118 "To Thomas Jefferson from Richard Douglas, 18 January 1809," *Founders Online, National Archives*. http://founders.archives.gov/documents/Jefferson/99-01-02-9575.

119 At https://www.monticello.org/site/jefferson/all-my-wishes-end-monticello.

120 Oran Follett and Thomas Corwin, *Selections from the Follett Papers* (Cincinnati, 1915), Vol. 12, 137.

121 Oran Follett and Thomas Corwin, *Selections from the Follett Papers* (Cincinnati, 1915), Vol. 12, 136-37.

122 R. Whitworth, *Narrative of Facts, Relating to what is Called the Judges' House* (Stafford, 1811), 27.

123 Benjamin Trumbull, *Complete History of Connecticut* (New Haven, 1818), Vol. 1, 172.

124 *Records of the Colony of New Plymouth, in New England*, Vol. 1, 110.

125 Wilkes Allen, *History of Chelmsford* (Massachusetts, 1820), 115.

126 *Acts and Laws of the State of Connecticut*, 300.

127 William Leggett, *Plaindealer* (New York, 1836), Vol. 1, 326.

128 Subsequent citations from newspaper pages found in *Chronicling America: Historic American Newspapers* (LOC database), unless otherwise indicated.

129 *Congressional Globe, Appendix (1857-1858)*, 306; also 270, 311.

130 Citations from *Chronicling America* (CA). Any titles and dates not footnoted provided in text.

131 CA, *Highland Weekly news* (Hillsborough, Highland County, Ohio), June 23, 1859.

132 CA, *Ashland Union*, June 6, 1860.

133 *Reports, Supreme Judicial Court of Massachusetts*, Vol. 84 (1866), 146.

134 *Reports, Supreme Judicial Court of Massachusetts*, Vol. 84 (1866), 146.

135 *Atlantic Monthly*, Vol. 8 (1861), 239.

136 Newspaper citations from *Chronicling America*; issue dates in text.

137 CA, *National Republican* (Washington, D.C.); *Evening Star* (Washington, D.C.); *Charleston Daily News*; *New Orleans Republican*.

138 *Laws, Mississippi*, 66.

139 *Laws, Mississippi*, 67.

140 *South-Atlantic*, Vol. 2 (1878), 163-164.

141 *Chronicling America*. This and following quotations from *Jackson Standard* 10/18/1877.

142 *Addresses and Journal of Proceedings of the National Educational Association* (1873), 59.

143 *Pennsylvania State Constitutions*, "Texts of the Constitution," Article XVI, Section 3, 1874.

144 Newspaper citations from *Chronicling America*. Individual issues and dates in text.

145 *Annual Report of the State Superintendent of Public Instruction*, Vol. 38 (1892), 318.

146 *Senate Journal of the Third Legislature of the State of Washington* (Olympia, Washington, 1893), 28.

147 *Official Gazette of the U.S. Patent Office*, xiv (1898), 659.

148 *United States Supreme Court Reports*, Vol. 44 (1900), 120.

149 *United States Supreme Court Reports*, Vol. 44 (1900), 120.

150 *Lawyers Reports Annotated*, Vol. 21 (1909), 609.

151 *Canadian Bill of Rights*, 1960. At http://www.irb-cisr.gc.ca/Eng/BoaCom/references.

152 *Parliamentary Practice of New Zealand*, Chapter 45, 605. At https://www.parliament.nz/resource.

153 *Report of the Second National Commission on Labour* (2001), 32-33. http://www.prsindia.org/uploads/media/1237548159/NLCII-report.pdf.

154 *Jamaica*. Chapter III, 13. (2). (b) http://laws-lois.justice.gc.ca/eng/acts/C-12.3/FullText.html.

155 Brenda Danet and Bryna Bogoch, "From Oral Ceremony to Written Document," *Language & Communication* 12 (1992), 95-122.

156 Brenda Danet and Bryna Bogoch, "From Oral Ceremony to Written

Document," *Language & Communication* 12 (1992), 100.

157 Brenda Danet and Bryna Bogoch, "From Oral Ceremony to Written Document," *Language & Communication* 12 (1992), 99-101, 105.

158 Brenda Danet and Bryna Bogoch, "From Oral Ceremony to Written Document," *Language & Communication* 12 (1992), 97, 105.

159 *Three Coronation Orders*, https://archive.org/stream/coronationothree00leggrich/coronationothree00leggrich_djvu.txt.

160 http://www.british-gazette.co.uk/the-coronation-oath-act-1953.

161 *Works of Geoffrey Chaucer* (Boston, 1961), 245.

162 *Middle English Dictionary*, (1450) R Parl, 5.196b; Wycl. Lantern (Hrl 2324), 18/28; and Bk. Noblesse (Roy 18.B.22), 72. http://quod.lib.umich.edu/m/med.

163 *Magna Charta, Made in the 9th Year of K. Henry the Third, and Confirmed by K. Edward the First*, Edward Cooke, tr. (London, 1680), 66.

164 *General Index to . . . the Parliamentary or Constitutional History of England* (London, 1751), Vol. 5, 377.

165 Donald S. Lutz, *Colonial Origins of the American Constitution* (Indianapolis, 1998), 70-87; also, https://history.hanover.edu/texts/masslib.html.

166 http://avalon.law.yale.edu/18th_century/ratny.asp.

167 *Congressional Register, or History of the Proceedings and Debates of the First House of Representatives* (New York, 1790), Vol. 2-3, 226.

168 Sarah Benor and Roger Levy, "The Chicken or the Egg," *Language*, 82 (2006), 233-278; Sandra Mollin, "Revisiting Binomial Order in English," *English Language and Linguistics*, 16 (2013), 81-103.

169 John Churchill, *Collection of Voyages and Travels, Consisting of Authentic Writers* (London, 1745), Vol. 1, 46.

170 Edward Coke, *Fourth Part of the Institutes . . . Concerning the Jurisdiction of Courts* (London, 1797), 300; Daines Barrington, *Observations upon the Statutes* (London, 1766), 13-14; Oliver Goldsmith, *History of England* (London, 1771), 361; Frederick Hervey, *Naval History of Great Britain* (London, 1779), 85.

171 Samuel Johnson, *History and Defence of Magna Charta* (Dublin, 1769), 13.

172 *Trial of William Penn and William Mead at the Old Bailey*, 1670 (London, 1908). No author named.

173 John Rayner, *An Inquiry into the Doctrine, lately Propagated, Concerning Attachments of Contempt . . . particularly as They Relate to Prosecutions for Libels* (London, 1769).

174 Samuel Johnson, *History and Defence of Magna Charta* (Dublin, 1769), 183-233.

175 Eric Burns, *Infamous Scribblers* (New York, 2006), 6-7.

176 http://avalon.law.yale.edu/18th_century/pa08.asp.

177 *Publications of the American Jewish Historical Society* (Philadelphia, 1893), Issues 1-2, 108-110.

178 William P. Rudd, *Dongan Charter and Present Charter* (Albany, 1896), 12-15.

179 *Historical Collections of Private Passages of State* (London, 1721), Vol. 5, 529.

180 *Journals of the House of Commons*, Vol. 4 (1644-1646), 5.

181 John Stevens, *History of the Antient Abbeys, Monasteries* (London,

1722), Vol. 1, 305; William Bohun, *Privilegia Londini: Or, the laws, customs, and priviledges of the City of London* (London, 1702), 95; *Ecclesiastical Gazette* (London, 1839), Vol. 1, 163.

182 *Journals of the House of Lords*. Vol. 29. See 578, 587, 591, 609.

183 John Ayliffe, *The Antient and Present State of the University of Oxford* (Oxford, 1714), Vol. 1, 31, 32, 37, 67, 71, 72.

184 *Machiavel's Letter to the Lords and Commons of G*** B****, 35, 36, 39, 41.

185 Thomas Knox, George Grenville, and Thomas Whateley, *Controversy between Great-Britain and Her Colonies Reviewed* (London, 1769), 6, 21.

186 Thomas Knox, George Grenville, and Thomas Whateley, *Controversy between Great-Britain and Her Colonies Reviewed* (London, 1769), Appendix, xxxii, xxxix.

187 Noah Webster, *An Examination into the Leading Principles of the Federal Constitution* (Philadelphia, 1787), 35n.

188 Paul Rapin de Thoyras and Nicolas Tindal, *History of England*, 3rd ed. (London, 1743), Vol. 2, 294.

189 "Ratification of the Constitution by the State of New York; July 26, 1788." http://avalon.law.yale.edu/18th_century/ratny.asp.

190 "Ratification of the Constitution by the State of Virginia; June 26, 1788." http://avalon.law.yale.edu/18th_century/ratva.asp.

191 "Ratification of the Constitution by the State of North Carolina; November 21, 1789." http://avalon.law.yale.edu/18th_century/ratnc.asp.

192 William Prynne, *Opening of the Great Seale of England* (London, 1643), 29.

193 Francis Whyte, *For the Sacred Law of the Land* (London, 1652), 171.

194 *Journal of the First Session of the Senate of the United States of America* (Washington, D.C., 1820), 74.

195 "Ratification of the Constitution by the State of Rhode Island; May 29, 1790." http://avalon.law.yale.edu/18th_century/ratri.asp.

196 J. Austin Allibone, *Critical Dictionary of English Literature, and British and American Authors* (Philadelphia, 1859), 466-468.

197 Robert Charles Dallas, *History of the Maroons, from their Origin to the Establishment of their Chief Tribe at Sierra Leone* (London, 1803), Vol. 2, 388.

198 William D. Guthrie, *Lectures on the Fourteenth Article of Amendment to the Constitution of the United States* (Boston, 1898), 56.

199 Gail Collins, *When Everything Changed* (New York, 2009), 213.

200 *Miscellaneous Documents of the House of Representatives* (Washington, D.C., 1866), 209.

201 *Miscellaneous Documents of the House of Representatives* (Washington, D.C., 1866), 100.

202 *Miscellaneous Documents of the House of Representatives* (Washington, D.C., 1866), 673.

203 *Journal of the Senate of the United States of America* (Washington, D.C., 1865), 501.

204 George Washington Julian, *Speeches on Political Questions* (New York, 1872), 311.

205 George Washington Julian, *Speeches on Political Questions* (New York, 1872), 23; see also 44-46.

206 William D. Guthrie, *Lectures on the Fourteenth Article of Amendment to the Constitution of the United States* (Boston, 1898), 2.

207 Samuel Crook, Christopher Barker, and William Garrett, *Ta*

Diapheronta, or Divine Characters in Two Parts (London, 1658), 549.

208 Hippolyte Du Chastelet De Luzancy, *Treatise of the Two Sacraments of the Gospel, Baptism and the Lord's Supper* (London, 1701), 153.

209 *Collection of the Occasional Papers for the Year 1716* (London, 1716), 20-21.

210 *State Records of North Carolina* (Raleigh, 1886), Vol. 1, 552-554.

211 Matthew Hale and Sollom Emlyn, *Historia Placitorum Coronæ: The History of the Pleas of the Crown* (Savoy, 1736), 328.

212 Jonathan Elliott, *Debates of the Several State Conventions on the Adoption of the Federal Constitution* (Washington, D.C., 1836), Vol. 4, 604.

213 *Reports of Cases Argued and Determined in the Supreme Court of Judicature* (Philadelphia, 1839), Vol. 6, 236.

214 *National Magazine and Republican Review* (Washington, D.C., 1839), Vol. 1, 9.

215 *Pamphlets on the Concord Railroad Corporation* (Concord, 1841), 5.

216 *Reports of the Superior Court of New Hampshire* (Concord, 1854), 237-245.

217 *Reports of the Superior Court of New Hampshire* (Concord, 1854), 243.

218 *Journal of the Senate of the State of New York at their Sixty-Third Session* (Albany, 1840), 183.

219 *Journal of the Senate of the State of New York at their Sixty-Third Session* (Albany, 1840), 183-190.

220 *Journal of the Senate of the State of New York at their Sixty-Third Session* (Albany, 1840), 188.

221 Leo H. Hirsch, "The Slave in New York," *Journal of Negro History*, 16 (1931), 398-399.

222 Leo H. Hirsch, "The Slave in New York," *Journal of Negro History*, 16 (1931), 400.

223 *Southern Magazine and Monthly Review* (Petersburg, Virginia, 1841), 107.

224 *Southern Magazine and Monthly Review* (Petersburg, Virginia, 1841), 118.

225 *Southern Magazine and Monthly Review* (Petersburg, Virginia, 1841), i.

226 Harriet Beecher Stowe, *Dred, a Tale of the Great Dismal Swamp* (Boston, 1859), Vol. 2, 101-105.

227 Harriet Beecher Stowe, *Dred, a Tale of the Great Dismal Swamp* (Boston, 1859), Vol. 1, "Author's Preface," xiv.

228 *Congressional Globe* (Washington, D.C., 1844), 30.

229 *Congressional Globe* (Washington, D.C., 1844), 30.

230 *Brownson's Quarterly Review*, Vol. 3 (1846), 97.

231 *Reports of Cases Argued and Determined in the Supreme Court of Vermont*, 2nd ed. (St. Paul, 1889), 58.

232 Sandra Mollin, "Revisiting Binomial Order in English," *English Language and Linguistics*, 16 (2011), 85-90.

233 See Joanna Kopaczyk, *Legal Language of Scottish Burghs* (New York, 2013), "Scottish Medieval Laws," 13-14.

234 *Oyster Bay Town Records* (New York, 1916), Vol. 1, Appendix, 680.

235 "Proceedings of Congress," *American Museum*, Vol. 6 (1789), 8.

236 Charles Pigott, *Political Dictionary* (London, 1795), 106.

237 Joshua Kendall, *The Forgotten Founding Father* (New York, 2010); on Webster's spelling book, 105-106.

238 Noah Webster, *Dictionary of the English Language* (Hartford, Connecticut, 1817), 171.

239 Noah Webster, *American Dictionary of the English Language* (New York, 1828), Vol. 1, n.p.

240 Noah Webster, Chauncey Goodrich, *American Dictionary of the English Language* (Springfield, Massachusetts, 1854), 604.

241 William Carpenter, *Dictionary of English Synonymmes* (London, 1842), 21, 59, 92, 93, 175.

242 William Carpenter, *Dictionary of English Synonymmes* (London, 1842), 89.

243 John Platt, *Dictionary of English Synonymes* (London, 1845), 124.

244 John Trusler, *The Distinction between Words Esteemed Synonymous* (London, 1794), Vol. 1, 69.

245 John Trusler, *The Distinction between Words Esteemed Synonymous* (London, 1794), Vol. 1, 149.

246 George Crabb, *English Synonymes Explained* (London, 1816), 413.

247 George Crabb, *English Synonymes Explained* (London, 1816), 13.

248 George Crabb, *English Synonyms Explained* (London, 1818), 600.

249 "Draft of Instructions to the Virginia Delegates in the Continental Congress (MS Text of A Summary View, &c.), [July 1774]," *Founders Online, National Archives*. http://founders.archives.gov/documents/Jefferson/01-01-02-0090.

250 *Papers of George Washington*, LOC, George Washington to Senate, August 22, 1789, Negotiations with Southern Indians.

251 John Bouvier, *Law Dictionary* (Philadelphia, 1879), 720.

252 *Century Dictionary and Cyclopedia* (New York, 1895), Vol. 8, 6460.

253 Michael W. McConnell, "Origins and Historical Understanding of Free Exercise of Religion," *Harvard Law Review*, 103 (1990), 1488.

254 Suzanne Kemmer, *Words in English*, at http://www.ruf.rice.edu/~kemmer/Words04/meaning.

255 http://www.wordreference.com/definition/infringement.

256 "Win the Peace for Whom?" *Time*, 0040781X, 9/16/1946, Vol. 48, Issue 12.

257 "Southern Explosion," *Time*, 0040781X, 3/8/1948, Vol. 51, Issue 10.

258 "Kickbacks," *Time*, 0040781X, 1/7/1957, Vol. 69, Issue 1. For "left-wing fringe groups," see 1956. "Friends of China," *Time*, 0040781X, 2/27/1956, Vol. 67, Issue 9.

259 "Black Supremacists," *Time*, 0040781X, 8/10/1959, Vol. 74, Issue 6.

260 "Conservative King," *Time*, 0040781X, 8/8/1960, Vol. 76, Issue 6.

261 "Fluoridation Fails Again," *Time*, 0040781X, 3/24/1961, Vol. 77, Issue 13.

262 Chester Lewis, Godfrey Hodgson, Bruce Page, *American Melodrama* (New York, 1969), 280.

263 Chester Lewis, Godfrey Hodgson, Bruce Page, *American Melodrama* (New York, 1969), 702.

264 Some editions listed in O'Neill, 326-329; Vancil, 220-221; see also Kendall, 278n.

265 Alessandro d'Antoni, *Treatise on Gun-Powder*, Thomson, tr. (London, 1789), 188.

266 Alessandro d'Antoni, *Treatise on Gun-Powder*, Thomson, tr. (London, 1789), xxx.

267 *Selden v. Coalter*, No number in original. Supreme Court of Virginia. 4 Va. 533; 1818 Va. LEXIS 3; 2 Va. Cas. 533. 1818.

268 http://www.sparknotes.com/testprep/books/newsat/ chapter15section4.rhtml.

269 Rod Evans, *Artful Nuance* (New York, 2009), 125.

270 Martin Manser and Stephen Curtis, *Penguin Writer's Manual* (London, 2004).

271 "Impinge vs. infringe." http://grammarist.com/usage/impinge-infringe.

272 *Pocket Fowler's Modern English Usage* (Oxford, 2008), 352-353.

273 At https://www.law.cornell.edu/supct/html/07-290.ZS.html, 1-2.

274 At https://www.law.cornell.edu/supct/html/07-290.ZS.html, 25-26.

275 See for example at http://www.madisonbrigade.com/t_coxe.htm.

276 Tenche Coxe, *View of the United States of America, in a Series of Papers* (Philadelphia, 1794).

277 Tenche Coxe, *View of the United States of America, in a Series of Papers* (Philadelphia, 1794), 272, 273, 277.

278 Tenche Coxe, *View of the United States of America, in a Series of Papers* (Philadelphia, 1794), 459-466.

279 Tenche Coxe, *View of the United States of America, in a Series of Papers* (Philadelphia, 1794), 272-273.

280 Tenche Coxe, *Statement of the Arts and Manufactures* (Philadelphia, 1814), xlvii.

281 Saul Cornell, *Well Regulated Militia* (New York, 2006), 47.

282 Noah Webster, "A Citizen of America," October 1787. http://teachingamericanhistory.org/library/document/a-citizen-of-america-an-examination-into-the-leading-principles-of-america.

283 *Heller v. District of Columbia*, 2011. At https://www.cadc.uscourts.gov/internet/opinions.nsf/DECA496973477C748525791F004D84F9/$file/10-7036-1333156.pdf. 15.

284 Ibid., 17-18.

285 Ibid., 37.

286 Thomas Sergeant, *Constitutional Law* (Philadelphia, 1830), 306.

287 *Brian Wrenn, et al., appellees v. District of Columbia and Cathy L. Lanier, appellants*. 1:15-CV-162 (FJS). United States District Court for the District of Columbia. 107 F. Supp. 3d 1; 2015 U.S. Dist. LEXIS 71383.

288 Ibid., 11-12.

289 Ibid., 17.

290 Ibid., 15-16.

291 *Matthew Grace and Pink Pistols, Plaintiffs, v. District of Columbia and Cathy Lanier, in her official capacity as Chief of Police for the Metropolitan Police Department, Defendants*. Civil Case No. 15-2234 (RJL). United States District Court for the District of Columbia. 2016 U.S. Dist. LEXIS 64681.

292 Samuel Goodrich, *Young American* (New York, 1847), 43-44.

293 Samuel Goodrich, *Young American* (New York, 1847), 37.

294 Theodore Sedgwick, *Treatise on the Rules which Govern the Interpretation and Application of Statutory and Constitutional Law* (New York, 1857), 148.

295 John Reid, *Constitutional History of the American Revolution* (Wisconsin, 1996), ix, 5, 19, 42-42.

SELECT BIBLIOGRAPHY

ONLINE REFERENCES, DATABASES, WEB ARCHIVES

17th - 18th Century Burney Collection Newspapers. Database (Library of Congress, on site)

Accessible Archives. Database (Library of Congress, on site) http://www.accessible. com/accessible

American Archives: Documents of the American Revolutionary Period, 1774-1776. Northern Illinois University. University Libraries Digital Collections and Collaborative Projects. http://amarch.lib.niu.edu

America's Historical Newspapers, 1690-. Database (LOC on site)

Avalon Project: Documents in Law, History and Diplomacy. Yale Law School. Lillian Goldman Law Library. http://avalon.law.yale.edu

Brigham Young University-Google Books. Database. American English Corpus. British English Corpus http://googleBook.byu.edu/x.asp#

British History Online. U. of London. Institute of Historical Research. Statutes of the Realm. http://www.british-history.ac.uk/search/series/statutes-realm

Cambridge History of English and American Literature. http://www.bartleby.com/ cambridge

Centre National de Ressources Textuelles et Lexicales. http://www.cnrtl.fr

Chronicling America: Historic American Newspapers. Database. (LOC public access) http://chroniclingamerica.loc.gov

Elliot's Debates. https://memory.loc.gov/ammem/amlaw/lwed.html

"Exploring Binomials: History, structure, motivation and function." 18th International Conference on English Historical Linguistics. KU Leuven, Leuven, Belgium, 14-18 July 2014. http://www.arts.kuleuven.be/ling/ICEHL18/ workshops/exploring-binomials

Founders Online: Correspondence and other Writings of Six Major Shapers of the United States. National Archives of the U.S. www.founders.archives.gov

George Washington Papers at the Library of Congress. Manuscript Division, Library of Congress. American Memory Collection. http://memory.loc.gov/ammem/ gwhtml/gwhome.html

James Madison Papers, 1723-1836. Library of Congress. American Memory Collection. http://memory.loc.gov/ammem/collections/madison_papers/ index.html

John Adams Library at the Boston Public Library. Digitized collection, Boston Public Library. https://archive.org/details/johnadamsBPL

Johnson, Samuel. *A Dictionary of the English Language: A Digital Edition of the 1755 Classic by Samuel Johnson*. Ed. Brandi Besalke. Last modified: November 25, 2013. http://johnsonsdictionaryonline.com

Lexicons of Early Modern English (LEME). http://leme.library.utoronto.ca (Replaces the *Early Modern English Dictionaries Database* (EMEDD), Ed. Ian Lancashire.) http://homes.chass.utoronto.ca/~ian/emedd.html

Library Company of Philadelphia. http://www.librarycompany.org

Lincoln/Net. Northern Illinois University. University Libraries Online Digital Collections of Primary Source Materials. http://lincoln.lib.niu.edu

Middle English Dictionary. (MED) U. Michigan. http://quod.lib.umich.edu/m/med

North Carolina Digital History. http://www.learnnc.org/lp/editions/nchist-revolution/4332

Online Library of Liberty. http://oll.libertyfund.org

Oxford English Dictionary. http://www.oed.com.proxy-bc.researchport.umd.edu

Papers of Benjamin Franklin. American Philosophical Society and Yale University. Packard Humanities Institute. www.franklinpapers.org

Pennsylvania state constitutions. http://www.duq.edu/academics/gumberg-library/pa-constitution/texts-of-the-constitution

TEAMS Middle English Texts Series. Robbins Library Digital Projects. University of Rochester. http://d.lib.rochester.edu/teams

TeachingAmericanHistory.org http://teachingamericanhistory.org/library

Thomas Jefferson Papers, 1606-1827. Library of Congress. American Memory Collection. http://memory.loc.gov/ammem/collections/jefferson_papers

U.S. Department of State, Office of the Historian. *Historical Documents.* https://history.state.gov/historicaldocuments

Vile, John R. *Constitutional Convention of 1787: A Comprehensive Encyclopedia of America's Founding.* ABC-CLIO, 2005. Database (LOC on site).

_____. *Encyclopedia of Constitutional Amendments, Proposed Amendments, and Amending Issues, 1789-2010.* 3rd ed. ABC-CLIO, 2010. Database (LOC on site)

Wycliffe Bible. http://wesley.nnu.edu/fileadmin/imported_site/wycliffe/wycbible-all.pdf

BOOKS BY TITLE

Acts and Laws of the State of Connecticut. Hartford: Charles Babcock, 1830. PDF eBook.

Addresses and Journal of Proceedings of the National Educational Association. Peoria, Illinois: N. C. Nason, 1873. PDF eBook.

American Gazette [. . .] Authentic Addresses, Memorials, Petitions, and other Papers . . . of the Present Unhappy Disputes between Great Britain and her Colonies. London: G. Kearsly, 1770. PDF eBook.

Black's Law Dictionary. 7th ed. Ed. Bryan A. Garner. St. Paul, Minnesota: West Group, 1999.

_____. Revised 4th ed. Ed. Henry Campbell Black. St. Paul, Minnesota: West, 1968.

Century Dictionary and Cyclopedia. New York: The Century Company, 1895. PDF eBook.

Charters and General Laws of the Colony and Province of Massachusetts Bay. Boston: T. B. Wait and Company, 1814. PDF eBook.

Collections of the Vermont Historical Society. Vol. 2. Montpelier: Printed for the Society, 1871. PDF eBook.

Colonial Records of North Carolina. Ed. William L. Saunders. Raleigh: Josephus Daniels, 1890. Vol. 9. PDF eBook.

Congressional Globe. Vol. 30. Washington: Blair & Rives, 1844. PDF eBook.

_____. [Vol. 27.] Washington, D. C.: John C. Rives, 1858. PDF eBook.

_____. Vol. 61, Part 2. Washington, D. C.: Rives & Bailey, 1869. PDF eBook.

Constitutions des Treize Etats-Unis de l'Amérique. Philadelphia, Paris: Ph.-D. Pierres, 1783. PDF eBook.

Constitutions of the Several Independent States of America; the Declaration of Independence; the Articles of Confederation Between the Said States;

and the Definitive Treaty Between Great-Britain and the United States of America. New York: E. Oswald, 1786. PDF eBook.

Corpus Glossary. Eds. Wallace Martin Lindsay and Helen McMillan Buckhurst. Cambridge: Cambridge U. Press, 1921.

Critical Memoirs of the Times. London: G. Kearsly, 1769. PDF eBook.

Critical Review, or Annals of Literature. Ed. Tobias Smollett. London: A. Hamilton, 1774-. PDF eBook.

Debates and Proceedings in the Congress of the United States. Vol. 1. Washington, D.C.: Gales and Seaton, 1834. PDF eBook.

Documentary History of the Constitution of the United States of America, 1787-1870. Vol. 1. Washington, D.C.: U. S. Department of State, May, 1894. PDF eBook.

Documentary History of the Constitution of the United States of America, 1786-1870. [Vol. 1.] Washington, D.C.: U. S. Department of State, May, 1894. [February 1901] PDF eBook.

Documentary History of the First Federal Congress of the United States, March 4, 1789-March 3, 1791. Ed. Linda Grant De Pauw. Baltimore: Johns Hopkins U. Press, 1972.

_____. Vol. 1. *Senate Legislative Journal.*

_____. Vol. 3. *House of Representatives Journal.*

_____. Vol. 4. *Legislative Histories.*

_____. Vol. 11. *Debates in the House of Representatives.*

Documentary History of the Ratification of the Constitution. Eds. John P. Kaminski and Gaspare J. Saladino. Madison: State Historical Society of Madison, 1976.

Eighth-Century Latin-Anglo-Saxon Glossary. Ed. J. H. Hessels. Cambridge: Cambridge U. Press, 1890.

Essay on the Expediency of a National Militia. n.a. London: R. Griffiths, 1757. PDF eBook.

Federal Cases. Vol. 18. St. Paul: West Publishing Co., 1895. PDF eBook.

Federalist. Ed. Robert A. Ferguson. New York: Barnes & Noble Classics, 2006.

Gentleman's and London Magazine: or Monthly Chronologer. London: C. Ackers. PDF eBook.

Interesting Letters Selected from the Political and Patriotic Correspondence of Messrs. Wilkes, Horn, Beckford, and Junius. London: W. Nicoll, 1769. PDF eBook.

Journal of the House of Representatives of the United States: Being the First Session of the Thirty-Ninth Congress. Washington, D.C.: Government Printing Office, 1866. PDF eBook.

Journal of the Senate of the State of New York at their Sixty-Third Session. Albany: E. Croswell, 1840. PDF eBook.

Journal of the Senate of the United States of America, Being the First Session of the Thirty-Ninth Congress. Washington, D.C.: Government Printing Office, 1865 [1866]. PDF eBook.

Journals of the House of Commons. London: Parliament. House of Commons. PDF eBook.

Journals of the House of Lords. Great Britain House of Lords. H. M. Stationery Office. PDF eBook.

Justice and Necessity of Taxing the American Colonies, Demonstrated. Together with a Vindication of the Authority of Parliament. Vol. 24, Issue 8. n.a. London: J. Almon, 1766. PDF eBook.

Laws of the State of Mississippi. Jackson, Mississippi: Kimball, Raymond & Co., 1873. PDF eBook.

Lawyers Reports Annotated. Vol. 21. Rochester, New York: Lawyers Co-operative Publishing Company, 1909. PDF eBook.

Letter to the People of Great-Britain, in Answer to that Published by the American Congress. n.a. London: F. Newbery, 1775. PDF eBook.

Machiavel's Letter to the Lords and Commons of G*** B***. London: S. Garnsey, 1749. PDF eBook.

Massachusetts Reports: Decisions of the Supreme Judicial Court of Massachusetts, Volume 84. [Vol. 2.] Boston: Little, Brown, 1866. PDF eBook.

Miscellaneous Documents of the House of Representatives, Printed during the First Session of the Thirty-Ninth Congress. Washington, D.C.: Government Printing Office, 1866. PDF eBook.

Modest Address to the Commons of Great Britain: And in Particular to the Free Citizens of London; Occasioned by the Ill Success of Our Present Naval War with France, and the Want of a Militia Bill. n.a. London: J. Scott, 1756. PDF eBook.

National Magazine and Republican Review. Vol. 1. Washington, D. C.: Fulton & Smith, 1839. PDF eBook.

Official Gazette of the U.S. Patent Office. Washington, D.C.: U.S. Patent Office, 1898. PDF eBook.

Oxford History of English Lexicography. Ed. A. P. Cowie. Oxford: Clarendon Press, 2009.

Pamphlets on Scottish History: 1706-1797. n. p., n.d. PDF eBook.

Pamphlets on the Concord Railroad Corporation. Concord: Asa McFarland, 1841. PDF eBook.

Parliamentary Debates in 1610. Ed. Samuel Rawson Gardiner. Camden Society, 1862. PDF eBook.

Pocket Fowler's Modern English Usage. 2nd ed. Ed. Robert Allen. Oxford U. Press, 2008.

Reconstruction: A Herald of the New Time. New York: Reconstruction Publishing Co., February, 1919. PDF eBook.

Records of the Colony of New Plymouth, in New England: Acts of the Commissioners of the United Colonies of New England, 1643-1679. Boston: Press of William White, 1859. PDF eBook.

Records of the Federal Convention of 1787. Ed. Max Farrand.

_____. Vol. 1. New Haven: Yale U. Press, 1966.

_____. Vol. 2. Yale U. Press, 1966.

_____. *Appendix A: Supplementary Records of Proceedings in Convention*. Vol. 3. Yale U. Press, 1966.

Reports of Cases Argued and Determined in the Superior Court of . . . New Hampshire. Vol. 3. [Vol. 23] Concord: B. W. Sanford, 1854. PDF eBook.

Reports of Cases Argued and Determined in the Supreme Court of New York. Vol. 6. Philadelphia: E. F. Backus, 1859. PDF eBook.

Reports of Cases Argued and Determined in the Supreme Court of Vermont. 2nd ed. St. Paul: West Publishing Co., 1889. PDF eBook.

Reports of Cases Argued and Determined in the Supreme Judicial Court of Massachusetts. Boston: Little, Brown. PDF eBook.

Rights of the Sailors Vindicated. London: G. Kearsly, 1772. PDF eBook.

Rover: A Weekly Magazine. Ed. Seba Smith. New York: S. B. Dean & Co., 1844. PDF eBook.

Scots Magazine. Edinburgh: Murray and Cochran, 1774- . PDF eBook.

South-Atlantic: A Monthly Magazine of Literature, Science and Art. Wilmington, North Carolina: Jackson & Bell, 1878. PDF eBook.

Southern Magazine and Monthly Review. Petersburg, Virginia: Edmund and Julian C. Ruffin, 1841. PDF eBook.

Southwestern Reporter. Vol. 236. St. Paul: West Publishing Co., 1922. PDF eBook.

State Records of North Carolina. Vol. 1. Ed. William L. Saunders. Raleigh: P. M. Hale, 1886. PDF eBook.

Statutes at Large . . . From Magna charta to 1800. Vol. 7. London: Mark Basket, et al., 1764. PDF eBook.

_____. Vol. 28. Danby Pickering, ed. PDF eBook.

Trial of William Penn and William Mead at the Old Bailey, 1670. Repr. London: Headley Brothers, 1908. PDF eBook (Stanford Law Library).

United States Supreme Court Reports. Vol. 44. Rochester, New York: Lawyers Co-operative Publishing Co., 1900. PDF eBook.

BOOKS BY AUTHOR

Adams, John. *Defence of the Constitutions of Government of the United States of America.* Philadelphia: Hall and Sellers, 1787. PDF eBook.

Adams, John and Charles Francis Adams. *Works of John Adams, Second President of the United States.* Boston: Little, Brown, 1850. PDF eBook.

Allibone, J. Austin. *Critical Dictionary of English Literature, and British and American Authors.* Philadelphia: Childs and Peterson, 1859. PDF eBook.

Almon, John. *Collection of Interesting, Authentic Papers, Relative to the Dispute between Great Britain and America.* London: J. Almon, 1777. [n. a.] PDF eBook.

Ames, James. *Typographical Antiquities: Being an Historical Account of Printing in England.* London: W. Faden, 1749. PDF eBook.

Beeman, Richard. *Plain, Honest Men: The Making of the American Constitution.* New York: Random House, 2009.

Blackstone, William. *Analysis of the Laws of England. By Sir W. Blackstone.* 2nd edition. Oxford: Clarendon Press, 1757.

_____. *Commentaries on the Laws of England.* London: W. Strahan, 1783. PDF eBook.

_____. Oxford: Clarendon Press, 1768. PDF eBook.

_____. *Discourse on the Study of the Law; Being an Introductory Lecture.* Oxford: Clarendon Press, 1758. PDF eBook.

Boswell, James. *Scots Magazine.* Edinburgh: Sands, Brymer, Murray and Cochran, 1767-. PDF eBook.

Bouvier, John. *Law Dictionary: Adapted to the Constitution and Laws of the United States of America.* Philadelphia: J. B. Lippincott & Co., 1879. PDF eBook.

Boyd, Julian P., and Gerard W. Gawalt, eds. *Declaration of Independence: The Evolution of the Text.* Hanover and London: U. Press of New England, 1999.

Bradford, Alden. *History of Massachusetts, Vol. 1, From 1764, to July, 1775.* Boston: Richardson and Lord, 1822. PDF eBook.

Bradley, Francis Henry. *Middle-English Dictionary: Containing Words Used by English Writers from the Twelfth to the Fifteenth Century.* Norfolk, U.K.: Lowe and Brydone, 1974. Repr.

Brodhead, Jacob. *Constitutions of the Sixteen States, Which Compose the Confederated Republic of America.* Boston: Manning & Loring, 1797. PDF eBook.

Burgess, Thomas. *Considerations on the Abolition of Slavery and the Slave Trade, Upon Grounds of Natural, Religious, and Political Duty.* 1789. PDF eBook.

Burkett, Eva M. *Study of American Dictionaries of the English Language before 1861.* Nashville: George Peabody College, 1936.

Burns, Eric. *Infamous Scribblers: The Founding Fathers and the Rowdy Beginnings of American Journalism.* New York: Public Affairs (Perseus), 2006.

Burroughs, Jeremiah. *Moses His Choice.* London: John Field, 1650. PDF eBook.

Chaucer, Geoffrey. *Works of Geoffrey Chaucer.* New Cambridge Edition, ed. F. N. Robinson. Boston: Houghton Mifflin, 1961.

Chester, Lewis, Godfrey Hodgson, Bruce Page. *An American Melodrama.* New York: Viking, 1969.

Coke, Edward. *First Part of the Institutes of the Lawes of England.* Ed. Thomas Littleton. London: E. and R. Nutt et al., 1738. PDF eBook.

_____. *Second Part of the Institutes . . . Containing the Exposition of Many Great and Other Statutes.* London: E. and R. Brooke, 1797. PDF eBook.

_____. *Fourth Part of the Institutes . . . Concerning the Jurisdiction of Courts.* London: E. and R. Brooke, 1797.

_____. *Magna Charta, Made in the Ninth Year of K. Henry the Third . . .* London: Thomas Simmons, 1680. PDF eBook.

Collier, Christopher and James L. Collier. *Decision in Philadelphia: The Constitutional Convention of 1787.* New York: Ballantine, 2007.

Collins, Gail. *When Everything Changed: The Amazing Journey of American Women from 1960 to the Present.* New York: Little, Brown, 2009.

Cornell, Saul. *Well-Regulated Militia: The Founding Fathers and the Origins of Gun Control in America.* New York: Oxford U. Press, 2006.

Cowley, John D. *Bibliography of Abridgments, Digests, Dictionaries and Indexes of English Law to the Year 1800.* (Selden Society.) Holmes Beach, Florida: Wm. W. Gaunt & Sons, 1979.

Coxe, Tench. *View of the United States of America, in a Series of Papers, Written at Various Times, between the Years 1787 and 1794.* Philadelphia: William Hall, 1794. PDF eBook.

_____. *Statement of the Arts and Manufactures of the United States [. . .] 1810.* Philadelphia: A. Cornman, 1814. (Book 2 of the Third Census of the United States.) PDF eBook.

Curry, John. *Historical and Critical Review of the Civil Wars in Ireland.* Dublin: Luke White, 1786. PDF eBook.

Dallas, Anne B. *Incidents in the Life and Ministry of the Rev. Alex. R. C. Dallas, A.M.* 2nd ed. London: James Nisbet, 1782. PDF eBook.

Dallas, Robert Charles. *History of the Maroons, from their Origin to the Establishment of their Chief Tribe at Sierra Leone.* Vol. 2. London: A. Strahan, 1803. PDF eBook.

D'Antoni, Alessandro Vittorio. *Treatise on Gun-Powder; A Treatise on Fire-Arms; and a Treatise on the Service of Artillery in the Time of War.* Tr. [Captain] Thomson. London: T. and J. Egerton, 1789. PDF eBook.

Flack, Horace E. *Adoption of the Fourteenth Amendment.* Baltimore: Johns Hopkins Press, 1908. PDF eBook.

Follett, Oran, and Thomas Corwin. *Selections from the Follett Papers, III.* Vols. 10-12. Cincinnati: Abingdon Press, 1915. PDF eBook.

Franklin, Benjamin. *Political, Miscellaneous, and Philosophical Pieces*. London: J. Johnson, 1779. PDF eBook.

_____. *Writings of Benjamin Franklin*. Albert Smyth, ed. Vol. 10. London: MacMillan, 1907. PDF eBook.

Friedenwald, Herbert. *Declaration of Independence: An Interpretation and an Analysis*. New York: Da Capo Press, 1974.

Goodrich, Samuel Griswold. *Young American: Or Book of Government and Law; Showing their History, Nature, and Necessity, for the Use of Schools*. 8th ed. New York: Mark H. Newman & Co., 1847. PDF eBook.

Gower, John. *English Works of John Gower*. Early English Text Society. Ed. G. C. Macaulay. London: Oxford U. Press, 1969.

Guthrie, William D. *Lectures on the Fourteenth Article of Amendment to the Constitution of the United States*. Boston: Little, Brown, 1898. PDF eBook.

Hale, Matthew, and Sollom Emlyn. *Historia Placitorum Coronæ: The History of the Pleas of the Crown*. Savoy: E. and R. Nutt, 1736. PDF eBook.

Hamilton, Alexander ['Camillus']. *History of French Influence in the United States*. Philadelphia: privately printed, 1812. PDF eBook.

Hervey, Frederick. *Naval History of Great Britain*. London: W. Adlard, 1779. PDF eBook.

Hickey, William. *Constitution of the United States of America; The Proximate Causes of Its Adoption and Ratification*. Washington: J. and G.S. Gideon, 1846. PDF eBook.

Hobbes, Thomas. *English Works of Thomas Hobbes of Malmsbury*. Ed. William Molesworth. London: John Bohn, 1839. PDF eBook.

_____. *Leviathan Or The Matter, Form, and Power of a Common-wealth, Ecclesiastical and Civil*. London: Andrew Crooke, 1651. PDF eBook.

_____. *Hobb's Tripos: In 3 discourses. The 1.: Humane nature, or the fundamental elements of policy . . . The 2.: De corpore politico, or the elements of law, moral and politick . . . The 3. Of liberty and necessity . . .* London: Gilliflower, 1684. PDF eBook.

_____. *Tracts of Mr. Thomas Hobbs of Malmsbury. Containing: Behemoth, the history of the causes of the Civil wars of England, from 1640. to 1660. printed from the author's own copy. . . An answer to arch-bishop Bramhall's book, called The catching of the Leviathan . . .* London: W. Crooke, 1682. PDF eBook.

Hooker, Richard. *Of the Lawes of Ecclesiastical Politie*. London: William Stansbye, 1636. PDF eBook.

_____. *Works of that Learned and Judicious Divine, Richard Hooker*. (2nd ed.) Oxford: Oxford U. Press, 1841.

_____. Hooker, Richard. *The works of that learned and judicious divine, Mr. Richard Hooker: in eight books of Ecclesiastical polity, completed out of his own manuscripts: with several other treatises by the same author, and an account of his life and death*. London: Printed by R. White, for Rob. Scot, Tho Basset, John Wright and Rich. Chiswel et al., 1676. PDF eBook.

Hopkins, Stephen. *Grievances of the American Colonies Candidly Examined*. London: J. Almon, 1766. PDF eBook.

Huellen, Werner. *English Dictionaries 800-1700: The Topical Tradition*. Oxford: Clarendon Press, 1999.

Hume, David. *Essays and Treatises on Several Subjects*. 2nd ed. London: A. Millar, 1758. PDF eBook.

_____. *History of England, from the Invasion of Julius Caesar to the Revolution in 1688*. London: A. Millar, 1767. PDF eBook.

_____. *History of England*. London: T. Cadell, 1782. PDF eBook.

_____. *Treatise of Human Nature*. London: Thomas and Joseph Allman, 1817. PDF eBook.

Hyamson, Albert Montefiore. *History of the Jews in England*. Forgotten Books, 2012. (1907.) POD.

James, Eldon Revare. *List of Legal Treatises Printed in the British Colonies and the American States before 1801*. (*Harvard Legal Essays*. Boston: Harvard U., 1934.) Union, New Jersey: Lawbook Exchange Ltd, 2002. PDF eBook.

Jefferson, Thomas. *Notes on the State of Virginia*. 2nd American ed. Philadelphia: Matthew Carey, 1794. PDF eBook.

Jensen, Merrill, and John P. Kaminski, Gaspare J. Saladino, et al. *Documentary History of the Ratification of the Constitution*. Madison: Wisconsin Historical Society Press, 1976- .

Julian, George W. *Speeches on Political Questions*. New York: Hurd and Houghton; Cambridge: Riverside Press, 1872. PDF eBook.

Kendall, Joshua. *Forgotten Founding Father: Noah Webster's Obsession and the Creation of an American Culture*. New York: Berkley Books, 2010.

Knox, Hugh. *Select Sermons on Interesting Subjects*. Glasgow: Robert & Andrew Foulis, 1776. PDF eBook.

Knox, Thomas, George Grenville, and Thomas Whateley. *Controversy between Great-Britain and Her Colonies Reviewed*. London: J. Almon, 1769. PDF eBook.

Kopaczyk, Joanna. *Legal Language of Scottish Burghs: Standardization and Lexical Bundles (1380-1560)*. New York: Oxford University Press, 2013.

Lambley, Kathleen. *Teaching and Cultivation of the French Language in England during Tudor and Stuart Times*. Manchester, London: U. Press and Longmans, Green, 1920. PDF eBook.

Larkin, James F., and Paul L. Hughes, eds. *Royal proclamations of King James I, 1603-1625*. Oxford: Clarendon Press, 1973.

Leggett, William. *Plaindealer*. William van Norden, 1836. PDF eBook.

Locke, John. *An Essay Concerning Human Understanding; with Thoughts on the Conduct of the Understanding*. Edinburgh: Mundell & Son, 1801. PDF eBook.

_____. *Letter Concerning Toleration*. London: Awnsham Churchill, 1689. PDF eBook.

_____. *Two Treatises of Government*. 7th ed. London: J. Whiston, et al., 1789. PDF eBook.

_____. and Pierre Maiseaux. *A Collection of Several Pieces of Mr. John Locke: Never Before Printed, Or Not Extant in His Works*. London: J. Bettenham, 1720. PDF eBook.

_____. and William Molyneux, Thomas Molyneux, Philippus van Limborch. *Some Familiar Letters, between Mr. Locke and Several of his Friends*. London: Printed at A. and J. Churchill at the Black Swan in Pater-noster Row, 1708. PDF eBook.

_____. *Works of John Locke Esq: In Three Volumes*. London: S. Birt, et al., 1751. PDF eBook.

Long, Edward. *History of Jamaica. Or, General Survey of the Antient and Modern State of that Island:: With Reflections on Its Situation, Settlements, Inhabitants, Climate, Products, Commerce, Laws, and Government*. London: T. Lowndes, in Fleet-Street., 1774. PDF eBook.

Lucas, Charles. *Political Constitutions of Great-Britain and Ireland, Asserted and Vindicated*. London: 1751. PDF eBook.

Lutz, Donald S. *Colonial Origins of the American Constitution*. Indianapolis, Ind.: Liberty Fund, 1998.

_____. *Preface to American Political Theory*. Lawrence, Kansas: U. Press of Kansas, 1992.

Matthews, P. H. *Oxford Concise Dictionary of Linguistics*. Oxford, New York: Oxford U. Press, 1997.

Middleton, Conyers. *Dissertation concerning the Origin of Printing in England*. Cambridge: W. Thurlbourne, 1735. PDF eBook.

Nash[e], Thomas, et al. (In) *Miscellaneous Tracts*. Ed. John Payne Collier. [1588] [London: for Shakespeare Society, 1842.] PDF eBook.

O'Neill, Robert K. *English-Language Dictionaries, 1604-1900*. New York, London: Greenwood Press, 1988.

Osselton, N. E. *Dumb Linguists. A Study of the Earliest English and Dutch Dictionaries*. Publications of the Sir Thomas Browne Institute, Leiden, Special Series 5. Leiden: n.p., 1973.

Parsons, Robert. *Conference about the Next Succession of the Crowne of Ingland*. N. p., 1594. PDF eBook.

_____. *Temperate Ward-Word*. 1599.

Penn, William. *Collection of the Works of William Penn*. London: J. Sowle, 1726. PDF eBook.

Perceval, John. *Full and Fair Discussion of the Pretensions of the Dissenters*. Oxford: D. Prince and J. Cooke, 1740. PDF eBook.

Rayner, John. *An Inquiry into the doctrine, lately propagated, concerning Attachments of contempt, the alteration of Records, and the Court of Star Chamber, upon the principles of Law, and the constitution, particularly as they relate to prosecutions for libels: With notes, references, and observations. By an English constitutional Crown Lawyer*. London: J. Williams, 1769. PDF eBook.

Reddick, Allen Hilliard. *Making of Johnson's Dictionary, 1746-1773*. Cambridge; New York: Cambridge U. Press, 1990.

Reid, John P. *Constitutional History of the American Revolution*. Abridged ed. Madison: U. Wisconsin Press, 1996.

Robertson, David. *Debates and Other Proceedings of the Convention of Virginia*. Richmond: Ritchie & Worsley, 1805. PDF eBook.

Schäfer, Jürgen. *Documentation in the OED: Shakespeare and Nashe as Test Cases*. Oxford: Clarendon Press, 1980.

_____. *Early Modern English Lexicography*. Oxford: Clarendon Press; New York: Oxford U. Press, 1989.

Sedgwick, Theodore. *A Treatise on the Rules which Govern the Interpretation and Application of Statutory and Constitutional Law*. New York: John S. Voorhuis, 1857. PDF eBook.

Sergeant, Thomas. *Constitutional Law*. Philadelphia: T. H. Nicklin & T. Johnson, 1830. PDF eBook.

Sidney, Algernon. *Discourses Concerning Government*. 2nd ed. London: J. Darby, 1704. PDF eBook.

Simpson, David. *Politics of American English, 1776-1850*. New York: Oxford U. Press, 1986.

Skeat, W. W. *Glossary of Tudor and Stuart Words*. Ed. A. L. Mayhew. Oxford: Clarendon Press, 1914.

Sledd, James H., and Gwin J. Kolb. *Dr. Johnson's Dictionary; Essays in the Biography of a Book*. Chicago: U. of Chicago Press, 1955.

Smalley, Vera E. *Sources of A Dictionarie of the French and English Tongues.* Baltimore: Johns Hopkins Press, 1948.

Smith, Adam. *Inquiry into the Nature and Causes of the Wealth of Nations.* London: Strahan and Cadell, 1776. PDF eBook.

Smollett, Tobias George. *Complete History of England,* Vol. 3. 1757. PDF eBook.
_____. *Complete History of England,* Vol. 5. 1758. PDF eBook.
_____. *Continuation of the Complete History of England.* London: Richard Baldwin, 1760. PDF eBook.
_____. *Critical Review: or, Annals of Literature,* Vol. 8. By a Society of Gentlemen. London: A. Hamilton, 1759. PDF eBook.
_____. *Critical Review, or Annals of Literature.* 1774. PDF eBook.

Starnes, De Witt, and Gertrude E. Noyes. *English Dictionary from Cawdrey to Johnson, 1604-1755.* Chapel Hill, N.C.: U. of North Carolina press, 1946.

Starnes, Dewitt T., and Ernest William Talbert. *Classical Myth and Legend in Renaissance Dictionaries; A Study of Renaissance Dictionaries in their Relation to the Classical Learning of Contemporary English Writers.* Chapel Hill, N.C.: U. of North Carolina Press, 1955.

Starnes, De Witt T. *Robert Estienne's Influence on Lexicography.* Austin: U. of Texas Press, 1963.

Storing, Herbert J. and Murray Dry, eds. *Complete Anti-Federalist.* Chicago, Ill.: U. Chicago Press, 1981.

Strype, John. *History of the Life and Acts of the Most Reverend Father in God, Edmund Grindal.* London: John Wyat and John Hartley, 1710. PDF eBook.

Stuart, Gilbert. In Francis S. Sullivan, *Historical Treatise on the Feudal Law.* 2nd ed. London: Edward and Charles Dilly, 1776. PDF eBook.

Sullivan, Francis Stoughton, and Gilbert Stuart. *Lectures on the Constitution and Laws of England with a Commentary on Magna Charta.* London: Edward and Charles Dilly, 1776. PDF eBook.

Symons, L. Eleanor. *Bibliography of English-French and French-English Dictionaries to 1800.* London: U. of London, School of Librarianship and Archives, 1949.

Thomas, Isaiah. *History of Printing in America, with a Biography of Printers & an Account of Newspapers.* [Repr. of 1810 ed.] New York: Weathervane Books, 1970.

Thorpe, Francis Newton. *Constitutional History of the United States, 1765-1895.* Chicago: Callaghan & Company, 1901. (Three volumes) PDF eBook.
_____. *Federal and State Constitutions.* Washington, D.C.: Government Printing Office, 1909.

Trumbull, Benjamin. *Complete History of Connecticut: Civil and Ecclesiastical, from the Emigration of Its First Planters, from England, in the Year 1630, to the Year 1764.* Vol. 1. Maltby, Goldsmith and Co. and Samuel Wadsworth, 1818. PDF eBook.

Trusler, John. *Concise View of the Common and Statute Law of England.* London: W. Nicoll, 1781.
_____. *The Difference, between Words, esteemed Synonymous in the English Language, Pointed out, and the Proper Choice of Them Determined.* Second ed. London: Rivington, 1783. PDF eBook.
_____. 3rd edition. London: J. Parsons, 1794. PDF eBook.

Tyrrell, James. *Bibliotheca Politica: or, an Enquiry into the Ancient Constitution of the English Government, Both in respect to the just extent of Regal Power, and the Rights and Liberties of the Subject.* London: R. Baldwin, 1694. PDF eBook.

Vancil, David E. *Catalog of Dictionaries, Word Books, and Philological Texts, 1440-1900.* Westport, London: Greenwood Press, 1993.

Watson, David Kemper. *Constitution of the United States: Its History, Application and Construction.* Vol. 2. Chicago: Callaghan, 1910.

Watts, Isaac. *Logick: or, The right use of reason in the inquiry after truth, with a variety of rules to guard against error, in the affairs of religion and human life, as well as in the sciences.* London: T. Longman [et al.], 1745. PDF eBook.

White, George Starr, M.D. *Think.* Los Angeles: Phillips Printing Co., 1920. PDF eBook.

Winthrop, Adam, John Winthrop, Wait Still Winthrop. *Winthrop Papers.* Boston: Massachusetts Historical Society, 1889. PDF eBook.

Wootton, David, ed. *Essential Federalist and anti-Federalist Papers.* Indianapolis: Hackett Publishing, 2003.

Worrall, John. *Bibliotheca Legum Angliae . . . Catalogue of the Common and Statute Law Books of this Realm.* [1788] Union, New Jersey: Lawbook Exchange, 1997. Facs. repr.

Wrinkle, Barbara. *Language Dictionaries with an Emphasis on Military Dictionaries.* Carlisle Barracks, Pa.: US Army Military History Research Coll., 1971.

Zubly, John Joachim. *Law of Liberty: A Sermon on American Affairs.* Philadelphia, London: John Almon, 1775. PDF eBook.

ARTICLES

Bately, Janet. "Estienne, Harrison, and the First French-English Dictionary." *Notes and Queries* 57.3 (2010): 325-334.

Benor, Sarah, and Roger Levy. "The Chicken or the Egg? A Probabilistic Analysis of English Binomials." *Language* 82.2 (2006): 233-278.

Breeze, Ruth. "Lexical Bundles across Four Legal Genres." *International Journal of Corpus Linguistics* 18.2 (2013): 229-253.

Chrimes, S. B. "Constitutional Ideas of Dr. John Cowell." *English Historical Review* 64.253 (October 1949): 461-487.

Christianson, Paul. "Young John Selden and the Ancient Constitution, ca. 1610-18." *Proceedings of the American Philosophical Society* 128.4 (December 1984): 271-315.

Churchill, Robert H. "Gun Regulation, the Police Power, and the Right to Keep Arms in Early America: The Legal Context of the Second Amendment." *Law and History Review* 25.1 (Spring, 2007): 139-175.

Considine, John. "Narrative and Persuasion in Early Modern English Dictionaries and PhraseBook." *Review of English Studies* N.S. 52.206 (May 2001): 195-206.

Cope, Esther S. "Sir Edward Coke and Proclamations, 1610." *American Journal of Legal History* 15.3 (1971): 215-221.

_____. "Sir Edward Coke and Proclamations: A New Manuscript." *American Journal of Legal History* 15.4 (1971): 317.

Cornell, Saul. "Early American Gun Regulation and the Second Amendment: A Closer Look at the Evidence." *Law and History Review* 25.1 (Spring 2007): 197-204.

Danet, Brenda, and Bryna Bogoch. "From Oral Ceremony to Written Document: The Transitional Language of Anglo-Saxon Wills." *Language & Communication* 12.2: 95-122.

DeMaria, Robert, Jr., and Gwin J. Kolb. "Johnson's 'Dictionary' and Dictionary Johnson." *Yearbook of English Studies* 28 (1998): 19-43.

Devine, Francis Edward. "Absolute Democracy or Indefeasible Right: Hobbes Versus Locke." *Journal of Politics* 37.3 (August 1975): 736-768.

Dunbar, Leslie W. "James Madison and the Ninth Amendment." *Virginia Law Review* 42.5 (June 1956): 627-643.

Enos, Richard Leo and Tony M. Lentz. "Bibliographical Guide to English Linguistics, 1500-1800." *Rhetoric Society Quarterly* 6.4 (Winter 1976): 68-79.

Finkelman, Paul. "James Madison and the Bill of Rights: A Reluctant Paternity." *Supreme Court Review* 1990 (1990): 301-347.

Gerber, Scott D. "Roger Sherman and the Bill of Rights." *Polity* 28.4 (Summer 1996): 521-540.

Graber, Mark A. "Subtraction by Addition? The Thirteenth and Fourteenth Amendments." *Columbia Law Review* 112.7: 1501-1549.

Graham, Howard J. "Our 'Declaratory' Fourteenth Amendment." *Stanford Law Review* 7.1 (December 1954): 3-39.

Hamburger, Philip A. "Natural Rights, Natural Law, and American Constitutions." *Yale Law Journal* 102.4 (January 1993): 907-960.

Hofstadter, Richard. "William Leggett, Spokesman of Jacksonian Democracy." *Political Science Quarterly* 58.4 (December 1943): 581-594.

Holland, H. A. "English Legal Authors before 1700." *Cambridge Law Journal* 9.3 (1947): 292-329.

Howe, William Wirt. "Evolution of Amendment in the Constitution of the United States." *Sewanee Review* 1.2 (February 1893): 181-193.

Johnson, Claudia L. "Samuel Johnson's Moral Psychology and Locke's 'Of Power.'" *Studies in English Literature, 1500-1900* 24.3 (Summer 1984): 563-582.

Kolb, Gwin J., and James H. Sledd. "Johnson's 'Dictionary' and Lexicographical Tradition." *Modern Philology* 50.3 (1953): 171-194.

Kopaczyk, Joanna. "Latin and Scots Versions of Scottish Medieval Burgh Laws." *Scottish Language* 30: 1-18.

Lamy, Rudolph B. "Influence of History upon a Plain Text Reading of the Second Amendment to the Constitution of the United States." *American Journal of Legal History* 49.2 (April 2007): 217-230.

Lancashire, Ian. "An Early Modern English Dictionaries Corpus 1499-1659." *Digital Studies/Le Champ Numérique*. U. of Toronto, Toronto: *CHWP* B.17, publ. September 1996. 75-90. https://www.digitalstudies.org/ojs/index.php/digital_studies/article/view/101/134

Lemmings, David. "Blackstone and Law Reform by Education: Preparation for the Bar and Lawyerly Culture in Eighteenth-Century England." *Law and History Review* 16.2 (Summer 1998): 211-255.

Levy, Raphael. Review. "Sources of a Dictionarie of the French and English Tongues." *Modern Language Notes* 64.6 (June 1949): 431-432.

Lyman, J. Chester. "Our Inequalities of Suffrage." *North American Review* 144.364 (March 1887): 298-306.

Matthews, Brander. "Evolution of Copyright." *Political Science Quarterly* 5.4 (December 1890): 583-602.

McConnell, Michael W. "Origins and Historical Understanding of Free Exercise of Religion." *Harvard Law Review* 103.7 (1990): 1409-1517.

McDowell, Gary L. "Politics of Meaning: Law Dictionaries and the Liberal Tradition of Interpretation." *American Journal of Legal History* 44.3 (July 2000): 257-283.

McGlynn, Michael P. "Orality in the Old Icelandic Grágás: Legal Formulae in the Assembly Procedures Section." *Neophilologus* 93 (2009): 521-536.

Miwa, Nobuharu, and Du Dan Li. "On the Repetitive Word-Pairs in English, with Special Reference to W. Caxton." *Cultural Science Reports of Kagoshima University* 58 (2003): 49-66.

Mollin, Sandra. "Pathways of Change in the Diachronic Development of Binomial Reversibility in Late Modern American English." *Journal of English Linguistics* 41: 168-203.

————. "Revisiting Binomial Order in English: Ordering Constraints and Reversibility." *English Language and Linguistics* 16.1: 81-103.

Motschenbacher, Heiko. "Gentlemen before Ladies? A Corpus-Based Study of Conjunct Order in Personal Binomials." *Journal of English Linguistics* 41(3): 212-242.

Nădrag, Lavinia. "Teaching the Origins of English Legal Language." *Contemporary Readings in Law and Social Justice* 4 (2012): 603-609.

Nizonkiza, Deogratias. "Relationship between Lexical Competence, Collocational Competence, and Second Language Proficiency." *English Text Construction* 4.1 (2011): 113-146.

Omohundro Institute of Early American History and Culture. "A Note on Certain of Hamilton's Pseudonyms." *William & Mary Quarterly* 12.2 (April 1955): 282-297.

Pandora, Katherine. "The Children's Republic of Science in the Antebellum Literature of Samuel Griswold Goodrich and Jacob Abbott." *Osiris* 24.1 (2009): 75-98.

Peardon, Barbara. "Politics of Polemic: John Ponet's Short Treatise of Politic Power and Contemporary Circumstance 1553-1556." *Journal of British Studies* 22.1 (Autumn 1982): 35-49.

Plumb, Milton M., Jr. "The Bill of Rights Comes Home." *Quarterly Journal of Current Acquisitions* 2.3/4 (June 1945): 30-44.

Rakove, Jack N. "Words, Deeds, and Guns: 'Arming America' and the Second Amendment." *William and Mary Quarterly*, Third Series 59.1 (January, 2002): 205-210.

Roberts, Peter R. "Welsh Language, English Law and Tudor Legislation." *Transactions of the Honourable Society of Cymmrodorion* (1989): 19-75.

Sassi, Jonathan D. "Communications." *William and Mary Quarterly* 69.1: 196-201.

Sauer, Hans. "Twin-Formulae and More in Middle English: The Historye of the Patriarks, Caxton's Ovid, Pecock's Donet." *Studies in Middle English: words, forms, senses and texts.* Michael Bilynsky, ed. (Studies in Medieval Language and Literature, 44.)

Schaefer, Jurgen. "John Minsheu: Scholar or Charlatan?" *Renaissance Quarterly* 26.1 (Spring 1973): 23-35.

Simon, Jocelyn. "Dr. Cowell." *Cambridge Law Journal* 26.2 (November 1968): 260-272.

Starnes, D. T. "Bilingual Dictionaries of Shakespeare's Day." *PMLA* 52.4 (December 1937): 1005-1018.

Stein, Gabriele. "Lexicographical Method and Usage in Cawdrey's A Table Alphabeticall." *Studia Neophilologica* 82 (2010): 163-177.

Vázquez y del Árbol, Esther I. "Binomios, Trinomios y Tetranomios cuasi Sinonimos en los Poderes Notariales Digitales Britanicos y Norteamericanos." *Revista de Llengua i Dret* 61 (2014): 26-46.

www.ingramcontent.com/pod-product-compliance
Lightning Source LLC
Chambersburg PA
CBHW061740270326
41928CB00011B/2315